CISTERCIAN STUDIES SERIES: ONE HUNDRED FORTY-EIGHT

Thomas Spidlik

Drinking from the Hidden Fountain
A Patristic Breviary

Ancient Wisdom for Today's World

CISTERCIAN STUDIES SERIES: ONE HUNDRED FORTY-EIGHT

Drinking from the Hidden Fountain
A Patristic Breviary

Ancient Wisdom for Today's World

Thomas Spidlik

Translated by Paul Drake

Cistercian Publications
Kalamazoo, Michigan - Spencer, Massachusetts
1994

First published as *Breviario Patristico* by
Piero Gribaudi Editore, Turin, Italy
© 1971 Piero Gribaudi Editore Turin

First published in English in 1992
by New City, 57 Twyford Avenue, London W3 9PZ
© English translation New City 1992

First American publication 1993
by Cistercian Publications
WMU Station, Kalamazoo, Michigan 49008

*The work of Cistercian Publications is made possible in part
by support from Western Michigan University to
The Institute of Cistercian Studies*

(pb) ISBN 0 87907 348 9

Typeset by
Phoenix Typesetting, Burley-in-Wharfedale, West Yorkshire

Printed and bound by
McNaughton & Gunn, Inc.
Saline, Michigan

Library of Congress Cataloging-in-Publication Data

Breviario patristico. English.
   Drinking from the hidden fountain : a patristic breviary : ancient
wisdom for today's world / Thomas Spidlik.
     p.   cm. -- (Cistercian studies series : no. 148)
   ISBN 0-87907-348-9 (pbk. : alk. paper)
   1. Devotional calendars--Catholic church. 2. Fathers of the
church. 3. Catholic Church--Prayer-books and devotions--English.
I. Spidlík, Thomás. II. Title.   III. Series
BX2178.B7413 1993
242'.2--dc20   93-29885
                                                                         CIP

Printed in the United States of America

CONTENTS

PROLOGUE

Every believer is as 'amen' who will become an 'alleluia'

I am what my father thought, I am what my mother prayed for.

I am the labour of my forebears.

I am their hopes, their sicknesses, their healings.

I am their loves, their struggles, even their blasphemies and their sins.

I am their dawns and sunsets, their pitiless winters, their thrilling springtimes, their blazing summers, their tranquil autumns.

I am their births and their deaths.

Scientists at one time used to speak, perhaps they still do, about heredity and, I think, about chromosomes and genes. I am no expert in that field. But I am quite sure that in me, in my life and in my actions, there is present everything that those who existed before me ever did: all their struggles, their failures, their successes.

My freedom is tinged with the colour of their freedom, whatever it was like: more or less bright, more or less sombre, more or less filled with laughter.

When I make a choice, it is the latest choice, the most recent act of millions of people who form a single chain from far distant Adam right down to me.

In the cradle of my freedom are hatched the countless eggs of the lives preceding mine.

No one is an island. No freedom is isolated.

Christians bring the Church to birth

Each of us ought to realize this fact: each one of us is also the Church.

The Church belongs to the second Adam, the Christ. From his side dripping blood and water on the hill of the skull, God took the Church, while the eyes of the Crucified were closing for their three days' sleep.

When on the third day the New Adam awoke, he embraced the Church and made her fruitful with his Spirit.

From then on, the children of the Church are without number. They have overflowed the continents and the centuries.

From the beginning, they were conscious of being God's new prophets, called to populate the earth and to point the human race towards the 'last times'.

Their way of life was scandalous. Individualism was banned; their life was communal; private property, in many cases, disappeared; they proclaimed the News of Salvation with a joyful simplicity of witness, rejoicing in the persecutions they underwent for the sake of Jesus, and forgiving their enemies.

The first Christian group was the community in Jerusalem.

That group lived by the teaching of love. Everything was subordinated to love between fellow Christians and their love for everyone.

Listening to the Word, the use of money, the breaking of the Bread, the creation of ministers, visits between Christians and their going out in mission, everything, every decision had love as its paradigm.

It was in this way that Christians began to create the face of the Church. 'Made' by the Church they 'made' the Church.

'Our Mother the Church' was a phrase in use right from the earliest times. But with good reason Adriana Zarri also speaks of 'Our daughter the Church'. Indeed, Paul himself affirmed the same idea when he asserted that Christians 'build up' the Church.

8

The history of their continual giving birth to or building up of the Church shows us creativity and daring, along with all the sluggishness, the mediocrity and the sinfulness of the human race.

It is a history that is nicely poised on a knife-edge: with the temptation to look for other words than the Word of God, the temptation to listen to other teachers than to Jesus the Teacher, the temptation to assume power of whatever kind.

Rosmini, Dostoevsky and Kirkegaard have given lively descriptions of the thousand traps that the Church has had to avoid in order to survive to our day. Her clothes today are a little tattered, her face, to use the biblical image, is blackened and wrinkled. But she is still today possessed by Christ and by the Spirit. Still today, despite everything, she is guarding the truth.

More than that, she has an immense wealth handed down of prayer, meditation, contemplation, holiness. Millions of people have prayed, meditated, contemplated and reached holiness.

Their spiritual wisdom has penetrated the Word with a joyful labour in which were united head and heart, thought and actual experience.

They have loved knowledge and known love. 'In love they have experienced the truth', Paul would say.

Dwarfs on the shoulders of giants

And all that is present today. It is in us.

Granted, there is a certain amount of rubbish: the sins of the Church.

But above all else there is a crowd of wings fluttering in our hearts: the holiness of the Holy One, of God, and the holiness of Christians sanctified by mortification in their faith and their love.

We have the twenty centuries of the Church's life in our blood.

We are its heirs.

Not only in the sense that we possess an inheritance to administer, but in the sense that we are like we are, because our ancestors were like they were. Our faith has the stamp of their faith. Our hope has the strength of their hope. Our love has the intensity of their love. Our freedom is tinged with the colour of their freedom, whatever it was like: more or less bright, more or less sombre, more or less filled with laughter. We ought to know them in order to know ourselves better. We ought, as they used to say in the Middle Ages, to climb on their shoulders so as to see further.

We are dwarfs: they are giants.

For this very reason we need their shoulders.

By living the Word, they have scanned the horizon of God's plan for salvation. They can help us to see what they have seen.

Probably we shall see further than they did, thanks entirely to them. This is the miracle of the Christian tradition. By it we are re-united with the source, the Word, and we are nourished with the light and the witness of our predecessors.

Without the tradition we should be really and truly dwarfs. The tradition, if it is truly heard, gives rise to generations of believers whose spiritual stature is continually growing.

Scientists are studying why today children are usually taller than their parents. On the level of the Christian life that is not a problem. The parents feed their children with the struggles of their own faith.

Recapturing the experiences of the Church's youth

That is the reason for this book. We turn to the past, not to study archaeology, but to make progress. Not to waste time establishing how old the Church is, but to recapture the experiences of its youth.

We turn to the past, to the distant past, to the Church's infancy, putting forward a plan for meditation, during the course of a year, on the writings of the Fathers.

But, when does the age of the Fathers of the Church begin and end?

The apostles and the first disciples had the privilege of personal contact with Christ. These hearers of the incarnate Word deserve precedence over the rest. It is they who kept and handed on the words of the Word.

The age of the apostles and the other privileged witnesses ends with the death of John the Evangelist at the close of the first century. Immediately after that begins the so-called patristic period.

Some of the Fathers remembered John or Peter personally. They are witnesses who have a personal share in the transmission of the apostles' testimony. They did not see Jesus in the flesh. Yet they do not regret that fact – for two reasons.

The first is the consideration set out by Paul in the Second Letter to the Corinthians: it is of no importance to know Christ in the flesh. What matters is the certainty that, thanks to Christ and in Christ, we are new creatures, reconciled with the Father. What makes all the difference is the terrifying love of Christ which gives our hearts no rest.

The other reason is the evidence that the promise of the Lord is being fulfilled, the promise that the grace of the Spirit will be manifest to all peoples, that the Church born in Jerusalem will spread to all the nations.

From Abraham onwards, through many centuries, God has prepared the chosen people to receive the Messiah. Despite that, when the Messiah appeared, the greater part of the Jewish people rejected him.

In the Church of the Nations, that is to say, among the pagan peoples, the opposite happened. The soil that seemed to need more cultivation received the seed of the Gospel and brought forth the hundredfold.

Already, in the middle of raging persecutions, Christianity penetrated the worlds of Greece and Rome, of Syria and Egypt. The Christian message came into contact, or conflict, with popular thinking, with ancient cultures, with magical ideologies. The problem of the relation between reason and revelation appeared. And alongside serious attempts to translate faithfully the revealed Word into philosophical categories or contemporary expression, there occurred corruptions and ambiguities.

From that stemmed arguments about fundamental themes such as Christology and the doctrine of the Trinity. Leaflets were written, pamphlets published, treatises composed, councils called together.

Between the opposing views and contrasting styles of life it seemed utterly impossible to find a harmony that was not a distortion, or even some dialogue. Yet the Church succeeded. In the great councils of Nicaea, Ephesus and Chalcedon, the bishops managed to preserve the unity of the faith, and the possibility of the Gospel and culture illuminating one another.

The title that the bishops in these councils held is the same as today: Fathers.

The Fathers of the Church were, first of all, bishops, the defenders of orthodoxy. Associated with the bishops, under the same title are all the other Christian writers of the first centuries, the witnesses to the one faith. Often they are writing to attempt a solution to theoretical or practical problems worrying their contemporaries.

Often they are commenting on the Scriptures, a few with weighty erudition, the majority with a deeply prayerful spirit and a sharp sense of practicality.

This last characteristic stands out particularly in the homilies of pastors. The pastors often seem, more than teachers, to be the mouthpieces of a people reflecting on the Word and shaping their lives in its light. As servants of their community, right to their very finger tips, the pastors manifest the faith, a faith which seeks complete fidelity.

So we do not find in them a theology manufactured out of thin air at a desk, an ascetic and lifeless theology, or worse than that, affected and alienating. We find a theology of suffering, endured and tested by a whole people, an authentic popular theology, an authentic ecclesial theology.

Probably, it is specially through their attitude of service that the Fathers have come to enjoy such enormous prestige, their words even coming to acquire a similar authority to the words of Scripture. The fact is that every believer recognizes himself or herself in what they say.

The golden period of patristic literature runs from the fourth to the sixth century. By convention, the age of the Fathers of the West is reckoned to end in the year of the death of Isidore of Seville in 636, and the age of the Fathers of the East with the loss of John Damascene which occurred in 749.

We are God's workshop

Reading the patristic texts is not always easy. And sometimes, at first sight, it seems disagreeable.

The view of the physical world is rudimentary, simplistic. Some dissertations on the human faculties, on the five senses or on the structure of the body are deadly boring. Certain 'genealogical trees' of the virtues, certain 'slotting-in games' of the vices are even irritating. Certain notes on clothes and certain rules of behaviour are a nuisance or make us smile a little today.

We could go on, if instead of a simple introduction we were to write a treatise. But the remarks so far made are enough to prepare our reading of this 'Patristic Breviary'. They are sufficient, that is, to help peel the skin off the texts presented and to reach the kernel itself. It is a rich kernel full of nourishment. A description of its value would need a number of pages far in excess of those necessary for an analysis of the occasional unpleasantness of the skin, which, in any case, always depends on the culture and the mentality of each age.

One thing we have already said about its value: the search for the proper connection between reason and revelation, and the practical and popular character, in the highest sense of these terms, that a great part of patristic theology possesses.

Now for a moment let us pause to consider another aspect. The Fathers never dreamt of constructing a 'Summa' in which they included 'everything – and, indeed, more than everything' as has been written with a certain ironic humour.

To classify the visible and the invisible, created things and uncreated, so as to achieve a perfect combination, rather like a crossword, means to fossilize the Christian vision: to distort and then fossilize it, not realizing that in it both complexity and unity are possible. This is no thanks to any philosophical system but because complexity and unity are in the indefinable, indeed unfathomable mystery, of which we can catch a few tremulous glimpses.

While the Fathers made no claim to dismember and re-assemble the totality, this totality is the background against which they see each particular dimension of humanity, of the world, of God. Whatever subject they tackle, they invariably place it against the wider vision from which the subject draws its full significance.

This vision is the divine plan of universal salvation, which, if it is lost sight of, leaves only a philosophical position or some form of humanism left.

The Fathers look at this divine plan in its development through time. It is not so much a matter of a theoretical scheme worked out in the mind of God, as of a God who actually puts it into effect.

'My Father is working still, and I am working' (John 5:17). This sentence spoken by Jesus in St John's gospel opens out to the Fathers the prospect of an incredible dynamism: the universe and the heart of every human being, the infinitely great and the infinitely small, are a unique workshop in which the Father and the Word fashion a new creation. It is a creation of blessedness, glorious and glorifying, where God will be 'all in all', where he will no longer be called God, but 'God-with-us'.

The finest exposition of the Bible is our life

This God of the new creation is the God who is working today and who was at work in the original creation. And the Word into whose image we shall be transfigured is the same Word who presided over the birth of the universe and who unceasingly stirs up in us the birth of the 'interior person'.

This is the background against which the Fathers range any problem. At root it has the unity of the Pauline theology, which is reflected, for example, in what Augustine said: 'As Christ is the Word of God, every action of the Word is for us a word.'

History is an activity of humanity 'activated' by God. And God's activity is his manifold speaking: challenging and scandalizing, appealing and testing.

15

In this is revealed the action, or rather, the personality of God, in the life of each individual and in the life of the universe. And in this God ratifies the Scriptures for us, since they are the book in whose words the Word became incarnate to enter the world.

For the Fathers, the book of nature, the book of history and the book of the Bible are not three documents but one revelation. A single activity is unveiled thereby. The result of it depends on the readiness of the human heart to understand. 'The Word of God is in your heart. The Word digs in this soil so that the spring may gush out,' says Origen.

The reading of the Bible, therefore, is neither a work of erudition nor an excuse for pious transports of the soul. It is the reception of the Word that digs into us and saves us. As Jerome affirmed: 'You are reading? No. Your betrothed is talking to you. It is your betrothed, that is, Christ, who is united with you. He tears you away from the solitude of the desert and brings you into his home, saying to you, "Enter into the joy of your Lord." '

Certainly, the Fathers did not have at their disposal the critical and scientific armoury that we possess today, and which we have the right and the duty to use. But their spiritual reading of the Bible, a reading understood as a means to salvation, as an initiation into the Light, as an approach to communion with the Living One, teaches us to be on our guard against two dangers. On the one hand, to beware of the dryness of a certain biblical exegesis today which offers, or claims to offer, exactness at the expense of the living nature of the message. On the other, to beware of the subjectivism which merely comes down to a certain virtuosity in playing the strings of the human psyche, giving the believer the suggestion of 'doing the truth in love' without giving any love for the truth, still less the truth itself.

16

The Fathers think that the reading of the Bible is not only an intellectual activity; it is going to school with the Spirit. Gregory Thaumaturgus writes: 'The one who prophesies has as much need of grace as the one who listens. No one can understand the prophets if the prophetic Spirit does not give them the ability to receive their meaning. The Bible, in fact, says that only the one who shuts is able to open, and it is the divine Word who opens what was closed, making mysteries intelligible.'

The Fathers also think that the reading of the Bible should have an effect on daily life, into which the Scriptures must be translated. Gregory the Great, for instance, says at the beginning of his homilies on the Book of Job: 'Anyone who speaks of God ought to think about the need for some sort of thought that will make the hearers better.'

In the last analysis, for the Fathers the finest exposition of the Bible is the life of the believer.

Some things will pass away: some remain

An introduction only allows us to make brief comments. And their conclusion, in this case, can only be a wish. A threefold wish.

A wish that every reader may rediscover that the thought and the witness of the Fathers is in his or her blood, as they are in the blood of the whole Church.

A wish that every reader may be referred by the Fathers back to the Bible. They are simply the shoulders of giants onto which we can climb to gain a deeper perception of the Old and New Testaments.

A wish that every reader may learn from the Fathers that the Bible is the book of life and that all life is discipleship in the school of the Word.

In the end, human words, even those of exegesis, will pass away, as will all our struggles to be an 'Amen', that is to be believers who live the faith in unconditional obedience to the will of the Father.

In the end, all that will remain in the sight of the Father will be the Eternal Word, the glorified Christ, and the 'Amens' transfigured into 'Alleluias'.

ABBREVIATIONS

PG *Patrologia Cursus Completus*, Series Graeca, J-P Migne, Paris

PL *Patrologia Cursus Completus*, Series Latina, J-P Migne, Paris

SC *Sources Chrétiennes*, Les Éditions du Cerf, Paris

Harvey *S. Irenaei V libri adversus haereses*, W. Wigan Harvey, Cambridge 1887

Stählin *Geschichte der alterchristischen Literatur*, Otto Stählin, Munich 1926

Nota Bene:

The Fathers numbered the Psalms according to the Greek Septuagint, followed also by the Latin Vulgate, but this does not correspond to the numbering in the original Hebrew Bible and the translations that follow it. Text references in the footnotes of the present work follow the latter numbering which occasionally conflicts with the Fathers' own ascriptions.

WILLIAM OF SAINT THIERRY (died 1148) A native of Liège and student in the school of Reims. William entered the Benedictine abbey of St Nicaise in Reims and became abbot of the monastery of St Thierry outside the city. An admirer of the Cistercian monastic reform and the biographer of Saint Bernard, he resigned his office in 1135 to enter the newly founded Cistercian abbey of Signy. His advice on *lectio divina* was directed to novices at the Charterhouse of Mont-Dieu.

Lectio divina

At fixed hours time should be given to certain definite reading. Haphazard reading, constantly varied and lighted on by chance does not edify but makes the mind unstable. Taken into the memory lightly, it leaves it even more lightly. You should concentrate on certain authors and let your mind grow used to them....

Some part of your daily reading should be committed to memory every day, taken as it were into the stomach, to be more carefully digested and brought up again for frequent rumination—something in keeping with your vocation and helpful to concentration, something that will take hold of the mind and save it from distraction.

The reading should also stir your affections and give rise to prayer, which should interrupt your reading—an interruption which should not so much impede the reading as to restore to it a mind ever more purified for understanding.

For reading serves the purpose of the intention with which it is done. If a reader truly seeks God in the reading, everything he reads tends to promote that end, making the mind surrender in the course of the reading and bring all that is understood into Christ's service.

William of Saint Thierry
The Golden Epistle 1.120-124

January

*Life, the heart's
first love*

1st January

Seek to be like God

The main aim of all rational creatures, defined by
many philosophers as the greatest good, is to become
like God. Actually this is not so much a discovery
of the philosophers as something derived from Holy
Scripture. The book of Genesis illustrates it when it
describes the original creation of the human race in
the words: 'God said, "Let us make human beings in
our image and likeness." So God created human beings
in his own image, in the image of God he created them;
male and female he created them.'

Notice that it says: 'God created human beings in his
image' and says nothing about likeness.

This means that the human race received the dignity of
God's image at the beginning of its creation, whereas the
perfection of God's likeness is reserved for the end. Human
beings must achieve it by imitating God in his works. The
possibility of perfection is there right at the beginning by
virtue of the image. In the end, human beings will reach
perfect likeness by means of their works.

This idea has been put forward in a clearer form by the
Apostle John. 'Beloved, we are God's children now; it does
not yet appear what we shall be, but we know that when
he appears we shall be like him, for we shall see him as
he is.' [1 John 3:2] He refers to the end of all things and,
while simply admitting that the end is as yet unknown,
he expresses the hope that we shall be made like God by
virtue of our good deeds. Thanks to his intercession for
us, we shall proceed from likeness to unity, since in the
end 'God will be all in all'. [1 Cor. 15:28]

Origen
Principles, 3, 6 (PG11, 333)

2nd January

The Christian is Body, Soul and Holy Spirit

The human being, who conforms to the model of the Son, gives glory to God because of having been made by the Father by means of the Son and of the Holy Spirit.

Therefore, the whole person is like God and not just a part: the whole person, soul and body, receives the Spirit of the Father. This is the perfect human being.

When the Spirit is united with the soul and with the body, then we have the spiritual person, the perfect person, the human being in the image and likeness of God.

If, on the contrary, the soul does not have the Spirit, we would have a carnal and imperfect being. Such a person in having been created would be in the image of God, but would have no likeness to him.

Likeness to God comes only from the Spirit.

Irenaeus
Against Heresies, 5, 6 (Harvey II, p.333)

3rd January

God does not Need us, But He Longs to Shower us with Gifts

God created Adam in the beginning, not because he needs the human race, but so that he might have a recipient of his generosity.

Moreover, God commanded us to follow Christ, not because he has any need of our service, but because he wants to give us salvation. To follow the saviour is to share in salvation, just as to follow the light is to gain the light.

People who are in the light do not themselves provide the light but are illuminated and made bright by it; they do not contribute anything to it but, by being illuminated, they receive the benefit of the light.

Similarly, to serve God does not mean giving him any gift, nor has God any need of our service. On the contrary, it is he who gives to those who serve him life, immortality and eternal glory. He rewards those who serve him without deriving any benefit himself from their service: he is rich, he is perfect, he has no needs.

God requests human obedience so that his love and his pity may have an opportunity of doing good to those who serve him diligently. The less God has need of anything, the more human beings need to be united with him. Consequently, a human being's true glory is to persevere in the service of God.

Irenaeus
Against Heresies, 4, 25 (Harvey II, p.184)

4th January

Growing up in the Word

'Could not God make people perfect right at the beginning?' someone may ask.

Take the example of a very small child. The mother can give her baby grown-up food, but the baby is still unable to take adult nourishment. Similarly, God could have given humanity perfection right at the beginning, but humanity could not have received it because it was only a child.

For that reason Our Lord, who sums up all things in himself, when he came on earth in these last days, came not in the full glory which he could have done, but in a form we could see. Certainly, he could have come in his imperishable glory, but we should not have been able to bear the greatness of his majesty.

Therefore, like giving milk to infants, the perfect Bread of the Father revealed himself to us on earth in human form, so that we might be nourished by his Word like babes at the breast and so by degrees become strong enough to digest the whole Word of God.

Irenaeus
Against Heresies, 4, 62 (Harvey, p.292)

5th January

Humanity as Witness to the Unknown

When we consider how human beings are made, we are filled with wonder at the wisdom of the Creator that is revealed in us.

Suffice it to observe the different functions of the senses which all stem from one centre, the brain, and report back to it all sorts of perceptions: sight, smell, taste, touch . . . , and also to observe the other organs of the body both internal and external; and the memory, that recalls numerous disparate elements without confusing or altering them; and the number of thoughts which do not cancel each other out but reappear at the right moment.

We cannot refrain from exclaiming with the Psalmist: 'Such knowledge is too wonderful for me, O Lord; it is high, I cannot attain it.' [Ps. 139:6]

In fact, no one will ever succeed in explaining completely the harmony that is displayed in our bodies or the subtlety that is apparent in our souls. Innumerable thinkers have written on this point. Even so, what has been said is but a small part of what remains to be said, for human reason cannot attain to divine wisdom.

So this is the Psalmist's attitude: he praises God for what he understands but confesses himself overwhelmed by it; it is not possible for him to encompass all the marvels which are to be seen in humanity.

Such an admission is in itself an appropriate hymn of praise.

Theodoret
The Cure of Pagan Diseases, 5, 81 (SC57, p.252)

6th January

The Great Little King

Just as a craftsman in ordinary life makes a thing in a shape suitable for its intended use, so the Master Craftsman has fashioned our nature to be a fitting instrument for the exercise of sovereignty over the universe, by providing it with spiritual gifts and a bodily shape fit for a king.

The soul's exalted and royal nature is shown to be far removed from submissiveness by the fact that it is free and independent and acknowledges no master: it has been provided with its own unchallenged power of choice. What is more characteristic of a king than this? Moreover the fact that it has been made as a copy of the Nature that governs the universe shows that it was created in the first place with the nature of a king.

Those who paint portraits of rulers in ordinary life copy the details of their form and underline their kingly importance by dressing them in purple so that the portrait is recognized as that of a king by its composition. In the same way, human nature by virtue of its likeness to the King of All, who created it to rule others, is seen to be a living portrait of him: the portrait has a part in the title and importance of its Maker.

It is not dressed up in purple nor does it show its importance by a sceptre or a crown – the Original does not have these either – but it is clothed in virtue, which is in truth the most royal of all garments, instead of a purple robe. It relies on the blessedness of immortality instead of a sceptre. In place of a kingly crown it is adorned with the garland of righteousness.

Thus the acoutrements of kingship show it to be

in all respects an accurate copy of the form of the Original.

Gregory of Nyssa
The Creation of Man, 4 (PG44, 136)

7th January

Mystery within Us

The Apostle Paul says: 'Who has known the mind of the Lord?' [Rom. 11:34]

To this I would add, 'Who knows his own mind?'

Let those who pretend that God's nature is within their comprehension explain their own nature. Do they understand the functioning of their own mind? It has many parts and many components. How does it comprehend knowledge? How are its different elements brought together? The mind is a single entity, not a compound. How is it divided among the various senses? How does this diversity in unity arise? How unity in diversity?

I know the solution to this problem. I have recourse to the pronouncement of God when he said: 'Let us make human beings in our image and likeness.'

As long as a copy in no respect departs from the intentions of the original, it is a proper copy. Insofar as it falls short of likeness to the original, it is not, to that extent, a copy. Therefore, since one of the qualities reckoned to belong to the divine nature is its incomprehensibility, there is no escape from the conclusion that in this respect the copy must have the same quality as the original.

If the nature of the copy was thought to be intelligible while the original was beyond comprehension, when you saw the two together you would discover that a mistake had been made. Since the nature of our intellect, like that of its Creator, is beyond understanding, its own incomprehensibility gives an accurate picture of the original. It remains a mystery.

Gregory of Nyssa
The Creation of Man, 11 (PG44, 153)

8th January

The Two Faces of the Human Race

What is the origin of the passions? We have no right to blame our human nature for their origin, because it was formed in God's likeness.

The animals came into this world before we did and we have inherited some of their qualities. This is the spring from which our emotions are derived. Those qualities which secure self-preservation in animals have been transferred into human life and become passions.

For instance, a fighting spirit keeps some animals alive; the pleasure of sex produces fertility; cowardice saves the timid animal; fear keeps the vulnerable animal safe from stronger predators; gluttony preserves the obese. Animals are unhappy when they fail to obtain any pleasure they are seeking. These qualities have found their way into the human condition from the animal creation.

But the likeness of God is not revealed by a fighting spirit in the human race. The supreme nature is not characterized by the pleasure of procreation, or by cowardice, greed, or dislike of inferiority. These passions are very far from being marks of divinity.

So let me illustrate humanity's dual nature by an

analogy. A creative artist may mould two different faces on one sculptured head to arrest the spectator's attention. Human nature is like that. It has a double likeness. In the drive of the passions it reproduces the signs of the animal creation, but in the soul it has the features of the divine beauty.

Gregory of Nyssa
The Creation of Man, 18 (PG44, 192)

9th January

Better not to be Born?

Homer says that humanity is weak and worried. Theognis, the Sicilian, cries out: 'The best fate for a person would be not to be born, not to see the rays of the sun.'

Euripides is fully in agreement with them: when someone is born, everyone ought to join together in weeping for him. How much misery he has come to suffer! On the other hand, the one who dies is freed from care. We ought to accompany him to the grave with songs of joy and of congratulation!

Herodotus recalls that the Athenian Solon asserted: 'The life of human beings is all a game of chance.'

Pythagoras and Plato maintain that there exists a population of souls without bodies. Some souls, they say, which have fallen into sin in some way, are sent for punishment into bodies. That is why Plato in his *Cratilus* says that 'soma' is 'sema', that is, the body is a tomb in which the soul must remain buried for a certain period.

However, Plato goes on to say the opposite in the third book of his *Republic*: there he maintains that we need to take care of the body so that it may be in harmony with the soul.

So it is clear that the philosophers contradict themselves. We, on the other hand, can demonstrate the strength of the teachings given by the Prophets and the Apostles.

Theodoret
The Cure of Pagan Diseases, 5, 11 (SC57, 229)

10th January

Free Will, not Fate

We are directed by free will and not, as some say, subjected to the compulsion of inescapable fate.

That is why God has given us the promise of his kingdom but also threatened us with punishment. He would not have done that to people in the toils of necessity. He would not have laid down laws, he would not have given us exhortations if we had been prisoners of destiny.

We are free and the masters of our fate. Just because we can grow evil from lack of effort or virtuous by striving, he uses the medicine of the fear of punishment to correct our course and the attraction of the hope of heaven to steer us towards wisdom.

Not only from this argument but from the way we normally behave, it is clear that our lives are not directed by fate.

For if fate were the cause of our actions rather than our free will, what justification have you for whipping the slave who is a thief? Why, if your wife has committed adultery, do you take her to court? When you do stupid things, why are you ashamed? Why are you intolerant of accusations and regard it as an insult if anyone calls you an adulterer or a fornicator or a drunkard or suchlike?

The myth of a compelling destiny is nonsense. Our lives are subject to no unavoidable fate. Everything, as I have argued, points to the beauty of free will.

John Chrysostom
Homily on Divine Love, 3 (PG56, 282)

11th January

Life is a Dream with Many Changes of Scene

I am not telling a lie: human life is a dream.

In our dreams we look without seeing, we listen without hearing, we taste and touch without tasting or touching, we speak without saying anything, we walk without moving. We seem to be moving normally even though we stay still and to be making our habitual gestures even though we are not. The mind invents realities that are entirely imaginary.

When we are awake, our thoughts are like these dreams. They come and go. They meet and part. They fly away before we can catch them.

Nor is our body any different from a dream. Is not its beauty likely to go rotten before it is ripe? Is not its health continually being threatened with illness? How little it takes to destroy its strength! How easily its senses deteriorate!

Our careers are no less precarious. Often a single day is enough to scatter a great work to the winds. Many people who are held in respect and honour with a sudden change of events fall into disgrace. The greatest kingdoms on earth have been destroyed in a short time.

35

If we have so many changes of scene in life, and so many dark experiences, we ought to learn to distinguish what is virtuous from what is base, what is good from what is bad, what is just from what is unjust.

I give you an example of what I mean. Do you possess a lot of money? If so, give it away because the beauty of riches consists not in money-boxes but in helping the poor. Are you short of money? Be careful not to envy the rich. And don't despair, because human affairs are always changing into their opposites.

Philo of Alexandria
cf. C. Cajetanus, Thesaurus Patrum VII, pp.4155ff.

12th January

The Search for Long Life

Augustine said:

'Wicked persons are allowed to go on living so that they may be reformed, or so that by means of their wickedness the virtuous may be put to the test.'

Jerome said:

'The shortness of this life is the penalty for people's sins. With all your might, hate what the world loves. Be dead to the world and let the world be dead to you. During your life despise what you cannot possess after your death.'

Isidore said:

'Only in this life can you do good. What is awaiting you in the future life is not the opportunity of doing good but the reward of having done it.

'Anyone who reflects on his own life in the light of its end, rather than the passing of the days, perceives how wretched and short it is.

'If you are seeking long life, you ought to be seeking that life through which you come close to Christ, that is, eternal life. That life is real life: this life is only mortal life.

'Ignorance of the end of life causes the individual to die at the moment he was least expecting it. So let all hasten to become free from their own wickedness. As long as we are alive Satan sets us on fire with desire for what is wrong: no sooner are we dead than he hurls us into the torments of hell.

'In this world nothing is long lived, nothing lasts long, everything comes to an end quickly.'

Cyprian said:

'Time on this earth means nothing to the person who is waiting for eternity.'

Defensor Grammaticus
Book of Sparkling Wisdom, 80 (SC86, pp.301ff.)

13th January

Has the Lord Abandoned us after Telling us to Set Sail?

In all his dealings with us the Lord teaches us how to live on this earth.

There is not a person in this world who is not a voyager, even if not all are anxious to return to the homeland.

In the course of this voyage the waves and the storms make us seasick. But at least we are in the ship. Outside the ship death would be inevitable. When one is swimming among the breakers, however energetic one's arms are, sooner or later one is defeated by the size of the ocean and allows oneself to drown. To complete the crossing, therefore, it is essential to remain in the ship, to be supported by its planks.

The plank that supports our weakness is the cross of Our Lord. He keeps us safe from the world that threatens to drown us. We suffer because we are tossed about by the waves, but the Lord himself supports us.

The Gospel tells us that Jesus left the crowd and went up a mountain to pray. That high mountain is a symbol of heaven. The head of this body which is the Church takes his place upon high in order that all his members may follow him. With that intention he prays – he intercedes on our behalf.

Insofar as the ship is carrying his disciples, it may be called the Church. The storm of temptations assail it, the contrary winds disturb it: that is, the devil opposes the Church and tries to stop it reaching its haven.

But we have a powerful intercessor. The Lord who has told us to set sail and to voyage towards our homeland surely will not allow his Church not to reach its haven.

Augustine
Sermons 75, 2-4 (PL38, 475 6)

14th January

Life's Journey

We read in the Book of Psalms: 'Blessed is the one who walks not in the counsel of the wicked, nor follows in the way of sinners.'

Life has been called a 'way' because everything that has been created is on the way to its end.

When people are on a sea voyage, they can sleep while they are being transported without any effort of their own to their port of call. The ship brings them closer to their goal without their even knowing it. So we can be transported nearer to the end of our life without our noticing it, as time flows by unceasingly. Time passes while you are asleep. While you are awake time passes although you may not notice.

All of us have a race to run towards our appointed end. So we are all 'on the way'.

This is how you should think of the 'way'. You are a traveller in this life. Everything goes past you and is left behind. You notice a flower on the way, or some grass, or a stream, or something worth looking at. You enjoy it for a moment, then pass on. Maybe you come on stones or rocks or crags or cliffs or fences, or perhaps you meet wild beasts or reptiles or thorn bushes or some other obstacles. You suffer briefly then escape. That is what life is like.

Pleasures do not last but pain is not permanent either.

The 'way' does not belong to you nor is the present under your control. But as step succeeds step, enjoy each moment as it comes and then continue on your 'way'.

Basil the Great
Commentary on Psalm 1, 4 (PG29, 220)

15th January

Before the Ship Sinks

An illness that has become chronic, like a habit of wrong-doing that has become ingrained is very hard to heal. If after that, as very often happens, the habit turns into second nature, a cure is out of the question.

So the ideal would be to have no contact with evil. But there is another possibility: to distance yourself from evil, to run away from it as if from a poisonous snake, once you have experienced it.

I have known some unfortunate people who in their youth let themselves slide into evil habits which have held them enslaved all their lives. Like pigs wallowing continually in the mire and becoming increasingly filthy, such sinners as these multiply their shame every day with fresh sins.

So, blessed is the one who has never thought of evil. However, if through his wiles the suggestions of the Enemy have found a foothold in your heart, do not remain inactive in the toils of sin.

Be careful not to be utterly overcome by it. If the sin is already weighing you down, if the dust of riches has already settled on you, if your soul has been dragged right down by attachment to material things, then before you fall into utter ruin get rid of the heavy burden. Before the ship sinks, follow the example of sailors and cast overboard the possessions you have accumulated overmuch.

Basil the Great
Commentary on Psalm 1, 6 (PG29, 224ff.)

16th January

Is it Possible not to be Afraid of Death?

What makes up this life that we love so much? Wishes and fears, hopes and disappointments, sufferings and sadness, genuine sorrows and counterfeit joys, prayers and supplications, anxieties and temptations. What sort of a life is that? And yet we love it.

And the other life? What makes up eternal life? The words of the Psalmist suffice to describe it: 'I will sing praises to my God while I have my being.' [Ps. 146:2]

Just because they loved the other life, the martyrs endured death, they endured and despised it.

The present life is ugly and painful, and yet it is so dear to us that without the help of the One who commanded them to despise it, even the martyrs would not have been strong enough to despise it for love of truth and eternal life. Anyone who despises death for the love of God, cannot do it without God's help.

You, no doubt, despise death, you love and long for eternal life. But 'Happy is he whose help is the God of Jacob.' [Ps. 146:5] Take away that help and you will be no better than a deserter.

Augustine
Serm. Morin, 31, (Miscellanea Agostiniana 560-2)

17th January

The Soul's Dizziness

There are two different roads, one broad and easy, the other hard and narrow. And there are two guides vying with each other to attract the traveller's attention.

Now that we are grown to years of discretion we see that life is an amalgam of vice and virtue. The soul by casting its gaze first on one and then on the other can calculate the consequences of each.

The life of the sinner presents all the pleasures of the present moment; the life of the righteous points to future benefits.

The easy undisciplined way of life leads to pleasure to be enjoyed now, not later; the way of salvation is hard in the present, but promises a beautiful future.

The soul is confused and dithers in its calculations. It prefers pleasure when it is looking at the present; it chooses virtue when its eye is on eternity.

Basil the Great
Commentary on Psalm 1, 5 (PG29, 221ff.)

18th January

Be Hard on your Heart

Avoid flattery. Flattery confirms sinners in their evil desires by giving them praise. Avoid flatterers. Flatterers' tongues rivet souls to their sins.

Not only do we normally steer clear of anyone who is in a position to reprimand us, we look for someone to heap praises on us. Whereas we ought to pray with the Psalmist: 'Let a good person strike or rebuke me in kindness.'[Ps. 141:5] Look for reproof, rather than praise. If your friend is good and kind, when he sees you are set to commit a sin, he will correct you in his kindness.

It is the Lord who deigns to speak through the one who corrects his brother or sister. He speaks so that the brother or sister who is reproved may not be lost.

The one who reprimands another does not hate. Indeed, he reprimands precisely because he does not hate. What then is the result? Listen to Scripture: 'Reprove a wise person and he will love you.' [Prov. 9:8]

Do not therefore covet praise which can make you a sinner; you will only collect contempt in the end if you do. It is better to love a good person who reproves you in his kindness.

Augustine
On Psalm 140, 13 (PL37, 1 815)

19th January

Only I can do Evil to Myself

Was it an altogether evil fate that befell Abel? He was felled by the hand of his brother and underwent a premature and violent death. Yet he benefited from it; he received his due reward.

Was it an altogether evil fate that befell Jacob, who was persecuted by his brother and went wandering to distant lands and even fell into slavery?

Was it an altogether evil fate that befell Joseph? He too was an exile without a home, a prisoner and a slave, exposed to the gravest dangers, reckoned a stranger by his own family, the victim of slanders.

Was it an altogether evil fate that befell Moses who was stoned by an enormous crowd, and that on account of the good he had done them?

Was it an altogether evil fate that befell Job, who was attacked by the devil with a thousand stratagems?

And the three young men? And Daniel robbed of his liberty and face to face with death?

Was it an altogether evil fate that befell Elijah, who was reduced to extreme poverty, always on the run, compelled to live in the desert?

And was it an altogether evil fate that befell David, who had to endure harsh treatment at the hands of Saul and later at the hands of his own son? His virtues stood out more clearly in the midst of such miseries than if his life had been passed peacefully.

And was the fate of the martyrs an altogether evil one? They were tormented by a thousand trials, but is it not perhaps because of this that their light shines so brightly?

John Chrysostom
On Providence, 16 (SC79, p.221)

20th January

Tears, not Sorrows

When you hear me speak of tears, you need not think of sorrow. The tears of which I am speaking bring more joy than all the laughter of the world can gain for you.

Do you doubt my words? Then listen to St Luke who tells us how the apostles, after being beaten with rods by order of the Sanhedrin, were filled with joy. [Acts 5:41]

Clearly that joy was not the effect of the rods. They cause pain, not pleasure. What rods cannot do, however, faith in Christ can. Faith triumphs over the nature of events. The beatings endured for Christ were springs of joy. Is it surprising, then, if the same effect is produced by tears shed for the selfsame Lord?

That is the reason why Jesus says on the one hand that the way is narrow, but on the other hand his yoke is sweet. [Matt. 7:14; 11:30]

John Chrysostom
On Virginity 54, 1ff. (SC125, p.331)

21st January

It Depends How You Use It

There are good things, bad things and things that are indifferent. Some of the things that are indifferent people consider to be good or bad while in reality they are neither. I will give you an example, to explain my meaning more clearly.

Poverty is in general thought to be an evil. Not so: if someone who is poor practises watchfulness and wisdom, poverty itself can completely overcome evil.

On the other hand, wealth is regarded as a good thing by most people. But that is not entirely true: it depends how you use it. If wealth were a good thing in itself and on its own account, then everyone who possesses it ought to be good. Yet not all rich people are virtuous, only those who manage their money in a responsible way. Therefore wealth is not a good thing in itself, it is only an instrument for doing good.

So with regard to indifferent things: they are either good or bad according to the use that is made of them.

John Chrysostom
Commentary on Isaiah, 3ff. (PG56, 146)

22nd January

Joy an Uneasy Bedfellow

Augustine said:

'The world's joy is vanity. We long for it to come, but when it has come we fail to hold on to it. Better the sorrow of the one who suffers unjustly than the joy of the one who acts unjustly.'

Jerome says:

'The wise person curbs the smile on his face by the gravity of his behaviour.

'If fortune smiles on you do not brag about it; and if misfortune happens to you do not be discouraged.'

Gregory said:

'If some joy befalls you in this present life, you need to accept it in such a way as never to forget the judgment to come.'

Basil said:

'Do not give way to vulgar laughter. Joy is more appropriately registered by a simple smile.

'Anyone who gives himself up to coarse laughter and immoderate jests does not leave himself room for penitence.'

Defensor Grammaticus
Book of Sparkling Wisdom, 55 (SC86, pp.142ff.)

23rd January

God's Anger is Worst when He does not Show It

Augustine said:

'Anyone who has not earned a flogging in this life will undergo torment in hell. But if we humbly receive whatever punishment God may give us, with a grateful heart, we obtain forgiveness for our sins and everlasting happiness.'

Jerome said:

'Whoever has received his share of troubles in this life, after death will not have to suffer the tribulations he has suffered already.

'God's anger is worst when God does not show he

is angry: the doctor stops treating you because he has given up hope of curing you.'

Isidore said:

'Earthly punishments contribute to our salvation: so that the righteous should be happy to suffer, and the evil-doer unhappy in prosperity.

'Punishment only wipes out our guilt if it reforms our way of life.'

Defensor Grammaticus
The Book of Sparkling Wisdom, 50 (SC86, pp.114ff.)

24th January

Bitter Roots Bear Sweet Fruits

In all our actions and in all our circumstances we ought to hold submission to God before our eyes.

When that is rooted in the soul, not only comfort, honours and rank, but also slanders, injuries, tortures, in fact everything, will produce in us fruits of joy.

The roots of a tree are bitter but the fruit is sweet. In the same way afflictions, when they are in accordance with God's will, will provide us with immense joy. Those who have often prayed and shed tears of suffering know what joy they have afterwards reaped. They feel their conscience purified, they are buoyed up with relief and the strength of hope.

It is not from external circumstances but from internal attitudes that sorrows and joys are born. As far as the soul is concerned, everything depends on the will.

So you want peace of heart? Then do not seek health, nor wealth, nor fame, nor power, nor luxury. Seek wisdom in God's sight, stick to the virtues, and nothing will be able to make you sad.

What do I mean, make you sad? That which makes the rest of the human race sad, will make your joy greater.

John Chrysostom
To the People of Antioch, 18, 3ff. (PG49, 185)

25th January

Martyrdom throughout the Length of Days

Martyrdom means bearing witness to God. Every soul that seeks in pureness of heart to know God and obeys the commandments of God is a martyr, bearing witness by life or by words.

In fact even if it is not a matter of shedding blood, the soul is pouring out its faith because it is by faith that the soul will be separated from the body before a person dies.

That is why, in the Gospel, the Lord praises the person 'who has left house or brothers or sisters or mother or father or children or lands for my sake and for the Gospel.' That person is blessed because he too is going to meet martyrdom simply by living in a way that is different from the crowd, because he is following the rule of the Gospel for love of his Lord.

The truly righteous are set apart from the world because they produce the fruits of grace in their actions. They do this because they have been able to become a friend of God and to obtain a place at the right hand of the Father, as the Apostles have done.

Clement of Alexandria
Miscellaneous Studies, 4, 4, 15 (Stählin II, p.255)

26th January

Salvation Depends on Mutual Help

We cannot be saved by seeking just our own individual salvation; we need to look first to the good of others.

In warfare, the soldier who takes to flight to save his own skin brings disaster on himself as well as on the others, whereas the good soldier who takes up arms on behalf of his comrades saves his own life along with theirs.

Our life is a warfare, the bitterest of battles. So in loyalty to our King let us draw up the lines of battle ready for blood and slaughter, with our eyes on the salvation of all, encouraging the stalwarts and stirring up the laggards.

Many of our brothers and sisters have fallen in this battle, wounded and covered with blood, with no one to care for them. There is no one to look after them, no layman, no priest, no comrade, no friend, no brother, because we are all of us seeking our own individual salvation, and thereby spoiling our chance of attaining it.

True freedom and glory come from not being concerned with ourselves. We are weak and vulnerable to the devil's attacks because we are not doing this. We are not standing shoulder to shoulder in the fight. We are not fortified with the love of God. We are not using the shield of brotherly love. On the contrary, we are seeking friends and comrades from very different motives: either because of family ties, or from habit, or because we live nearby, instead of the search for sanctity.

All our friendships ought to be cemented with this one bond, the desire to help one another.

John Chrysostom
On the Gospel of St Matthew, 59, 5 (PG58, 581)

27th January

Childishness or the Spirit of Childhood?

Jesus says: 'Let the children come to me, and do not hinder them; for to such belongs the kingdom of God.' [Luke 18:16]

If that is how things are, growing up means loss. Why should I desire to grow up if adulthood deprives me of the right to the kingdom? Can you explain why God should have given us physical development which favours vice, not virtue? And for what reason did the Lord not turn to children but to grown men when he was choosing his Apostles? In brief, why does he say that children are fit to enter the kingdom?

Someone will suggest this reason: because children do not bear malice, they do not know how to swindle their neighbour, they are not vindictive, they do not desire wealth, they do not covet honours.

Maybe: but virtue is not founded on ignorance. Still less is self-control praiseworthy if it is only due to impotence.

Therefore the Lord is not offering us childhood as our example but the goodness that imitates the simplicity of childhood. He does not put before us inability to sin – which would not be virtue – but the will not to sin, a steady will not to sin, for which we ought to take childhood as our model.

For the rest, the Lord himself says: 'Unless you turn and become like children, you will never enter the kingdom of heaven.' [Matt. 18:3]

Ambrose
On the Gospel of St Luke, 8, 57ff. (PL15, 1782)

28th January

The Conception and Birth of our Spiritual Being

The foetus already has all the parts of its body, but it cannot use them inside its mother's womb. When it is born into the world, the body develops in its senses and parts and acquires the ability to use them. Physically, it is in the world that the human being comes to perfection.

The same is true for our spiritual being. It begins as a foetus. Then it leaves the womb and bit by bit it develops until it comes 'to mature manhood, measured by the stature of the fullness of Christ.' [Eph. 4:13]

The foetus is formed from the seed and the ovum; our spiritual being is conceived in the waters of Baptism and thanks to the fire of the Spirit.

The foetus in the realm of nature passes from non-being to being; the foetus in the spiritual realm passes from not having divine sonship or daughterhood to the condition of being a child of God.

The foetus in the realm of nature develops slowly; our spiritual being, once it has been conceived as a child of God, grows in the world as if in the womb, according to the measure of justice in this world.

Finally, the foetus in the realm of nature leaves its mother and is born into the world; the foetus in the spiritual realm, when it has fulfilled all justice according to the law of the world, leaves the world to be born again.

It enters then into another world, which is the world of Christ's justice.

Philoxenus of Mabbug
Homily 9, 26off. (SC44, pp.247ff.)

29th January

God makes Good Loans, But do We make Good Investments?

According to the parable of the Lord [Luke 19:12-27], the first of ten servants told his master when he returned from a long journey, 'Lord, your pound has made ten pounds more.' That servant's single pound bore interest tenfold. A second servant's pound bore fivefold. A third servant's pound bore no interest at all.

'Why did you not put my money into the bank?' The Lord asks for the profit on his own money, not ours. The third servant explains that he kept it hidden in the ground. That means that he has wasted his intellect on earthly pleasures and buried his reason, which was given him in the image and likeness of God, in the pit of lasciviousness.

The parable says nothing about the other seven servants. They are debtors who squandered the money they received.

Matthew also makes a similar comparison, observing that the rich man who does not distribute his goods to the poor is seriously at fault. But equally at fault is anyone who could distribute the truth but keeps it to himself.

Ambrose
On the Gospel of St Luke, 8, 91 (PL15, 1792)

30th January

When the Play is Over

Think of actors: they wear masks, they dress up. One looks like a philosopher while not being one; another seems to be a king but is no king; another appears to be a doctor and has not the faintest idea how to cure the sick; another pretends to be a slave despite being free; still another plays the part of a teacher yet does not even know how to write.

They do not appear as they are, they appear to be something else. The philosopher is a philosopher only because of his abundant but false wig, the soldier is a soldier just because he sports a military uniform. These disguises help to create an illusion, to hide the reality.

The world is a theatre too. The human condition, richness, poverty, power, subjection are merely the pretences of actors.

But when the day is done and the night falls (which, however, we ought to call day: it is night for sinners and day for the just), when the play is over, when we all find ourselves confronted with our own actions and not with our riches or dignity or the honours we have had or the power we have wielded, when we are asked to give an account of our lives and our works of virtue, ignoring both the feats of our opulence and the humility of our need, when we are asked: 'Show me your deeds!', then the disguises will fall and we shall see who is truly rich and who is truly poor.

John Chrysostom
Homily on Lazarus, 6, 5 (PG48, 1034)

31st January

Hope Lessens the Labour

The Psalter begins with the words: 'Happy is the one who does not take the counsel of the wicked for a guide.'

These words immediately show us our final end, which is happiness. The hope of future goods, therefore, can help us to accept willingly the sufferings of life.

For anyone travelling along an impassable road, the hope of a comfortable hotel is a relief. Merchants have to face many risks, and they find courage in the thought of making a profit. Farmers find the hope of the harvest cheers up their labours.

In the same way the great Master, who is Truth leading the life of every human being to a good end, first of all shows us our reward, so that our gaze may go beyond the tribulations of the present and our spirit hurry towards the eternal joys.

'Happy is the one who does not take the counsel of the wicked for a guide.' Yes, happy because he will enjoy God who is happiness *par excellence*.

God in fact is perfectly good. He is the One towards whom all things tend. His nature is unchangeable, supreme dignity, superabundant love, an inexhaustible treasure.

Basil the Great
Commentary on Psalm 1, 3 (PG29, 213)

February

*My body is where
God plans to meet me*

1st February

From Adam and Adam's Rib Came a Perfect Human Being

Adam was formed from clay by the hands of God, so he became a perfect human being, endowed with a living soul, not by carnal intercourse and not by seed. In the same way the Word also became human without carnal intercourse and without seed.

In the Old Testament we read that God made a deep sleep fall upon Adam; then he took one of his ribs and formed a woman from it. In consequence, God the Word took a body with a soul from the actual rib of Adam, that is, from the woman, and built it into a perfect human being. In this way he became truly the child of Adam. In making himself a human being, becoming like us in everything except sin, the Word joined the human family.

On the other hand, he was at the same time human and God, so that his soul and body were holy, and more than holy. He was, he is, and he always will be God the Holy. The Virgin too is holy, without spot, just as the rib taken from Adam was holy.

As regards the rest of the human race they are, according to the flesh, really part of the same family; they are their brothers and sisters. Nevertheless, because of their nature they remain earthly and do not suddenly become holy.

But if God has himself been made a human being and has deigned to be called the brother of the human race, we ought to be born again, in water by the grace of the Holy Spirit.

Simeon the New Theologian
Theological and Ethical Treatises, 13, 130ff.
(SC129, p.411)

2nd February

The Body was Made by One who Knows What He is Doing

Look within yourself. From your own nature you can learn something of your Maker.

There is nothing to be ashamed of in your body. If you are in control of its members, they are not in the slightest evil. Adam and Eve in paradise were naked at first and their bodies did not appear shameful or disgusting. Our limbs do not cause sin, but the wrong use of them does. The Creator of our bodies knew what he was doing.

Who makes the secret parts of the mother's womb able to bear children? Who gives life to the lifeless fruit of conception? Who shapes the sinews and bones, who covers all with flesh and skin? When the baby comes to the light, who gives the milk that it can suck? How does the newborn infant grow to become a child, then an adolescent, then an adult, and then in the end an old person?

Who imposes on the heart the regularity of its beat? Who protects so skilfully our eyes with their eyelashes? Who makes our whole bodies able to be kept alive by our breathing?

Look at your Maker. Admire your wise Creator. The greatness and the beauty of his creatures will help you to contemplate him.

Cyril of Jerusalem
Catecheses, 9, 15 (PG33, 653)

3rd February

A Talented Musician Needs an Exceptional Instrument

You could say that the body has been constructed like a musical instrument.

Musicians often cannot give adequate proof of their talent because the instrument they are playing is unfit for use: it is either spoilt with age, or damaged by being dropped, or completely ruined through damp or rust. If you put it in the hands of an artist of the first rank, such an instrument does not respond to his skill.

The same thing happens with the spirit. It functions through the body to display its skill in a spiritual way. But the spirit cannot exercise its normal activity except with an instrument which conforms to the order of nature.

Our spirit is fashioned in the image of the perfect Good. As long as it remains with the good, it keeps its likeness to the Model. When it strays from the good, it loses its original beauty.

Therefore, just as the spirit takes its proper perfection from its likeness to the beauty of the universal Model, so the body, ruled by the spirit, finds its proper embellishment in the beauty of the spirit.

Gregory of Nyssa
The Creation of Man, 12 (PG44, 161)

4th February

Beyond Medical Knowledge

Even without anyone to instruct us we are quite able, on the basis of what we see, live and feel, to understand how our body is formed. Its own nature teaches us.

It may be useful, nonetheless, to consult experts to have a clearer idea. The science of anatomy has allowed us to know the positions of the individual parts of the human body. Other sciences help us to grasp their uses.

In a detailed study we must examine the organs as having three kinds of function: life, enjoyment and conservation.

The organs without which it is impossible to have life are three: the brain, the heart, the liver.

Then there are the gifts that nature gives to the human being to make life pleasant: the senses. The lack, which is not infrequent, of one or other of them does not result in death, but without being able to use them life is less enjoyable.

Finally, we should recall those organs which have no purpose in themselves but are useful to conserve life, for example, the stomach and the lungs.

The true and perfect life, however, is that of the soul. In the soul is found the beauty of the likeness of God, who created humanity with the words: 'Let us make human beings in our own image, after our own likeness.'

Gregory of Nyssa
The Creation of Man, 30 (PG44, 240)

5th February

To Despise the Body is Blasphemy

The Creator of the human body's members was not ashamed to assume the flesh they are made from. As God himself asserts:

'Before I formed you in the womb I chose you as my prophet, before you were born I consecrated you.' [Jer. 1:5]

It is God who fashions every infant in the womb. As Job says:

'Like clay you have moulded me, like milk you have poured me out, like cheese you have curdled me. You have clothed me in flesh and blood, knit me together with bones and sinews.' [Job 10:9-11]

There is therefore nothing disgraceful in the composition of the human body, provided only that it is not polluted by adultery or lasciviousness.

The One who created Adam created also Eve. Male and female were formed by God's hands, and no member of the body was created sinful.

Thus those who despise the body should keep quiet: they despise Christ himself who made it.

Cyril of Jerusalem
Catecheses, 12, 26 (PG33, 757)

6th February

It is not the Body that Sins

Do not believe anyone who maintains that our bodies have nothing to do with God. I might say in passing that people who regard the body as corrupt most often defile it with impure actions.

But what can possibly be wrong about this marvellous body of ours? Look at the beauty, the harmony of it.

The eyes are shining, the ears are placed in the most convenient position for catching sounds. The nose is capable of distinguishing smells and the tongue is useful both for tasting and for speaking. Internally the lungs breathe in the air, the heart beats without intermission, the blood flows through countless veins and arteries, the bones are all connected with one another.

Never say the body is responsible for sin.

It is not the body that sins, but the soul. The body is only an instrument; it is like the outward clothing of the soul. It becomes impure if it is used for fornication, but it becomes the temple of the Holy Spirit if it is united to his sanctity.

These are not my words. The Apostle Paul says them: 'Do you not know that the body is the temple of the Holy Spirit within you?'

Cyril of Jerusalem
Catecheses, 4, 22ff. (PG33, 484)

7th February

When Grace takes Possession of the Pastures of the Heart

Grace carves the laws of the Spirit in the hearts of the children of light. They have no need, as a result, to look for a safe guide only in the Bible, written in ink. The grace of God carves the laws of the Spirit, and the divine mysteries too, on the tablets of the heart.

Then from the heart grace takes charge of the whole body. Indeed, when grace has taken possession of the pastures of the heart, it is supreme over all the limbs and all the imagination. It overflows onto them from the heart.

If someone loves God, God's love is united with that person. If someone believes in God, God instils faith into him. So there is a two-way movement. You offer your limbs to God and God enters into communion with you by offering you what we can call his limbs, supposing he had any.

From that moment onwards you can do everything in sincerity and purity.

The dignity of the human person is therefore beyond imagining. Look at the sky and the earth, the sun and the moon, and admire their grandeur. Yet the Lord condescended to rest, not in them, but only in the human heart.

Pseudo-Macarius
Homilies, 15, 20ff. (PG34, 589)

8th February

The Temple of the Ape God

It is not your outward appearance that you should beautify, but your soul, adorning it with good works. Although the body, to be precise, should be made beautiful, though in a measured way.

Women who make make their outward appearance beautiful but leave the soul ugly are unconsciously copying Egyptian temples. Around the temples we see stairways, porticoes, sacred groves, lawns with fountains. The outer walls sparkle with rare stones and paintings and glitter with gold and silver.

But if you penetrated to the enclosure, seeking the god who inhabits the temple, a priest looking solemn and chanting a hymn in Egyptian might draw aside the curtain for you to see the god and give you instead a good laugh. You would not find the god you were looking for, but a cat or a crocodile or a local snake, some animal more fit for a bog than a temple. The Egyptian god is a beast draped in purple.

Certain women are like that. They curl their hair, rouge their cheeks, underline their eyes and devise all manner of tricks. But if you were to lift this outer veil you would be horrified. You would not find our God dwelling there, but an ape adorned with finery which has taken over the shrine.

Clement of Alexandria
The Teacher, 3, 2 (PG8, 560)

9th February

Our Mind is like a Flute

The Creator has bestowed divine beauty on us by adding, to his own image in us, the likeness of the qualities he himself possesses. This beauty brings with it other benefits with which God has generously enriched our human nature.

For instance we ought to consider our minds as far more than a gift. They are a way of sharing the mind of God. But the mind by itself, because it is incorporeal, cannot communicate with other beings: it does not have any means of displaying its proper nature.

So God created an instrument, the vocal chords, which the mind strikes like a plectrum, and so by using different sounds it can share its own internal world.

The mind is like a competent musician who relates with the public on the flute or the lyre. The mind is full of a thousand ideas that otherwise would remain hidden, and it lavishes them upon the minds of others in a way that they can understand by means of sound.

Therefore from the human body flows music as if the flute and the lyre were playing together, creating a unique harmony. The same lips now open, now closed, are like fingers running swiftly over musical instruments.

Gregory of Nyssa
The Creation of Man, 9 (PG44, 149)

10th February

The Importance of Keeping Healthy

When the body is ill, the soul is badly affected. In the great majority of cases, in fact, our spiritual capacities behave according to our physical condition; illness lays us low and makes us different, almost unrecognizable from when we are well.

If the strings of an instrument give a feeble or false sound because they are not taut enough, the artist has no way of displaying any particular talent: the defect in the strings defeats all skill. It is the same with the body. It can do a great deal of harm to the soul.

So I ask you: take care that your body stays fit, safeguard it from illness of any sort.

I am not telling you either to let it waste away or to let it grow fat. Feed it with as much food as is necessary for it to become a ready instrument of the soul.

If you stuff it with delicious dainties, the body is incapable of resisting the impulses that attack it and weaken it. A person may be very wise and yet, if he abandons himself without restraint to wine and the pleasures of the table, it is inevitable that he will feel the flames of inordinate desire blazing more fiercely within him.

A body immersed in delights is a body that breeds lust of every kind.

John Chrysostom
Homily on the Epistle to the Hebrews, 29, 3ff.
(PG63, 207)

11th February

Sport is Good for You But Digging is Better

Physical exercise is good for the health. But not only that: while it stimulates the desire to care for bodily vigour, it stimulates the same desire for vigour of soul. Exercise is extremely useful therefore, assuming it does not distract us from more important activities.

Some enjoy wrestling, others like to play ball in the sunshine. For some it is enough to go for a walk in the countryside or the city. If they were to wield a spade, however, they would be doing an exercise that is useful even from an economic point of view.

The King of Mitylene would grind grain; it was one way, a tiring one, of practising gymnastics. Other ways would be to draw water or chop wood.

Wrestling, it goes without saying, should not simply be a matter of competition, but a way to make you work up a sweat.

In any case, we must always keep a balance: neither doing nothing nor killing ourselves with exhaustion.

Clement of Alexandria
The Teacher, 3, 10 (PG8, 620)

12th February

Using Illness Well

When you are ill, you can call the doctor. Not for nothing have there always existed in nature medicines from which human experimentation has derived healing.

If you are too preoccupied with your physical illnesses, however, it is a sign that your soul is still too enslaved to the body. Your soul is mourning for the time when everything was going well; it considers it a great misfortune that illness prevents its tasting the pleasures of life.

If, on the other hand, the soul accepts suffering by giving thanks to the Lord, you could say it has reached the point almost of mastering the feelings, of hardly noticing the physical illness any more.

Then the soul is ready to accept with joy even the fact of eventual death, knowing that after death there awaits a more real life.

> **Diadochus of Photica**
> *Spiritual Works*, 53 (SC 5b, p.115)

13th February

The Right Use of Doctors

Medicine is a gift from God even if some people do not make the right use of it.

Granted, it would be stupid to put all hope of a cure in the hands of doctors, yet there are people who stubbornly refuse their help altogether.

Not infrequently, illness is an opportunity to correct one's faults.

Their correction, though, is an image and symbol of the improvements due to the soul.

We ought not to reject medical skill *en bloc* but we ought not to trust ourselves completely to it either.

Just as we till the ground but at the same time ask

God to make it fertile, just as we leave the guidance of the ship to the steersman but at the same time pray God to save us from the perils of the sea, so we ought to go to the doctor for help without abandoning our faith in the Most High.

Basil the Great
The Greater Rules, 55 (PG31, 1048)

14th February

The Right Use of Medicine

All the different sciences and techniques have been given us by God to make up for the deficiencies of nature.

Agriculture is an example, because the produce of the ground does not spring up in sufficient quantity all on its own. The art of weaving is another, because we need clothing both to cover ourselves decently and to protect ourselves from the bite of the cold.

The same holds good for medicine.

The body is subject to innumerable ills. Sometimes it lacks food, at other times it has too much. So God the governor of life has made us the gift of medicine, the skill to remove what is superfluous and to supply what is lacking, and in this way to be a symbol of the art of healing our souls.

Not by chance does the earth produce plants that have healing properties. It is clearly evident that the Creator wants to give them to us to use.

So much then for doctors and their prescriptions. The Christian, in accepting their healing, knows how they

71

reveal the glory of God and sees in them a mirror of the healing that is needed by the soul.

Basil the Great
The Greater Rules, 55 (PG31, 1044)

15th February

Let the Body be no Hindrance to the Soul

God has placed the spirit in the body. The more the body puts on weight, the more it drags the soul down; it transfers its own heaviness to the soul and impedes its flight.

If, on the contrary, an individual by the steady practice of self-control lessens the weight of the flesh, he finds he has been purified. That is to say, the body on the one hand gives clarity and joy to the soul, on the other hand it is readily obedient to the wishes of the soul.

The soul in fact takes the body where it likes and the body does not resist: more than that, its weight does not prevent it from making its abode wherever it pleases the soul.

Philoxenus of Mabbug
Homily 10, 357ff. (SC44, pp.324ff.)

16th February

The Stomach's Hypocrisy

I doubt if anyone will achieve freedom from gluttony this side of the grave.

Gluttony is the hypocrisy of the stomach which complains of being empty when it is well fed, and bellows that it is hungry when it is full almost to bursting.

If a person swallows too much food, he is inviting impure thoughts. If he mortifies the stomach, he is creating pure thoughts.

Often a lion if it is caressed becomes domesticated, whereas the more you coddle the body, the more it goes wild.

Master gluttony before it masters you!

John Climacus
Stairway to Paradise, 14 (PG88, 854)

17th February

At Table

We give up a diet that is over-full and too refined to hold at bay the body which behaves like a champing stallion pawing the ground and quivering. As a result, we have a surplus of food which we can distribute to the poor: a sign, this, of authentic love for our brothers and sisters.

The individual who gives thanks to God and eats and drinks everything that is prepared and served up to him at table is not going against true wisdom, because everything God made 'is very good'. [Gen. 1:31]

73

But the individual who voluntarily gives up what he likes shows an even greater wisdom. He is only able to do it, provided he has first tasted how sweet the Lord is.

If the body is weighed down with too much food, it makes the mind tired and sluggish; if it is weakened by excessive abstinence it generates in the soul melancholy and an indifference to the divine Word.

There is therefore great need of a balance: moderate the appetite when the body is vigorous, give it more nourishment when the body is weak.

Diadochus of Photica
Spiritual Works, 43ff. (SC56, pp.110ff.)

18th February

Living to Eat?

Some people live to eat, just as the animals do 'whose life is no more than filling their stomachs'.

But our Teacher exhorts us to eat in order to live. Nourishment is not what we are here for, nor is pleasure our purpose in life. We only use them during our sojourning here as the Word instructs us, and he chooses our nourishment with immortality in view.

Clement of Alexandria
The Teacher, 21, 1 (PG8, 377)

19th February

Sister Flesh and Brother Wine

Many people eat plenty and grow fat on it. Others abstain from some kinds of food in order to practise asceticism, and condemn those who eat. Put shortly, they have only hazy ideas why they should eat or why they should abstain.

We, on the other hand, when we fast, give up wine and meat, not because we detest them, as though using them were a crime, but because we are hoping for an eternal reward. We willingly go without things that please the senses in order to be able to enjoy the pleasures of the spiritual table: we sow in tears today in order to be able to reap in joy tomorrow.

Do not despise those who eat, when they are eating in order to keep their strength up. Do not condemn those who drink wine in moderation; it does their stomachs good. Never regard meat as an evil in itself. Paul has taken issue with certain people 'who forbid marriage and enjoin abstinence from foods which God created to be received with thanksgiving by those who believe and know the truth.' [1 Tim. 4:3]

If you abstain from those foods, do not do so as if they were unclean. Rather think of them as a good thing which you are content to give up for love of a far greater spiritual benefit.

Cyril of Jerusalem
Catecheses, 4, 27ff. (PG33, 489)

20th February

Neither Slaves of the Passions nor too Strict in Mortification

Do not devote yourself entirely to disciplining your body. Arrange a programme that is within your capability and then concentrate on your spiritual work.

Those who do not know how to walk in the way of the Spirit are likely to fail to keep a watchful eye on the passions that rage within them, and let themselves be entirely taken up with the body. They then reach one of two opposite states. Either they become gluttonous, profligate, miserable, choleric, full of rancour, and this quenches their spirit, or they overdo the mortification and lose their clarity of thought.

Not one of the things God has put at our disposal is forbidden in Scripture. The Bible limits itself to reproving excess and correcting what is unreasonable.

For example, there is no need to avoid eating, having children, possessing wealth and administering it with justice; only avoid gluttony, luxury, and so forth.

There is a further point. There is no need to avoid dwelling on these matters in your thoughts, they exist because we have thought of them in the first place, avoid only dwelling on them with immoderate eagerness.

Maximus the Confessor
Centuries on Charity, 4, 63ff. (SC9, pp.165ff.)

21st February

A Flood of Alcohol

When the ground has been watered enough it produces good grain in abundance. If, on the other hand, it is sodden through a flood, it sprouts only thorns and thistles.

It is the same with the ground of our soul. If we use wine with frugality, alcohol helps the soul to make what the Holy Spirit has sown in it grow luxuriantly.

Instead, a bout of unrestrained drinking makes the ground of the soul slushy and incapable of producing any thoughts but thorns and thistles.

Diadochus of Photica
Spiritual Works, 48 (SC5b, p.112)

22nd February

The Young People's Drink and the Drink of the Elderly

'Take a little wine for your stomach's sake,' says the Apostle to Timothy who was drinking only water. [1 Tim. 5:23] In saying this he was offering welcome help to Timothy's weak and disease-ridden body. Note that he says 'a little' for fear that the cure by reason of excess should make another cure necessary.

Water is the natural non-alcoholic drink for anyone who is thirsty. Water streaming from the rock is what the Lord provided for the Hebrews of old to drink, a simple sober drink, and the wanderers very much needed to keep sober.

Only later came the fruit of the vine, when the

travellers had been taught how to rest from their journeying. The prophetic grape-bunch, the Holy Vine, specially crushed for us, is the Word, and the Word has ordained that the blood of the grape should be mixed with water just as his blood is blended with water for salvation. To drink the blood of Jesus is to partake of the Lord's immortality.

I admire people who have undertaken a life of austerity and seek water as the medicine of temperance, people who flee as far as they can from wine, as though from the threat of fire. I am glad that young men and women keep off this drug. It is not good to pour wine, the most fiery of liquids, onto the ardour of youth, lest it inflame their burning desires, and kindle their wilder instincts.

But for those of a more advanced age for whom the fires of youth have cooled off, taking wine is a happier recommendation. They are less likely to be bowled over by the billows of drunkenness. They have age and reason to secure them. Even so, for them too there should be a limit, so that their mind remains clear, their memory continues to work, and their body is unaffected by the wine.

Clement of Alexandria
The Teacher, 2, 2 (PG8, 409)

23rd February

The How and Why of Taking a Bath

There are four reasons why people go to the baths: for cleanliness, for warmth, for health, for pleasure.

Over-use of bathing saps one's strength. Furthermore, it is not always a good moment to enter the water;

immediately after having eaten or on an empty stomach are two moments when it ought to be avoided. And of course we must consider the age of the individual and the time of year.

Our standard should be moderation, which ought to accompany all our days. In this way we will not stay so long in the baths that they have to drag us away by force, nor will we go there with the same ease with which we go to chat with our friends in the town square.

Certainly there immediately springs to mind the most beautiful bath of all: that which washes off the stains of the soul, the spiritual bath of which prophecy speaks: 'The Lord will wash away the filth of the daughters of Israel, he will cleanse them from blood', [cf. Isa. 4:4] that is, from the blood of iniquity and of the prophets they have killed.

> **Clement of Alexandria**
> *The Teacher*, 3, 9 (PG8, 617)

24th February

At Least Wear a Fig Leaf!

When we go bathing let us be careful not to copy Adam's nakedness which was not exactly praiseworthy. Let us at least wear a fig leaf!

In our flight from corruption we ought by means of the chastity of the body to achieve the beauty of temperance. Our spirit is formed in God's image and the body is its home. Ever since the sin of Adam, not only has the soul been contaminated, the body also tends gradually towards corruption.

The holy Word of God became incarnate therefore and, being himself also God, communicated to us the water of salvation in baptism.

Through the medium of water, under the action of the Spirit who is holy and who gives life, we have in consequence become regenerate; we have been purified both in body and soul.

Diadochus of Photica
Spiritual Works, 52ff. (SC5b, pp.114ff.)

25th February

Fresh for the New Day

The life of the body is one of flux and change. The human being cannot exist except in ceaseless motion like the flow of a river.

To relax tension we have sleep. When we wake up, the motion starts up again. Neither of the two states lasts very long. But it is thanks to their alternation that we are refreshed.

A constant tension would provoke a collapse: a continuing relaxation would result in the dissolution of the individual. The regular change at the right moment from the one state to the other is the secret of preserving human vitality.

So, if the body is tired, sleep takes over. Just as horses that have competed in the hippodrome are allowed to rest, so sleep is granted to us to restore us, relax us, and make us fresh for the new day.

Gregory of Nyssa
The Creation of Man, 13 (PG44, 165)

26th February

When you Sleep do not Leave your Light Outside

After our meal, we thank God for our share in the good things he has given us and for the day that is past. Then our thoughts turn to sleep.

For some people expensive mattresses, pillows shot with gold, valuable blankets, thick purple rugs and soft bed-clothes are sweeter than sleep itself. They sleep on such floppy feather-beds that the body sinks into them as if in a ditch. They cannot even turn over because the mattress keeps lifting up all over the place. Anyone who has a harder bed sleeps better and is more rested on the following day.

Falling asleep is a bit like the fall into death: emptiness of mind, loss of feeling. The closed eyelids shut out the light.

Yet we are children of light, so let us not leave our spiritual light outside the door. Let us try not to sleep too much, especially when the days are short. Let us wake up early, perhaps to dedicate some time to reading.

Sleep is like the tax-collector; it robs us of half our life.

Clement of Alexandria
The Teacher, 2, 9, 77 (Stählin, I, p.204)

27th February

Courage and Humility Defeat Death

Isidore said: 'The one who is faithful to God ought not to trust in God's own faithfulness: nor should the one who sins against God despair of God's mercy. In the heart of both are hope and fear side by side: hope of forgiveness which inspires courage, and fear of punishment which rouses humility.

'It is necessary that the penitent never feel secure with regard to their sin, because such a feeling of security produces carelessness, and carelessness takes them back unawares to their past life.

'We do not know how long our life may last. We ought therefore to be in a hurry lest death overtake us unexpectedly while we are delaying.'

Caesarius said: 'The surer we are of the past, the more careful we must be of the future. All our sins come back to us quickly if we do not fight them every day with good works.'

Defensor Grammaticus
Book of Sparkling Wisdom, 23 (SC77, pp.326ff.)

28th February

When our Winter is Past

Use your body, I beseech you, with moderation. Remember, with this body you will be raised from death when you come to be judged.

Perhaps you have some doubt whether this could happen. If so, reflect in detail on what has already happened within your own self. Tell me, where were you a hundred years ago? Cannot the Creator who gave existence to a person that did not exist bring to life again a person that did exist but is now dead?

Every year he makes the corn spring to life that had withered and died after it was sown. Do you suppose that he who raised himself from the dead for our sake will have any difficulty in raising us to new life?

Or look at the trees. For a number of months they remain without fruit, even without leaves. But once the winter is past, they become green all over, new, as if risen from the dead. With better reason, and with greater ease, shall we be called to new life.

Do not listen to those who deny the resurrection of the body. Isaiah testifies: 'The dead shall live again: the bodies of those who have died shall live.' [Isa. 26:19] And according to the word of Daniel, 'Many of those who sleep beneath the earth shall awaken, some to life eternal, the rest to eternal ruin.' [Dan. 12:2]

Cyril of Jerusalem
Catecheses, 4, 30ff. (PG33, 492)

March

O Lord, let your grace
pour down on me

1st March

I must Address the Problems and the Secrets of my Soul

Now that I am old, at the end of my life, I recognize my duty to dedicate myself to the soul's study. In fact, I have a soul that is intelligent, immortal and sacred, in which I am the image of my Creator, and in this soul I attain to his likeness, which is the taste of the dignity of reason.

It seems to me advisable first of all to know myself clearly. Why am I, who am the image of God, bound to the earth?

By what divine purpose was the human race formed after all the other creatures had been brought to life?

Humanity, clearly, was made to stand in the midst of the other beings, to stand between two extremes, linking high and low because it shares in the nature of each. The fusion in humanity of matter and spirit gives unity to elements which, by their nature, are very far from one another.

I also ought to investigate my faculties. What are their movements, what is their function according to the divine plan? How does the intellect work? By what means does the soul lose its way, and by what means does it return to the right road?

It is my duty to tackle these problems and many other secrets also. Right from the beginning, in fact, I can trace within me a mystery: I have been created by God, I have received my being from him.

Niceta Stethatus
Treatise on the Soul, 1 (SC81, pp.64ff.)

2nd March

Does the Soul Exist?

Since some people do not realize it quite clearly enough, it is necessary to demonstrate briefly that every human being has a rational soul. Some deny this truth, convinced that human beings consist only of their bodies.

A good argument is the following. Only the human being manages to think of objects outside its own body and to meditate upon things it does not see. Furthermore, the human being reflects upon its own reasonings, judges and chooses the most logical set of reasoning.

Anyone trying to be objective must realize that human intelligence is distinct from the senses: it evaluates their perceptions, it remembers them and it shows to the senses what is the best thing.

The eye is able to see, the ear to hear, the mouth to taste, the nose to smell, the hand to touch. But to decide what must be seen, heard, touched, tasted, smelt, is not the task of the senses but of the soul and its intelligence.

Another argument may be convincing. Why does the human being think of immortality if the body is by nature mortal? And how can you explain that often it will be willing to suffer death out of love for virtue?

Athanasius
Against the Heathen, 30ff. (PG25, 61)

3rd March

The Right Use of the Word 'Soul'

If someone shows us a real loaf, the word 'loaf' is used in its proper sense. But suppose instead that we are shown a loaf made out of stone, carved by an artist. The appearance is the same, it is the same size, the colour is similar, almost all its characteristics seem the same. Yet such an object cannot feed you. So, that stone can only be called a loaf improperly, not in its rightful meaning.

It is the same with the soul. Its perfection lies in its being intelligent and gifted with the power of reason. Where this characteristic is missing, the word 'soul' can only be used by analogy. It is referring, quite simply, to vital energy which, because it is called by the same name, is seen as like the soul. It is no more than the functioning of the animals' senses.

I mention this by way of warning to people who love the things of the flesh. I should like to persuade them not to let themselves be deceived by external appearances, but to devote their lives to the good things of the soul. Only they possess a soul; the senses they have in common with the animals.

Gregory of Nyssa
The Creation of Man, 15 (PG44, 176)

4th March

The Dignity of the Soul is to do Everything According to Reason

Many arguments can show that the soul is rational.

In the first place, it was the soul that invented the techniques that have so many benefits for life. If these techniques are so useful, if that which is useful is praiseworthy, and if that which is praiseworthy conforms to reason, then it follows that our soul is rational.

Moreover, let us think of the senses. They are not able to understand things: their perception is insufficient, indeed they can be deceived. The senses, which are irrational, generate a false perception of things in us.

We must therefore think in the following way: are things understandable or not? If they are, it must be another faculty that is more able than the senses to penetrate to the reality of things.

Now, things are understandable, as we can see by the fact that we use each thing according to what it can do. But if things are understandable and the senses judge falsely because they are irrational, it must be the mind that discerns all these things and that grasps what they are really like. The mind is the rational part of the soul. Conclusion: the soul is rational.

The dignity of the soul consists in doing everything according to reason.

Maximus the Confessor
Treatise on the Soul (PG91, 359)

5th March

Is the Soul Immortal?

The body is moved by the soul and is animated by it from within.

The soul is not added to the body as one stone cast next to the other, nor are the two mixed together. If this were the case, the soul would be made up of parts, and it would not be intrinsically one and simple.

The soul, however, is simple and consequently immortal.

Just think, what is it that suffers corruption and dies? Answer: that which is made up of parts which exist in a state of tension with one another, tending to divide themselves up. The soul, since it is not composite, is indivisible in its very nature, and therefore it cannot suffer corruption: in other words, it is immortal.

Maximus the Confessor
Treatise on the Soul (PG91, 355)

6th March

The Five Powers

The spirit is of divine origin. It has its own energy. It is the source of ideas. It orders reason, if reason accepts it as guide.

The mind is the faculty which originates thoughts.

Judgment is the appreciation of the thoughts originated: positive if they are good thoughts, negative if they are otherwise.

Imagination is the ability to picture something to

ourselves. It is a mistake to say that everything we can picture to ourselves is on that account true. It may be true or it may be false. And it can happen that the mind, if it lacks discrimination, can take the false for true.

Sensitivity is the reaction following the judgment of good or bad thoughts.

In this way, the powers of the human soul are distinguished, and this is how they act when they are true to their nature.

To live in accordance with their nature is good: it means to win salvation.

To live in opposition to their nature is shameful: it means to prepare oneself for punishment.

To live on a higher plane than the natural is splendid: it means to deserve every commendation.

Niceta Stethatus
The Spiritual Paradise, 5 (SC8, pp.70ff.)

7th March

What Happens in the Crossroads of the Spirit

It is the task of the hands to find food for the body's necessities, and the task of the mouth to give service to the word. This particular organ is ours so that we can emit sounds, and we have another organ to receive them. The two activities are not muddled up, every organ carries out its own specific function without disturbing the one next to it. Hence the ear does not have to speak, nor does the tongue have to listen.

Imagine a big city welcoming its visitors by many different gates. Not every one goes to the same part. Some go to the market, some to their homes, some to the public halls, some to wide streets, some to narrow alley ways, and some to the theatre, each according to his preference.

Something similar takes place in the city of the spirit, the city within us.

The doors of the various senses are filled with many things. The spirit examines these, it distinguishes between them and sorts them out, sending each one to the place where it will be dealt with appropriately.

This is what happens in the crossroads of the spirit.

Gregory of Nyssa
The Creation of Man, 10 (PG44, 152)

8th March

Conscience, a Spark of Life

When God made human beings, he put in them a kind of divine faculty, more alive and splendid than a spark, to illuminate the spirit and show it the difference between good and evil. It is the conscience with that law which is part of its nature.

The patriarchs and all the saints were able to please God by obeying the law of conscience. But people trampled on it and muddied it with their sinfulness. As a consequence we needed a written law, we needed the prophets, we needed the actual coming of our Lord Jesus to rediscover, to re-awaken, to rekindle in us the spark which had been smothered.

So now it depends on us whether we smother it again or allow it to shine out and give us light through our obedience.

If our conscience tells us to do something and we do

it, our conscience is still alive. If we do not do what it tells us, we trample on it again and bit by bit yet again we smother it. In the end it will no longer be able to speak plainly to us because of the clods of earth we throw on it. Like a dirty light it will show us things half in shadow, so that we cannot see clearly.

Just as in muddy water you cannot recognize your face, so we will gradually discover that we cannot perceive what our conscience is telling us. In fact, we might even imagine that we have no conscience at all.

But there is no one without a conscience. It is, as we said previously, a divine faculty and it never dies.

Dorotheus of Gaza
Teachings, 3 (SC92, pp.209ff.)

9th March

Threefold Obedience to Conscience

To keep our conscience clear must inspire all our dealings with God, our neighbour and material things.

In the first place, in relation to God: we must take care never to go against his commandments, even in things that nobody will ever see. For instance, we must keep a watch over our thoughts, and when an impure desire comes into our hearts we must overcome it quickly instead of consenting to it. We may see our neighbour do something odd and judge him guilty in our minds, thus offending against charity. We must be careful about everything we do in secret.

Then, in relation to our neighbour: we must never do anything that, in our opinion, may upset or offend, whether it be in our acts, our words, our attitudes or our expressions. I repeat, even a look can be offensive. Every time we know we are behaving with the intention of hurting or making another feel bad, we defile our conscience because we are aware of this intention.

Finally, in relation to material things: we should be careful not to make bad use of them, losing them or wasting them, even if they are things of little value. Treating our clothes badly, not being happy with sufficient food to satisfy the necessities of the stomach but seeking always more refined and costly delicacies, all of this goes against our conscience.

Dorotheus of Gaza
Teachings, 3 (SC92, pp.215ff.)

10th March

A Mirror with which to See Inside Ourselves

Holy Scripture is presented to the mind's eye like a mirror in which the appearance of our inner being can be seen.

In this mirror we can see both the ugliness and the beauty of our soul. We can tell what progress we are making or whether we are making any progress at all.

Holy Scripture recounts the good deeds of the saints and encourages the hearts of the weak to imitate them. In recording the prowess of the saints, Scripture also underlines our weakness in the face of the onslaught of the vices. But its words ensure that the more the soul sees of the triumphs of so many heroes of the faith, the less it is alarmed in the midst of its own battle.

Sometimes, however, Holy Scripture does not only record the victories of the saints but also mentions their defeats, so that we may see from their failures what we ought to be afraid of, besides learning from their triumphs what we ought to aim at. For example, Job is described in the Bible as being exalted by temptation, whereas David is represented as humiliated by it.

By this means, our hopes may be nourished by the valour of people in the past, while because of their weakness we may gird on the protection of humility. The victories of the saints give our spirits wings through the joy they cause; their failures give us pause through fear.

From Scripture the soul of the reader learns the confidence of hope and the humility of fear. Thanks to the weight of the fear, it does not have the temerity to be proud; but this fear does not cast it into utter despair, because the soul is fortified in the strength of hope by the examples of valour.

Gregory the Great
Commentary on the Book of Job, 2, 1 (SC32, p.180)

11th March

Freedom or Responsibility

God created human beings to have free will. He honoured them with reasoning and wisdom and placed before their eyes the choice between life and death. If by their free choice they walk the way of life, they can live for ever. But if by choosing evil they tread the road to death, they will be punished in eternity.

The features of our human nature that we cannot alter deserve neither praise nor blame. No one was ever accused in court of being white or black skinned, or tall rather than short, because we have no choice in these matters. It is to what we can freely choose that punishment and praise belong.

In either case there is need, on the one hand, of our choice and our will, and on the other hand, of God's co-operation and help. If one of these is missing, the other is useless.

So far as God is concerned, he never violates our liberty. Our free will is never over-ridden or crushed. Furthermore, we have received from God commandments which can make us to be like him, by helping us to lead sinless lives and become like angels among our fellow human beings. [cf. Deut. 30:19]

Niceta Stethatus
The Spiritual Paradise, 2 (SC8, pp.61ff).

12th March

When we Speak of Truth and when Truth Speaks for Itself

The Greek culture that preceded the proclamation of the Gospel was not given by God to people as the only thing to think about. He gave it as the rain falls on fertile ground.

Only in this way does the grain grow. True, weeds grow at the same time, but these either wither or are pulled out. We can see the application of the Lord's parable here.

When I speak of Greek culture, I am referring to all the good things that have been said by the various schools of thought.

However, it is one thing to speak about the truth and

quite another to see the Truth who teaches us himself. One thing is the copy and the other is the original. The former is given by study, the latter by faith.

Clement of Alexandria
Miscellaneous Studies, 7, 1 (SC30, p.73)

13th March

How can we Satisfy our Need to Know?

True knowledge is the light whereby we can infallibly distinguish good from evil.

That limitless light illumines the way of righteousness which leads the mind towards the Sun himself. In that light the mind strives with all its energy after divine charity.

Our longing for true knowledge is satisfied by spiritual discourse, provided it comes from God through the exercise of charity.

The intellect ceases to be tormented as it concentrates upon the Word of God.

Whereas previously it was troubled and made wretched by its worries, now the exercise of love expands the compass of its reflections.

Diadochus of Photica
Spiritual Works, 6, 7 (SC5b, pp.87ff.)

14th March

Knowledge is no Good without Charity

If you have received from God the gift of knowledge, however limited, beware of neglecting charity and temperance. They are virtues which radically purify the soul from passions and so open the way of knowledge continually.

The way of spiritual knowledge passes through inner freedom and humility. Without them we shall never see the Lord.

'Knowledge puffs up whereas charity builds up.' [1 Cor. 8:1] Therefore unite knowledge with charity and by being cleansed from pride you will become a true spiritual builder. You will build up yourself and all those who are your neighbours.

Charity takes its power to build up from the fact that it is never envious nor unkind. It is natural for knowledge to bring with it, at the beginning anyway, some measure of presumption and envy. But charity overcomes these defects: presumption because 'it is not puffed up' and envy because 'it is patient and kind.' [1 Cor. 13:4]

Anyone who has knowledge, therefore, ought also to have charity, because charity can save his spirit from injury.

If someone is judged worthy to receive the gift of knowledge but allows his heart to be full of bitterness or rancour or aversion to another, it is as if he had been struck in the eye by a thornbush. That is why knowledge is no good without charity.

Maximus the Confessor
Centuries on Charity, 4, 57 ff. (SC9, pp.164ff.)

99

15th March

The Presumptuous Bat

The light allows the eye to distinguish, for example, gold from silver, copper from iron and tin. Moreover, it allows us to note the difference between colours and shapes, between the plants and between the animals. But only for those who have sound eyesight. The blind gain no advantage from the rays of the sun: they do not even see the brightness of the light!

There are people who do not want to open their eyes to the light of truth but are quite happy to live in darkness. They are like the blind. They are like the birds that fly by night and take their name from it, night-jars, or like bats.

It would be stupid to be angry with these animals. Nature has assigned them that destiny. But human beings who purposely choose the mirky gloom, what reason can they give to justify themselves?

What prevents them removing the mist from their eyes is arrogance. They fancy they know the truth better than others because they have studied a lot. But they are like fish in the sea: they live in salt water, but, nevertheless, once they have been caught they still need to be salted.

Theodoret
The Cure of Pagan Diseases, 2, 1 ff. (SC57, p.136)

16th March

More True than the Truth?

Some people abandon the teachings of the Church and fail to understand how a simple and devout person can have more worth than a philosopher who blasphemes without restraint. Heretics are like that.

Heretics are always wanting to find something more true than the truth. They are always choosing new and unreliable ways. But like the blind led by the blind, they will fall into the abyss of ignorance by their own fault.

The Church is like paradise on earth. 'You may eat freely of the fruit of every tree in the garden,' says the Spirit of God. In our case he means: Feed on the whole of Scripture, but do not do it with intellectual pride, and do not swallow the opinions of the heretics. They pretend to possess the knowledge of good and evil, but they are impiously elevating their own intelligence above their Creator.

Beware! By devouring the ideas of the heretics we banish ourselves from the paradise of life.

Irenaeus
Against Heresies, 5, 20 (Harvey II, p.379)

17th March

God Tests us by our Conscience

The tree of life represents the Holy Spirit dwelling in the hearts of the faithful, as St Paul says: 'Do you not know that your body is a temple of the Holy Spirit within you?' [1 Cor. 6:19]

The tree of knowledge of good and evil represents our senses which produce contrasting fruits: pleasure and pain.

Each of these is divided again into two: there is pleasure arising from natural needs, and there is pleasure resulting from debauchery; then there is pain consisting of fear and sorrow, and there is pain coming as a consequence of struggle and spiritual burdens. The fruits are good if we pluck them, keeping close to nature at the right season.

God has planted this tree in our hearts, this sense of good and evil, for a good purpose: to test us, to make trial of our obedience, to give us the opportunity to live in accordance with nature or not, as we choose, and to follow what leads to perfection or what leads to imperfection.

Niceta Stethatus
The Spiritual Paradise, 5 (SC8, pp.40ff.)

18th March

The Wolves of Anger

Jerome said:

'Loss of temper is the beginning of anger. Real anger arises when bad temper gives place to the desire for revenge.'

Gregory said:

'The devil has a habit of making the heart of an individual angry and quarrelsome when he sees another person concerning himself with him in an act of love.'

In the *Book of Clement* it is said:

'There is a kind of anger that upsets the mind and makes it lose its equilibrium in argument. But there is a right and proper anger: if one is angry with oneself and accuses oneself of one's own mistakes and one's own false acts.'

In the *Lives of the Fathers* it is said:

'Sullen angry eyes betray the anger of the heart. In the soul that keeps the score of evils done to it, there dwell wolves.

'Just as smoke hurts the eyes, so the memory of these injuries hurts one's prayer. The prayer of an angry person is abominably turbulent. The psalm singing of someone who is irritated is a disagreeable noise.'

Defensor Grammaticus
Book of Sparkling Sayings, 19 (SC77, pp.292ff.)

19th March

Loose Words lead to Lewd Acts

Filthy talk makes us feel comfortable with filthy action. But the one who knows how to control the tongue is prepared to resist the attacks of lust.

We have to be clear as to what is filthy or lustful.

The parts of our body involved in sexual union are not base, the embrace of the married couple is not base, nor are the words that talk about all this. The human organs, including the genitals, deserve respect and are not base. Their use is base, if we use them in a disordered way. Only malice is base and what is done with malice.

Thus speech becomes dirty if it treats these subjects in a malicious way.

103

We should avoid useless chatter, because 'when there is much talk, offence is never far away.' [Prov. 10:19] Garrulousness harms, in the first place, the garrulous: 'One is thought wise for keeping silent, while another is detested for being too talkative.' [Eccles. 20:5]

Clement of Alexandria
The Teacher, 2, 6 (PG8, 451)

20th March

We need Guidance on the Way

In the Book of Proverbs we read: 'Where there is no guidance, a people falls like leaves, but in an abundance of counsellors there is safety.' [Prov. 11:14]

You see the force of this saying, brothers and sisters. You see what the sacred scripture is teaching us. It is ensuring that we do not trust in our own strength, that we do not consider ourselves experts, that we do not imagine that we can manage our own affairs.

In fact, we need help: we need guidance and the aid of God. There is nothing more miserable, nothing more risky than people having no one to guide them on the road to God. What does the Scripture say? 'Where there is no guidance, a people falls like leaves.'

The leaf at its beginning is always green, fresh and delightful. Then by degrees it dries up and falls, and after that it is disregarded and trampled on. Anyone without a guide is like that. At first he is always enthusiastic for fasts and vigils, for tranquillity of mind and for obeying his conscience in everything. Then by degrees that enthusiasm wanes, and because he has no director to feed and rekindle that flame, he dries up without anyone noticing, he falls down and from then on becomes prey to his enemies who do what they like with him.

It is different, however, with those who share their thoughts with others and only act after taking the advice: 'In an abundance of counsellors there is safety.' It does not mean by 'an abundance of counsellors', that one should consult everyone, but that one should always seek advice from those whom one trusts most, and not keep silent about some things while speaking of others.

Woe to those who say one thing and do another! One should bring everything out into the open and consult, as I said, about everything. There is safety then, meaning salvation, precisely in the abundance of counsellors.

Dorotheus of Gaza
Teachings, 5 (SC92, pp.251ff.)

21st March

Made in the Image of the Trinity we can Attain to his Likeness

The image of God is revealed in us by means of the threefold division of our internal make-up.

The Godhead is adored in three Persons: Father, Son and Holy Spirit. Similarly, three parts can be seen in the image formed in accordance with this model, namely in the human being who adores him, who has made everything from nothing, with soul, mind and reason.

Just as the three Persons are co-eternal and consubstantial and at the same time God is distinct in three persons, though indivisible, so in the image of God there are three parts co-existent and consubstantial. From them human beings take their characteristic form of the image: by means of them they are the image of God, albeit, as we say to avoid misunderstanding, we are talking of an image made from clay.

The soul, the mind and the reason make up a unique and undivisible nature, co-existent and consubstantial, because the mind and the reason are part of the soul which is incorporeal, immortal, divine. These faculties are co-existent and consubstantial with the soul, inseparable one from the other, just as the Father, the Son and the Holy Spirit are consubstantial and co-existent, and, being indivisible, constitute a single Godhead, the Godhead who gave existence to the universe.

So much for the nature of the image. As to the likeness, it consists in justice, in mercy, in communion, in love for others. People in whom these qualities are alive and active allow us to see clearly both the image and the likeness of God.

Niceta Stethatus
Treatise on the Soul, 21 (SC81, pp.82ff.)

22nd March

The Willing Slave of the Spirit

The soul is a marvellous divine invention and it deserves our admiration. When he made it, God put no vice in its nature, but created it in the image of the virtues of his Spirit. He gave it knowledge, discernment, wisdom, faith, love and all the virtues.

So long as the soul keeps knowledge, love and faith, it reveals the nature of the Lord.

He also put in it intelligence and free will, and he included in its nature another great subtlety. He made it extremely mobile, able to travel in imagination there and back instantly, ready like a willing slave to do the bidding of the Spirit.

God in fact created the soul in such a way as to be like a wife and companion to him, to be united with him in one spirit, as St Paul puts it: 'He who is united to the Lord becomes one spirit with Him.' [1 Cor. 6:17]

The glory that Moses bore on his face was an image of the true glory. The Jews at that time could not bear to look at Moses' face. Nowadays Christians receive the light of that glory in their souls and the powers of darkness are dazzled by it and put to flight.

The Jews were God's chosen people and the outward sign by which they were recognizable was circumcision. Nowadays, however, God's special people receive the sign of circumcision in the soul, internally. The heavenly knife amputates any superfluous pride, the foreskin of impurity which is sin.

With the Jews, the flesh was sanctified in baptism. With us, the soul is sanctified by baptism of the Lord in the Spirit. [cf. Matt. 3:11]

Pseudo-Macarius
Homily 46, 5ff. (PG34, 796)

23rd March

Who is Unaware of the Stream?

You would be a blasphemer if you were to say that every believer receives and possesses the Spirit without knowing or recognizing the fact.

Yes, you would! You would be accusing Christ of lying when he said: 'The water that I shall give will become in him a spring of water welling up to eternal life.' and again: 'Out of his heart shall flow rivers of living water.' [John 4:14 & 7:38] When a spring wells up, when rivers gush out from a spring, how is it possible to look at it and not to recognize it?

If all that were to happen without our knowledge, clearly we should not have the slightest idea of eternal life that flows from it and dwells in us, nor should we be able to see the light of the Holy Spirit. We should remain like the dead, blind and unconscious. Our hope would be vain, our efforts useless.

But it is not so, not at all! The Father is light, the Son is light, the Holy Spirit is light: one light, timeless, indivisible, inconfusible, eternal, uncreated, illimitable, invisible, lacking nothing, above and beyond all things, a light no one can ever behold without first being purified. And by contemplating it, we can receive it.

Simeon the New Theologian
Theological and Ethical Treatises, 10, 501ff. (SC129, pp.297ff.)

24th March

One Heart that Seems Two

How is it possible for sin and grace to dwell in the same heart, as if there were two different hearts?

The illustration of a fire may help. If you have a fire below a vessel and you put some wood on it, the fire flares up and the water in the vessel heats up and boils. But if you fail to put more wood on the fire it begins to fade gradually and goes out.

In our hearts is the heavenly fire of grace. If we pray

and meditate on the love of Christ, we add wood to the fire and our hearts burn with longing for God.

If, on the contrary, we are negligent and give our attention to worldly affairs, vice enters the heart, takes it over and torments us.

Nevertheless, the heart remembers the peace which it tasted earlier and begins to repent, to direct itself afresh towards God. On the one hand, then, peace is brought nearer, on the other, we are seeking it fervently in prayer. It is like stirring the fire which is warming the heart.

The vessel of the heart is very deep, so deep that the Bible says God searches the abyss of it. If a person deviates from the way of God's commandments, he puts himself under the power of sin. And because the heart is a deep abyss, sin goes right down into it in order to take over its territory. So it is necessary for grace also, slowly, to descend to those depths.

Pseudo-Macarius
Homily 40, 7ff. (PG34, 765ff.)

25th March

The Reins of Power

In certain cases, the spirit follows the inclinations of nature like a slave.

The body takes the upper hand, rouses the passions and drives us to demand selfish pleasure. Then the spirit gives in to the body and even supplies it with the necessary means to satisfy its lusts.

This is not the experience of everyone. Those who are holy do not behave like that. In them it is the spirit that gives the orders and chooses what is truly useful and has the upper hand over the body.

Gregory of Nyssa
The Creation of Man, 14 (PG44, 174)

26th March

You are Utterly Fair, my Love, and There is no Flaw in You

You can see that a city is prosperous by the wealth of goods for sale in the market. Land too we call prosperous if it bears rich fruit. And so also the soul may be counted prosperous if it is full of good works of every kind.

But first of all it has to be farmed energetically. Then it must be watered by abundant streams of heavenly grace for it to bring forth fruit, some thirtyfold, some sixtyfold, and some a hundredfold. The soul only acquires goodness and the capacity of fulfilling its duties if it has the grace of God.

On the other hand, what is uglier or more disgusting than a soul given over to base passions? Look at the hot-headed person: he is like a wild beast. Consider the slave of lust or gluttony: who can bear the sight of him? Pity the victim of melancholy whose spirit is totally prostrated.

It is for us to seek to acquire beauty, so that the Bridegroom, the Word, may welcome us into his presence and say, 'You are utterly fair, my love, and there is no flaw in you.' [S. of S. 4:7]

Basil the Great
Commentary on Psalm 29, 5 (PG29, 316)

27th March

The Secret of the Peace we Need

Those who are engaged in spiritual warfare must always keep their hearts tranquil. Only then can the mind sift the impulses it receives and store in the treasure house of the memory those that are good and come from God, while rejecting altogether those that are perverse and devilish.

When the sea is calm, the fishermen's eyes can see the movements of the fish deep down, so that hardly any of them can escape. But when the sea is ruffled by the wind, the turmoil of the waves hides from sight the creatures that would easily have been seen if the sea wore the smile of calm. The skill of the fisherman is of little use in rough weather.

Something of the same sort happens with the soul, especially when it is stirred to the depths by anger.

At the beginning of a storm, oil is poured on the waters to calm them, and in fact the oil defeats their commotion. In this way, when the soul receives the anointing of the gift of the Holy Spirit, it gladly gives in to this inexpressible and untroubled sweetness. And even if it is continually attacked by temptation it maintains its peace and joy.

Diadochus of Photica
Spiritual Works, 23 (SC5b, pp.27ff.)

111

28th March

It is Easy to Pass from Contemplation to Action but not Vice Versa

The one who, on the one hand, does not keep the commandments in the context of actual relationships with his neighbour and has even given up physical work and, on the other hand, remains alone in his room without even working spiritually, is lazy, lazy in both aspects.

The person who is used to spiritual activity does not find any difficulty in following the divine commandments also on the physical plane. Indeed, he finds it easier. The person who, instead, burns up all his energy in external activities, if he interrupts them, is not able to carry out internal activities. He is like someone who holds in his hands tools and materials to build something but does not know how to go about it. He cannot exercise the art and even less can he perfect it; he can do nothing that has any value.

For this reason all the Apostles and all those who have brought God into the world gave first place to solitude with respect to activity.

Simeon the New Theologian
Theological and Ethical Treatises, 15, 95ff. (SC129, p.451)

29th March

When the Mind is Well Disposed

So perhaps Abraham had some priest at his disposal? Some expert? Perhaps he had heard some teaching, some preaching, some wise counsel? But no written documents existed in those days, no Law, no Prophets, nothing of that sort at all.

He successfully sailed a sea that was not favourable to him in the slightest. He traversed a road that was impassable, he who came from an idolatrous family. Nevertheless, these harsh conditions did not harm him.

On the contrary, his holiness achieved great splendour. By practising the virtues before anyone else did, he left an example of what was to be taught by the Law, by the Prophets, by Christ: an authentic and burning love, contempt of riches, concern for his children . . .

Yet this righteous man did not have a home. The roof over his head was the shade of the trees.

Although a stranger in an unfriendly country he eagerly practised hospitality; he welcomed and entertained the three who arrived in the middle of the day. He did the impossible for his nephew, although Lot did not behave as he ought to his uncle. Then, under pressure of famine, he went as an exile again to another country, without any uneasiness or anxiety. He showed the same submissiveness, the same endurance of pain, the same patience.

What priest taught him all this? What expert? What prophet? None! It was because his own mind was so well disposed that he could cope with all these situations.

John Chrysostom
On Providence, 13, 1 (SC79, pp.189ff.)

113

30th March

'Pray for One Another'

You have written to me: 'Pray to God for my sins.'

I answer you: 'You must pray too for *my* sins.'

In fact we read in the Bible: 'Treat others as you would have them treat you.' [Luke 6:31]

I am the most wretched, the most miserable of all people myself. But to the best of my ability I make my own the words: 'Pray for one another, that you may be healed.' [Jas. 5:16]

Barsanuphius
Letters (ed. Nicodemo l'Agiorita, Venice 1816)

31st March

Progress in Self-Knowledge

I pray you, brothers and sisters: let us strive with every means at our disposal to know ourselves. Then each one of us, starting with this self-knowledge, will be able to discover what is too high for us.

We need to know ourselves so well that we can say like David: 'I am a worm and no man' [Ps. 22:7] or like Abraham: 'I am dust and ashes.' [Gen. 18:7] Otherwise it will be impossible to understand even the smallest part of the Word of God, to interpret it in a spiritual way worthy of the Spirit of wisdom. Without humility it is not possible to become the recipient of the gifts of the Spirit.

When souls undergo purification through penitence and the practice of the commandments, they receive grace to discover themselves completely and to know what is beyond their reach. By intensifying their purification, by deepening their humility, they begin gradually to understand, albeit in obscure fashion, the things of God and what belongs to God.

According to the measure of their understanding they increase their penitence, they become ever more humble, they consider themselves more and more unworthy of such knowledge and of the revelation of the divine mysteries.

Humility is a solid wall protecting them. If this understanding is like a house in which they have taken up residence, they can dwell there safe from any kind of arrogance.

Grow in this way from day to day in faith, hope and love for God, go ahead in knowledge and sanctification. Go ahead and he can clearly keep track of your progress.

Simeon the New Theologian
Theological and Ethical Treatises, 9, 440ff. (SC129, p.253)

April

*Ah, my heart
is a battlefield*

1st April

God has Created Nothing Evil

Never let us try to maintain that God has created anything that is intrinsically bad. We read in Scripture: 'And God saw everything that he had made and behold, it was very good.' [Gen. 1:31]

Perhaps someone is asserting that God created the devils as they are, or that right from the beginning he assigned them their role of deceiving and ruining human beings? If so, he is contradicting Scripture and insulting God by thinking of him as the inventor and creator of evil.

In reality, before forming the visible world, God made the spiritual powers of heaven so that they might unceasingly give thanks and praise to their Creator, knowing that they had been made from nothing and were destined for the glory of heavenly felicity.

In fact, the Lord himself says of these powers: 'When the morning stars sang together and all the sons of God shouted for joy.' [Job 38:7]

The beginning of every thing is Christ in whom the Father has created all that exists. We read in Scripture: 'All things were made through him, and without him was not anything made that was made.' [John 1:3] And again: 'In Christ all things were created, in heaven and on earth, visible and invisible . . . all things were created through him and for him.' [Col. 1:16]

Cassian
Conferences, 8, 6ff. (SC54, pp.14ff.)

2nd April

But Why does God Put up with Evil in the World?

Why does error have a free rein and why does God allow the wicked to disturb the existence of so many people?

First of all, before trying to understand, we need to put ourselves in front of the incomprehensible wisdom of God. One who is firmly anchored in God does not suffer any loss, even if attacked by a thousand waves and a thousand storms. On the contrary, he emerges stronger.

There is a reason, however, which I can venture to suggest.

In the first place, scandals are permitted so that the rewards of the righteous may not be diminished. That is why God said to Job: 'Do you not understand that I have treated you in this fashion so that your righteousness may be made manifest?' [Job 40:8]

But there is another reason why the wicked are left at large: so that they may not be deprived of the advantages of conversion from their evil ways, which certainly could not happen if they had been rendered incapable of doing evil. In this way, St Paul, the penitent thief, the prostitute, the tax collector and many others were saved.

You may speak to me about those who have been scandalized. Well and good. But I then speak to you about those who have benefited from the scandal by winning glory, and I repeat my point: the existence of careless and lazy people would not justify leaving in a state of inferiority keen and wide-awake people who are capable of richly deserving their eternal recompense. A great wrong would be done to them if they were not given the chance to strive.

John Chrysostom
On Providence, 12, 1 (SC79, pp.183ff.)

3rd April

Why does God allow Temptation?

One can distinguish five reasons why God allows the devils to attack us:

first, so that from attack and counter-attack we may become practised in discerning good from evil;

second, so that our virtue may be maintained in the heat of the struggle and so be confirmed in an impregnable position;

third, so that as we advance in virtue we may avoid presumption and learn humility;

fourth, to inspire in us an unreserved hatred for evil through the experience we thus have of it;

fifth, and above all, that we may attain inner freedom and remain convinced both of our own weakness and of the strength of him who has come to our aid.

Maximus the Confessor
Centuries on Charity, 2, 67 (SC9, p.114)

4th April

Sin is in no Way the Fault of our Nature

'I am the victim of violence in my nature,' you say. 'I love Christ, yet my nature compels me to sin.'

If you were in fact compelled to sin, if you were the victim of violence, then you would be forgiven for it. On the other hand, if you sin through idleness, do not expect forgiveness.

But let us look at the question a moment to discover if we do commit sins by compulsion, under pressure of violence, rather than through idleness or serious negligence.

It is written: 'Thou shalt not kill.'

But who compels you to kill? Who forces you to do it? On the contrary, you have to do violence to your own nature to kill someone. Which of us would light-heartedly cut a neighbour's throat? Who would gladly stain his hands with blood? No one. So the facts are the exact opposite of your contention. To sin, you have to force yourself.

God has given our nature the gift of mutual love as a result of which every living creature loves its own kind, every human being loves his neighbour. Do you see? Our nature predisposes us to virtue. It is the vices that are contrary to nature. If they win a victory, it is the fault of serious negligence on our part.

And adultery, what shall we say about that? What sort of necessity drives you to that?

You answer: 'The tyranny of desire.'

Why, I ask you? Can you not have intercourse with your spouse and in this way defeat that tyranny? 'But I am in love with someone else's spouse.' In this case there is no compulsion. Love cannot be compelled. You do not love because you are forced to love: you love spontaneously, of your own free will. Sexual intercourse may be an irresistible need, but love is a free choice.

The conclusion is clearly apparent: virtue is consistent with our nature whereas vice is opposed to it.

John Chrysostom
On the Letter to the Ephesians, 2, 3 (PG62, 20)

5th April

God does not Judge by Quantity

To steal or at any rate to covet another person's belongings is a sin whose seriousness is not lightened according to whether it is gold or silver that is at stake. In either case, it is the same attitude of mind that is at the root of it.

A person who steals a small object will not refuse to steal a big one. If he does not steal, it is because he has no opportunity, and that is no credit: it is the combination of circumstances.

You say to me: 'That ruler is robbing his subjects.' But you, tell me, do not you rob others yourselves?

It is no use your objecting that he is stealing money by millions and you are only taking a little. Think of the incident in the gospel when the woman gave two farthings to charity and yet acquired as much merit as rich people who offered gold. [Luke 21:1] Why is that? Because God sees the intention of the heart and is not interested in the amount of the offering.

If that applies to almsgiving, why should it be different with greed of gain?

Just as the woman who offered two farthings has as much merit thanks to her intention, so you who steal two farthings are no less to blame than thieves on a grand scale.

John Chrysostom
On the Second Letter to Timothy, 3, 3 (PG62, 617)

6th April

Accomplices

Inside us evil is at work suggesting unworthy inclinations. However, it is not in us in the same way as, to take an example, water mixes with wine. Evil is in us without being mixed with good.

We are a field in which wheat and weeds are growing separately. We are a house in which there is a thief, but also the owner. We are a spring which rises from the middle of the mud, but pours out pure water.

All the same, it is enough to stir up the mud and the spring is fouled. It is the same with the soul. If the evil is spread, it forms a unity with the soul and makes it dirty. With our consent, evil is united with the soul; they become accomplices.

Yet there comes a moment when the soul can free itself and remain separate again: in repentance, contrition, prayer, recourse to God. The soul could not benefit from these habits if it were always sunk in evil.

It is like marriage. A woman is united with a man and they become one flesh. But when one of them dies, the other is left alone.

But union with the Holy Spirit is complete. So let us become a single spirit with him. Let us be wholly absorbed by grace.

Pseudo-Marcarius
Homily 16, 1 (PG34, 613)

7th April

Right Use not Misuse

It is important to understand the right use of external objects and pictures of them in our imagination.

The reasonable use of them produces for its fruit the virtues of chastity, charity and right knowledge.

Their unreasonable use results in debauchery, hatred and ignorance.

It is through the measure in which we misuse the powers of the soul, namely its desire, emotion, reason, that the vices install themselves: ignorance and folly in the reasoning faculty, hatred and debauchery in the desires and emotions. Their right use, on the contrary, produces right knowledge and prudence, charity and chastity.

Nothing that God has created is in itself bad. Food is not bad, gluttony is; the procreation of children is not bad, lechery is; wealth is not bad, avarice is; glory is not bad, only vainglory is.

So you see nothing is bad in itself, only the misuse of it, which is the soul's negligence in cultivating its true nature.

Maximus the Confessor
Centuries on Charity, 3, 1 (SC9, p.123)

8th April

How Weak the Wicked Are!

See for a moment how weak the wicked are. They cannot even reach the spot to which instinct is leading and almost pushing them. What would happen if they lacked even this help from nature, so strong as to seem irresistible?

Look how impotent they are! They long for objects that are simple and of little account and yet they do not even succeed in attaining these.

They indeed lack any strength whatsoever.

Do they abandon virtue and run back to vice because they do not know what is truly good? Nothing is so weak as the blindness of ignorance.

Or perhaps they know very well what they ought to be seeking? Then it is the passions that lead them astray; it is lack of self-control that makes them too feeble to fight against vice.

Yes, they are able to do evil. But this ability comes not from any power they might have, but rather from their weakness.

Boethius
The Consolations of Philosophy, 4, 2 (PL63, 793)

9th April

Sin is a Contagious Disease

Doctors speak of an epidemic when a disease is caught by just one person or animal and then infects them all. It is like that with those who commit sin. They infect one another, they are ill together and they die together.

Look at the prostitutes who camp out in the squares. They despise sensible people and they talk about their degrading exploits as if they were things to be admired. Diseased creatures, they want to spread their own evil to others. They want many others to become like themselves, because the more people there are suffering from the very same illness, the less they feel guilty of anything shameful.

When a piece of material is inflammable, it is impossible to stop it catching fire, especially if the wind is blowing.

So it is with sin. It attacks a single individual first, but then the people nearby are bound to be infected. The fascination of evil attracts many, all except the very healthy.

Basil the Great
Commentary on Psalm 1, 6 (PG29, 235)

10th April

The Devil has not Full Power

Among the angelic powers the chief of the terrestrial order, the one to whom God had entrusted the task of looking after the earth, was not evil by nature, he had not received any trace of evil from his Creator. He was good.

However, he did not maintain the light and the honour that God had given him. By a deliberate act of his own free will he rebelled against the Creator. He turned his face away from goodness and fell into evil. Evil in fact is merely the absence of good, as darkness is the absence of light.

A host of angels placed under his command followed him in the fall. Despite their angelic nature, they also freely plunged from goodness down to evil and became wicked.

The devils cannot do anything against us without

God's permission. But with God's permission they are powerful. All wickedness, all the passions are inspired by them. But listen: God allows them to suggest sin to a person, but they cannot force him to do it. We ourselves are responsible for accepting or rejecting their seductive suggestions.

John Damascene
The Orthodox Faith, 2, 4 (PG94, 873ff.)

11th April

The Devil's Strategy

The devil demonstrates simultaneously his weakness and his wickedness.

He is unable to harm anyone who does not harm himself. In fact, anyone who denies heaven and chooses the earth is, as it were, rushing towards a precipice, even though running of his own accord.

The devil, however, starts working as soon as he sees someone living up to faith's commitments, someone who has a reputation for virtue, who does good works.

He tries to worm vanity into him, to make it possible for him to be puffed up with pride, become presumptuous, lose trust in prayer and not attribute to God the good that he does but to take all the credit himself.

Ambrose
On the Gospel of St Luke 4, 25

12th April

The Faithfulness of the Whore who Married the Governor

Abbot John the Dwarf said:

'If a king wanted to capture the town of his enemy, first of all he would cut off its water supply and prevent food from getting in. The enemies, dying of hunger, would surrender. In the same way we should treat the passions of the flesh. If someone lives in fasting and hunger, in a short while the enemies of his soul get exhausted.'

One day, speaking about conversion of the heart, the Abbot told this story to one of the brothers:

'Once there was a woman if ill repute in a city. She had many lovers. The governor approached her and said: "If you promise me you will behave properly, I will take you for my wife." She promised, he married her and took her to his own home.

'The lovers, who still wanted her, said: "That official has taken her. If we risk going into the palace, he'll catch us and punish us. But we'll get out of that. Let's go round the back and whistle to her. She'll hear it and come down, and then we'll be all right."

'But the woman, when she heard them whistling, blocked her ears, bolted the doors and hid herself in the innermost part of the house.'

The old man explained the story. The woman of ill repute is our soul. Her lovers are our passions. The governor is Christ. The innermost part of the house is our heavenly dwelling place. The whistlers are the devils. But the soul can always find refuge with its Lord.

Sayings of the Desert Fathers (PG65, 208)

129

13th April

Detach Passion from the Image

What keeps the spirit free in the face of external realities and of the images of them is spiritual love and the mastery of self.

The soul that loves God does not fight against these realities nor against their images which appear in the imagination, but against the passions that attach themselves to them.

For example, one is not seduced by a woman, nor bitter towards someone who has caused one to suffer, nor even troubled by the images that arise in the mind, but by the passions that attach themselves to these images.

External realities are different from the images of them, and the passions attached to them are different again. Thus, a man, a woman, money are material things. Merely to remember these things is to make an image of them in the mind. An unreasoning affection or a blind hatred for these same things is a passion.

A passionate image of them is a thought composed of an image and a passion; detach the passion from the image and there remains a simple thought.

How can we detach them? We have the weapons, if we have the will to use them: spiritual love and the mastery of self.

Maximus the Confessor
Centuries on Charity, 3, 38ff. (SC9, pp.136ff.)

14th April

The Three Stages

We must distinguish simple thoughts, that is, ones without passion, from passionate thoughts.

If we are examining the way in which sins of thought begin, we notice that the latter, namely passionate thoughts are accompanied by a large number of simple thoughts.

Let us take money as an example. Someone thinks of a sum of money belonging to someone else. His imagination urges him to theft, and in his spirit he has already sinned. At the same time as he is thinking of the money, he thinks also of the purse, of the bag, of the living quarters and what not.

Yet it is the thought of the money that is passionate. While, on the contrary, the thought of the bag or the living quarters was merely a simple thought, because the spirit feels no passion for these particular things.

So with other thoughts: vainglory, the opposite sex, and so on.

Thus in our moral development we can distinguish three very important stages:

firstly, never to commit a sin in our acts;

secondly, never to pause at a passionate thought;

and thirdly, to keep our peace of soul in the face of impure pictures or memories of offences received.

Maximus the Confessor
Centuries on Charity, 2, 84ff. (SC9, pp.118ff.)

15th April

One Vice leads to Another

Augustine said:

'None can find joy in God if they live in vice.'

Jerome said:

'We are so indulgent with our vices, inasmuch as they are things we like doing, because we attribute them to human nature.'

Isidore said:

'To renounce our vices completely we must avoid any opportunity to commit sin.

'Anyone who does something bad commits a double sin because he gives in to his own will and then reinforces it by persisting in his pride.

'The vices follow one another: as soon as one has gone another takes its place.

'Sometimes little vices ward off bigger ones. But you cannot heal vices with other vices; healing comes rather through the practice of virtues.'

Caesarius said:

'Our only enemies are our vices.'

Defensor Grammaticus
Book of Sparkling Sayings, 27 (SC77, pp.352ff.)

16th April

Just as Crabs

Just as a bundle of green logs suffocates and puts out a bonfire causing clouds of smoke, so excessive grief often surrounds the soul with thick cloud and dries up the fount of tears.

Just as a blind person is no use as an archer, so a disciple with the mania of contradiction will end in perdition.

Just as tempered metal can sharpen soft or rusty metal, so can a zealous brother set a tepid one on the right track.

Just as clouds hide the sun, so do vile thoughts darken the soul and lead to its destruction.

Just as iron, even without willing it, is drawn by a magnet, so is a slave to bad habits dragged about by them.

Just as the winds whip up the seas, so does anger stir confusion in the mind.

Just as crabs always stay in the same place because first they go forwards and then they go backwards, so does the soul make no progress if it vacillates, now laughing, now crying, now plunging into unrestrained merry-making.

Just as anyone who climbs a rotten ladder risks his life, so are honours and power a danger for humility.

John Climacus
Stairway to Paradise, 26, Appendix (PG88, 1085)

17th April

Idleness Contains All Sin

The cradle of all temptations and all useless and unhealthy thoughts is idleness. Idleness contains all sin.

The idle are never servants of God. Those who do not do what they must with fidelity and fervour, those who do not do it with the intention of serving God, are idle when they come to act.

And it is ridiculous to look for idle works to escape idleness. An idle work is one that has no usefulness or is done with no intention of becoming useful: useful in the first place to one's own conscience, enriching the heart's treasure.

Do you want to know what you should busy yourself with? Over and above daily prayer you need to work – in such a way, though, as to preserve, or rather, to increase your spiritual happiness.

Certainly, some kinds of heavy work distract the soul and weary it. All the more reason for you to have a sense of your own weakness and to have humility of heart.

Bernard of Clairvaux
Letters to the Brethren, 21 (PL184, 321)

18th April

The Worm of Pride

Augustine said:

'We must avoid pride. If it was able to deceive angels, how much more will it be able to scatter human wits.'

Ambrose said:

'Pride transformed angels into demons, humility makes human beings into saints. Pride leads you to despise God's commandments, humility urges you to follow them. The proud want to be praised even for what they have not done, the humble try to hide the good they do.'

Gregory said:

'The one who is in the first place can never learn humility if he does not overcome pride when he is in the last.'

In *The Lives of the Fathers* it is said:

'Fruit that is ruined is no use to the farmer; virtue that is proud is no use to God. Just as the weight of fruit breaks the branch, so pride smashes the beauty of the soul.'

Defensor Grammaticus
Book of Sparkling Sayings, 17 (SC77 pp.258ff.)

19th April

The New Pharisees

Christ himself accuses us of hypocrisy: 'This people honours me with their lips, but their heart is far from me. In vain do they worship me.' [Matt. 15:8-9]

Precisely these words that the Lord was speaking to reprove the Pharisees I feel he is speaking to us, the hypocrites of today who have been enriched with so much grace and yet have remained in a worse state than the hypocrites of yesterday.

Do not we also require others to carry crushing weights while we do not touch them even with a finger? Is it not possibly true that we too look for the best seats at banquets, the front places in meetings and like to be called experts? And do we not have a mortal hatred for anyone who does not offer us these honours?

Have not we too, perhaps, thrown away the key of true knowledge and shut the door of the kingdom of heaven in the face of other people, so that we neither enter it ourselves nor allow others to enter? [Luke 11:46, Matt. 23:6-7,13]

Maximus the Confessor
Ascetics, 35 (PG90, 940)

20th April

Three Kinds of Lies

There are three kinds of liar: those who lie with their thoughts, those who lie with words and those who lie with their very lives.

The liar of thought, for example, is the individual who is suspicious. If he sees two people talking, he immediately imagines they are talking about him. If they break off their conversation, he is convinced they are doing so because they have seen him coming. Whatever other people may say he interprets as an attack on himself. Such a person does not look for the truth but feeds on conjecture. Hence indiscreet curiosity, scandalmongering, the habit of eavesdropping, of picking quarrels, of making rash judgments.

The liar of the tongue, for example, is the lazy person who gets up late in the morning and instead of saying 'I'm sorry, I've been a fool,' spins a yarn about having been ill and unable to stand up properly. Or else it is the person who wants something but instead of saying 'I want one of those' makes a palaver of it with the words: 'I am feeling ill, I need this, or that . . . '

Lastly there are the liars with their lives: a profligate who pretends to be chaste, a miser who praises love for the poor . . . they are two-faced people, their outward appearance quite different from the inward reality. Their whole existence is duplicity, a kind of acting.

Dorotheus of Gaza
Teachings, 9 (SC92 pp.321ff.)

21st April

Few Manage to Stem the Gossiping Tongue

Garrulousness is the rostrum from which vainglory preaches itself.

Garrulousness is a proof of ignorance, the door to scandal-mongering, the handmaid of trifling scurrilities and the helpmeet of falsehood.

It destroys the spirit of penance, gives rise to boredom, predisposes to lethargy, destroys recollection, distracts attention, obliterates fervour and cuts off prayer.

Silence on the other hand is the mother of prayer. It frees the prisoner; it guards the divine flame; it watches over reasoning; it protects the sense of penitence.

Few are they who manage to dam the rush of water. Still fewer are they who are able to stem the gossiping tongue.

John Climacus
Stairway to Paradise, 11 (PG88, 852)

22nd April

Greed is never Satisfied

Ambrose said:

'Avarice and pride are so much the same evil that you cannot find someone who is proud but not avaricious nor someone who is avaricious but not proud.'

Isidore said:

'The greater our love for the things we possess, the greater our pain when we lose them.

'Greed is insatiable. The person who is afflicted with it always needs something else; the more he has, the more he wants.

'The powerful are nearly all so inflamed with a mad lust for possessions that they steer well clear of the poor. Small wonder that when they come to die they are condemned to the flames of hell, since they did nothing to put out the flames of greed during their lifetime.'

Defensor Grammaticus
Book of Sparkling Sayings, 30 (SC77, pp.374ff.)

23rd April

Anyone Given to Lust is Dead while Alive

Jerome said:

'Woe to those who put an end to lust only at the end of life.

'At banquets and in the midst of lustful pleasures, desire can take control even of an iron will. It is difficult to resist voluptuous delights and conserve modesty.

'Sensuality will rule beneath the luxurious clothing

and beneath rags; it fears not the purple of kings nor the squalor of beggars.

'Anyone given to lust is dead while alive, anyone given to drunkenness is dead and buried.'

Gregory said:

'The darts of lust are sharpened when the belly is full to bursting.'

Isidore said:

'A spirit inflated by pride leads to lust and prostitution; chastity is preserved by a humble mind.'

Defensor Grammaticus
Book of Sparkling Sayings, 21 (SC77 pp.310ff.)

24th April

Gluttony is the Snare of the Devil

The devil said to Jesus: 'If you are the son of God, command that these stones become bread.' [Luke 4:3]

Here we learn that there are three principal weapons that the devil likes to carry in order to wound our souls. They are gluttony, arrogance and ambition.

He begins with the weapon with which he has already been victorious. We likewise should begin to be victorious in Christ in the very same area in which we have been defeated in Adam: we should be wary of gluttony. The devious trap is set for us when the table is laid for a royal banquet; it is bound to weaken our defences.

See what weapons Christ uses to defeat the power of the devil. He does not use the almighty power he has as God: what help would that be to us? In his humanity he summons the help common to all – overlooking bodily hunger and seeking the word of God for nourishment.

Whoever follows the Word is no longer attached to earthly bread, because he receives the bread of heaven and knows the divine is better than the human, the spiritual is better than the physical. Therefore, because such a person desires the true life, he looks for that which fortifies the heart by means of its invisible substance.

Ambrose
On the Gospel of St Luke, 4, 17 (PL15, 1617)

25th April

Ridiculous Conceit

Scripture says: 'The voice of the Lord breaks the cedars.' [Ps. 29:5] Generally Holy Scripture praises the cedar on the grounds that it does not fall, it does not go rotten, it is fragrant, it offers good shelter. Here, however, it is attacking it: it does not produce any fruit, and its wood is hard to bend. In short, it is the perfect image for the wicked man.

'I have seen the wicked, the proud man, exalting himself like a cedar of Lebanon.' [Ps. 37:35] But, 'The Lord will break the cedars of Lebanon.' [Ps. 29:5]

The cedars of Lebanon represent people who make their way at others' expense and then boast about it. In fact these cedars, already tall in their own right, are standing on a mountain that makes them even more visible.

The sort of people who prop up their prestige with the corruptible things of the world are like them. Such people are proud of a position that does not belong to them, they are conceited and boastful and put themselves on a pedestal above ordinary mortals as if they were on the summit of Lebanon.

Basil the Great
Commentary on Psalm 28, 5 (PG29, 293)

26th April

Anything a Fool says is Rubbish

Jerome said:

'Stupid and tasteless words are not fitting for Christians. Their speech should always be in good taste so as to sound pleasing to the ears of other people.

'Anything a fool says is rubbish, just an empty din.'
Gregory said:

'Just as the ear does not understand food nor the throat take in words, so the fool does not comprehend the conversation of the wise.'

Isidore said:

'Nothing is worse than folly, nothing more reprehensible than stupidity, nothing more shameful than ignorance.

'Ignorance is the nurse of the vices, for it does not realize what deserves blame and what does not. The ignorant are easily led astray, and little time passes before the fool falls into vice.'

Defensor Grammaticus
Book of Sparkling Sayings, 24 (SC77, pp.336ff.)

27th April

The Attainment of Perfect Freedom

What are the external objects which rouse the passions in us? Chiefly the opposite sex, material possessions and fame. To avoid being overwhelmed by these passions, there are certain steps we can take.

As far as the opposite sex is concerned, it is enough to gain control of our own bodies by mortification. With respect to material possessions we must make a resolution to be content with the bare necessities. With regard to fame, let us try to experience the beauty of practising virtue in secret, seen only by God.

Anyone who behaves in this fashion will not despise anything that exists on the face of the earth.

At times it happens that someone who has not these conditions before his eyes is not disturbed by the passions and enjoys a partial freedom. Yet the moment a person of the opposite sex or wealth or fame crosses his path, the passions tear his spirit to pieces.

Do not delude yourself into thinking that you have perfect freedom of spirit if there is no external object disturbing you. Only if you remain untroubled at the appearance of such an object, only then have you attained perfect freedom.

Maximus the Confessor
Centuries on Charity, 4, 49ff. (SC9, pp.162ff.)

28th April

Let us Glory in Temptation

The devil does not have only one weapon. He uses many different means to defeat human beings: now with bribery, now with boredom, now with greed he attacks, inflicting mental and physical wounds equally.

The kind of temptation varies with the different kinds of victim. Avarice is the test of the rich, loss of children that of parents and everyone is exposed to pain of mind or body. What a wealth of weapons is at the devil's disposal!

It was for this reason that the Lord chose to have nothing to lose. He came to us in poverty so that the devil could find nothing to take away from him. You see the truth of this when you hear the Lord himself saying: 'The prince of this world is come and has found nothing in me.' [John 14:30] The devil could only test him with bodily pain, but this too was useless because Christ despised bodily suffering.

Job was tested by his own goods, whereas Christ was tempted, during the experience of the wilderness, by the goods of all. In fact, the devil robbed Job of his riches and offered Christ the kingdom of the whole world. Job was tested by vexations, Christ by prizes. Job the faithful servant replied: 'The Lord has given and the Lord has taken away.' [Job 1:21] Christ, being conscious of his own divine nature, scorned the devil's offering of what already belonged to him.

So let us not be afraid of temptations. Rather, let us glory in them saying: 'When I am weak, then am I strong.' [2 Cor. 12:10]

Ambrose
On the Gospel of St Luke, 4, 39 (PL15, 1625)

143

29th April

Tackle your Fears Head-On

Fear is a childish feeling of the adult but empty soul. Fear is really a lack of faith that becomes obvious when we think of what unforeseen things might happen. It is lack of trust in God.

The proud soul is a slave to fear precisely because it trusts in itself and so shudders at any noise or any shadow. Those who are contrite for their sins have no fear.

So if there are places where you are normally afraid to go, do not hesitate to frequent them even at dead of night, armed with prayer. Your fear is a childish and ridiculous thing, but if you give way to it only a little, it will take root in your heart and stay with you. So arm yourself with prayer and when you reach the spot lambast the enemy in the name of Jesus. There is no stronger weapon in earth or heaven than that.

And when you are cured of your fear, sing the praises of the One who has freed you. If you thank him, he will always protect you.

Sometimes only the body is afraid and the fear has not spread to the soul, then you are nearly cured.

The one who serves God, fears his Lord and no other. The one who does not fear his Lord is scared even of his own shadow.

John Climacus
Stairway to Paradise, 21 (PG88, 945)

30th April

Reach out to the Good in the Freedom of Love

Evil as a thing in itself does not exist. It has no being, if we think of it as completely separated from the highest Good. Nothing exists that does not participate in the Good. Evil is only a lack of Goodness, and nothing exists that is completely lacking in Goodness.

Divine Providence affects every being; there is no being that is outside its influence. When some evil happens, Providence kindly makes use of it for the benefit of the sinner or of other people, individually or as a community.

We cannot agree with the one who says that Providence ought to compel us to be good even against our will. What sort of Providence would it be that destroyed our human nature? Its function is rather to protect the nature of every being. Therefore, when dealing with beings that have been given free will, it acts taking account of this free will of theirs.

Evil is weakness, impotence, lack of knowledge, ignorance of what it is impossible not to know, insufficient faith, not enough desire for or doing of what is good.

The objection could be raised that weakness deserves forgiveness rather than punishment. If humanity had not been given any strength, that objection would be justified. But according to Scripture the highest Good gives each person the strength that is needed. Consequently we have no excuse for neglecting the good qualities we have received from him who is Goodness itself.

This Good is the beginning and the end of all things. It is involved in all existence. It creates from nothingness. It is the cause of all good without being the cause of evil. It is Providence and perfect Goodness. It transcends being and not-being. And it has the ability to turn evil into good.

We ought to reach out to it with all our might, with all the desire of love.

Pseudo-Dionysius the Areopagite
On the Divine Names 4, 33ff. (PG3, 812)

May

Come to me, O God,
that I may come to you

1st May

One Route but so Many By-Ways

Jerome said:

'There are many virtues which lead those who practise them to the kingdom of heaven. There is only one route but there are many by-ways.

'Whoever is anxious to make progress, even if he reaches a certain degree of perfection, can always find some need for improvement and become more proficient day by day.

'No one can enjoy a good reputation both for virtue and for a big bank balance.'

Ambrose said:

'The virtues cannot take command of the soul unless it has first shaken off the yoke of vice.'

Isidore said:

'We climb towards virtue only with effort: without any effort at all we fall into vice.

'If you want your virtues to increase, do not make them public.'

Gregory said:

'If you are still doing good only from fear, you have not altogether escaped from the clutches of evil. Vices we can restrain with fear, but virtues only grow in a climate of love: in faith and hope and love.'

Defensor Grammaticus
Book of Sparkling Sayings, 26 (SC77, pp.346ff.)

2nd May

The Spiritual Pilgrim's Guidebook

A firm faith is the mother of the renunciation of the world; the opposite, obviously, produces the opposite effect.

Unwavering hope is the door to the renunciation of every earthly affection; the opposite, obviously, produces the opposite effect.

The love of God is the basis of detachment from the world; and here too the opposite, obviously, has the opposite effect.

Self-control is the mother of spiritual health. The mother of self-control is the thought of death combined with the remembrance of the sharpness of the wrath of the Lord our God.

Solitude and silence help to maintain purity; fasting pours water on the fire of the passions.

Contrition is the enemy of evil and base thoughts.

The death of avarice is attained by faith and flight from the world.

Perseverance in prayer is the annihilation of sloth.

The thought of judgment stirs the will to good purpose.

Love of humiliation is the cure for anger.

Detachment from visible things is to open your eyes to the invisible.

Silence and solitude are the enemies of pride; if you are involved with people, keep an eye out for occasions of humiliation.

Visible pride is cured by an attitude that is empty of arrogance; invisible pride is cured by the Eternal Invisible.

John Climacus
Stairway to Paradise, 26, Appendix (PG88, 1084)

3rd May

All the Limbs Begin to Tremble

To fear God is not simply to say: 'I fear God,' as some who seem to fear God suggest. It is a fear that arises naturally in the soul and causes it to tremble, to such an extent that it makes the body tremble too.

The body is afraid of what can make it suffer; the soul is afraid of what can cause its death.

The body is afraid of wild beasts, of fire and sword, of drowning, of falling from a height; it is afraid of the law, handcuffs, torture, prison.

In the same way the soul is naturally afraid of the unseen judge and the punishments God has reserved for those who provoke his anger. The soul takes fright when it thinks about these.

It is not a reasoning fear that afflicts the body when it sees something that may make it suffer. The mere sight of it, or even the thought, makes it tremble instinctively.

The soul similarly when it looks with the eye of faith at the perils that may come to it and sees the terrible punishments that the word of the Judge has revealed, is immediately filled with fear and all its spiritual members, that is its thoughts, begin to tremble.

Philoxenus of Mabbug
Homily 6, 162ff. (SC44, pp.167ff.)

4th May

The Power of Faith

The power of faith is enormous. It is so great that it not only saves the believer: thanks to one person's faith others are saved also.

The paralytic at Capernaum did not have faith. But the men who brought him to Jesus and let him down through the roof had it. The soul of the sick man was ill as well as his body. That is made clear in the Gospel: 'And when Jesus saw their faith he said . . . , "Rise, take up your pallet and go home." ' The Gospel does not speak of 'his' faith but of 'their' faith. The stretcher-bearers believed and the paralytic had the benefit of being healed because of it. [Mark 2:1-11]

Then there is the death of Lazarus. Four days had passed. His dead body was already decomposing. How could one who had been dead for so many days believe and himself ask for the Deliverer? He could not possibly do so, but his sisters provided the faith for him. When they met the Lord, one sister fell down at his feet. He asked, 'Where have you laid him?' The other sister said, 'Lord, by this time there will be a bad smell.' Then the Lord said, 'If you believe you will see the glory of God.' As if to say, 'As regards faith, you must take the place of the dead man.' And the faith of the sisters succeeded in calling Lazarus back from the hereafter. [John 11:1-44]

So if these two women by believing in place of the other were able to secure his resurrection, how much more certainly will you be able to secure it for yourself by your own faith?

Perhaps your own faith is feeble. Nevertheless, the Lord who is love will stoop down to you, provided only you are penitent and can say sincerely from the depths of your soul: 'Lord, I believe. Help thou mine unbelief.' [Mark 9:23]

Cyril of Jerusalem
Catecheses, 5, 8ff. (PG33,516)

5th May

If you Believe, he who Welcomed the Thief will Welcome you Also

Faith is the assent of the soul to a truth. If you want to know what advantage the soul gains from it, listen to what the Lord says:

'Whoever hears my word and believes him who sent me, has eternal life; he does not come into judgment, but has passed from death to life.' [John 5:24]

How truly great is the goodness of God to the human race!

The righteous in ancient times, in order to find favour with God, had to struggle for many years. They achieved it after having served God for long and with heroic efforts; Jesus grants it to us in an instant.

It is true. If you believe that Jesus Christ is Lord and that God has raised him from the dead, you will be saved. Jesus on the cross on Calvary welcomed the thief to Paradise. He will welcome you also.

Cyril of Jerusalem
Catecheses, 5, 8ff. (PG33, 516)

6th May

Faith without Works is Dead

Someone may say: 'I have faith, and faith suffices for salvation.' St James gives him the answer: 'Even the demons believe, and shudder. Faith without works is dead.' [Jas. 2:17-19]

How can we speak of having faith in God and believing what he promises about the future when we do not even believe what he teaches us about the present, about our existence in time?

We have been ensnared by earthly things and we live absorbed in the flesh which makes war on the spirit.

True faith in Christ is what they had who welcomed the whole of it into their lives by means of the practical fulfilment of the commandments, saying in effect: 'I live, yes, but it is no longer I who live but Christ who lives in me; and the life I now live in the flesh I live by faith in the Son of God who loved me and gave himself for me.' [Gal. 2:20]

Maximus the Confessor
Ascetics, 34 (PG90, 940)

7th May

Prove your Faith by Your Trust

'Look at the birds of the air,' says Jesus. [Luke 12:24] What a splendid example for our faith to follow!

If God's providence bestows an unfailing supply of food on the birds of the air who neither sow nor reap, we ought to realize that the reason for people's supply running short is human greed.

The fruits of the earth were given to feed all without distinction and nobody can claim any particular rights. Instead, we have lost the sense of the communion of goods, rushing to turn these goods into private property.

The birds do not know famine because they do not claim anything specially for themselves and neither do they have any envy of others.

'Consider the lilies of the field: not even Solomon in all his glory was arrayed like one of these. If God so clothes the grass which is alive today and tomorrow is cast into the oven, how much more will he clothe one of you!' Listen to these stupendous and uplifting words.

With this parable of flowers and grass the Lord urges us to hope that God will also be merciful to us.

Nothing is more persuasive than a glance at unthinking creatures who have received such beautiful dress from providence. Surely we should be all the more ready to believe that human beings, if they entrust themselves completely to God and free themselves of all their worries, will not lack anything.

Ambrose
On the Gospel of St Luke, 7, 124ff.
(PL15, 1751)

8th May

Let Nothing Discourage You: Have no Fear!

In accordance with the words of the apostle, always maintain an attitude of thankfulness: 'Give thanks for all things.' [1 Thess. 5:18]

For tribulations, sufferings, anguish, illness, physical pain, for everything that happens to you give thanks to God. Indeed, 'Through many tribulations we must enter the kingdom of God.' [Acts 14:22] There we shall be freed from every evil.

Have no doubt, never be discouraged. Remember Paul's teaching: 'Though our outer nature is wasting away, our inner nature is being renewed every day.' [2 Cor. 4:16] Only by accepting suffering will you be able to share in the cross of Christ.

As long as the ship is far out to sea, it remains exposed to danger at the mercy of the winds. But when it reaches harbour there is no longer anything to threaten its safety, its tranquillity, its peace.

The same thing happens to you. During this life, you must expect pain and suffering and attack by spiritual storms. But when you arrive in harbour, you will have nothing else to fear.

Barsanuphius
Letters (ed. Nicodemo l'Agiorita, Venice 1816)

9th May

Purify the Roots and You will be Entirely Pure

Discipline of the body, if it is combined with peace of mind, purifies it from all material tendencies.

Discipline of the soul makes it humble and purifies it from the impressions that push it in a material direction.

Discipline effects the transition from the emotions of passion to the activity of contemplation, or, better, it raises the soul above all terrestrial objects and feeds it on contemplation. The spirit then is turned towards God by means of the vision of his ineffable glory, and it derives joy from the hope of its future state.

Discipline of the soul is a painful commitment of the heart to reach purity.

Between purity of mind and purity of heart there is the same difference as there is between a particular limb and the whole body. The heart is the central organ of the senses, it gives meaning to the senses, it is in fact their root.

St Paul's expression can be applied in this case: 'If the root is holy, so are the branches.' [Rom. 11:16]

Isaac of Nineveh
Philocalia

10th May

The Perfect Person's Rule of Life

The perfect person does not only try to avoid evil. Nor does he do good for fear of punishment, still less in order to qualify for the hope of a promised reward.

The perfect person does good through love.

His actions are not motivated by desire for personal benefit, so he does not have personal advantage as his aim. But as soon as he has realized the beauty of doing good, he does it with all his energies and in all that he does.

He is not interested in fame, or a good reputation, or a human or divine reward.

The rule of life for a perfect person is to be the image and likeness of God.

Clement of Alexandria
Miscellaneous Studies, 4, 22, 135ff. (Stählin II, p.308)

11th May

Weighing up our Actions

The Abbot Germanus said: 'We are perfectly convinced that the right judgment of our thoughts is the spring and the root of all the virtues. But we would like to know how to acquire that judgment, and also how it is possible to recognize its authenticity, that is to say, whether it comes from God.'

The Abbot Moses replied: 'Only by humility can true judgment be acquired. And the first test of humility is to submit to the opinions of the ancients not only what one ought to do but also what one ought to think.

'By this method a young person will learn to walk safely along the path of true judgment and to overcome the snares of the enemy without coming to any harm. There is no possibility of anyone being led astray if he seeks the inspiration of the ancients rather than acting on his own initiative.

'All the devil's enmity will not prevail over someone who does not hide the thoughts that spring up in his heart but submits them to the scrutiny of mature people to decide whether to accept or reject them. Besides, an evil thought loses its poison in the very moment that it is brought to the light.

'Humility is therefore indispensable for acquiring true judgment, that is to say, for saving us from the danger of exaggeration in one direction or the other.'

Cassian
Conferences, 2, 9ff. (PL49, 530)

12th May

Simplicity a Name for God

The complicated soul is continually at the mercy of opposing thoughts.

It speaks the truth one moment, tells lies the next. It approves, then rejects; it links and unlinks; it is like a bazaar stocked with a muddle of thoughts; it never stays long enough with one idea either to believe in it or to renounce it; it chooses something only to abandon it almost at once.

Simplicity, however, is exactly the opposite, as its name suggests; there is no confusion of thought at all.

159

Indeed, simplicity might well be another name for God. God is simple, that is, one, because there are no parts or divisions in him. In common parlance, similarly, we call someone simple if he does not act deceitfully nor lay traps for others; there is no stirring of the evil spirit in him.

Simplicity comes before faith; faith is the daughter of simplicity, not of complexity.

Simplicity exists in us long before we acquire complexity: children are rich in innocence, they are pure.

Philoxenus of Mabbug
Homily 4, 82ff. (SC44, pp.98ff.)

13th May

The New People are a People of Children

Paul shows great wisdom when he says: 'We never sought glory from people, whether from you or from others, though we might have made demands as apostles of Christ. But we were babes among you.' [1 Thess. 2:7]

A child is charming, gentle, simple-minded, without cunning or hypocrisy, in short, straightforward in thought and speech. He is therefore the personification of simplicity.

A child has a sensitive soul. We too are sensitive. We trust one another without reserve. We do good. We keep ourselves clear of rancour and crookedness.

Old people are often crooked and unforgiving. The new people are a people of children, lovable like children.

Paul who speaks of his own joy in 'a heart without malice' gives a definition of children in a certain sense when he writes: 'I would have you wise as to what is good and guileless as to what is evil.' [Rom. 16:19]

In this meaning of the word, we are always children, always sensitive, always new as those who share in the new Word.

Whoever has been called to eternal life ought to resemble the Incorruptible. For this reason, let our whole life be springtime; let the truth within us never grow old.

Clement of Alexandria
The Teacher, 1, 5, 19 (Stählin I, pp.101ff.)

14th May

Gentleness, the Face of Love

Just as water falling a drop at a time onto the fire in the end puts it out, so tears of sincere sorrow damp down in us the flame of anger and contempt. Then gentleness arrives, a deep tranquillity of soul, which is untroubled either by honours or by ridicule.

The first stage of this tranquillity consists in silencing the lips when the heart is excited. The second, in silencing the mind when the soul is still excited. The goal is a perfect peacefulness even in the middle of the raging storm.

Anger is a dislike hatched from the memory of offences received, a desire to hurt the people who have hurt us. The sweet scent of humility, however, makes it disappear, as the darkness scatters when the sun rises.

Some people with a hot temper do not worry about it and ignore the remedies that would heal them. They

161

forget, unfortunately, what is written: 'Surely anger kills the fool, and jealousy slays the simple.' [Job 5:2]

Anger is like the rapid revolution of the mill-wheel. It not only crushes but also scatters more grain than a reaper could do working a whole day.

It is also like an outbreak of fire when the wind is blustery: it scorches and burns up the field of the heart more disastrously than a slow fire would in a longer period.

The hot-tempered individual is like an epileptic: the disease takes him by surprise, shakes him up, flings him to right and left. He needs a great deal of humility because his anger is the result of an over-inflated opinion of himself.

On the other hand, gentleness attains its highest expression when we keep our heart calm in the face of someone who is provoking us, and actually show him our love.

John Climacus
Stairway to Paradise, 8 (PG88, 823)

15th May

Uphold the Living Rather than Hold the Dead

A monk, seeing two men carrying a dead body on a stretcher, said to one of them: 'Are you holding the dead? Go and uphold the living!'

An old monk received a visit from some thieves one day: 'We've come to strip your cell.' He answered: 'My children, all you like to take is yours.' The thieves cleared the place out and left. They forgot, however, a bag that was hanging on the wall.

The monk unhooked the bag and ran after them: 'My children, you've forgotten this!' They were astonished by the patience of the old man, and they went back and restored everything to its place in the cell, saying to one another: 'Here truly is a man of God.'

Another old monk knew one of the brothers who, when he came to his cell, would always take something. He realized what was going on, but did not rebuke him. 'Without doubt,' he thought to himself, 'he took it because he needed it.'

When the old monk was about to die, all the brothers were gathered round. He noticed the one who had so often stolen from him and called: 'Come closer!' Then he embraced the brother and said: 'I'm thanking these hands of yours because through their merits I am going to the kingdom of heaven.'

The brother did penance and became an excellent monk, thanks to the lesson he had received.

Two brothers lived in the same place. One day an old man turned up, anxious to test them. With his walking-stick he began to wreak havoc on the vegetable patch of the first brother.

This brother saw him and hid. But when there was only one cabbage left, he came out of hiding and said to the old man: 'Father, if you like, leave this one; I will cook it for you and we will eat it together.'

The old man bowed to the ground before him and exclaimed: 'The Holy Spirit is with you, brother, because of your forbearance!'

Sayings of the Desert Fathers nos. 204ff. (PG65, 79)

16th May

Patience is our Martyrdom

Gregory the Great said:

'You cannot acquire the gift of peace if by your anger you destroy the peace of the Lord.

'True patience is to suffer the wrongs done to us by others in an unruffled spirit and without feeling resentment. Patience bears with others because it loves them; to bear with them and yet to hate them is not the virtue of patience but a smokescreen for anger.

'True patience grows with the growth of love. We put up with our neighbours to the extent that we love them. If you love, you are patient. If you cease loving, you will cease being patient. The less we love, the less patience we show.

'If we truly preserve patience in our souls, we are martyrs without being killed.'

Defensor Grammaticus
Book of Sparkling Sayings, 2 (SC77, pp.74ff.)

17th May

Obedience is the Child of Trust

Obedience is the complete renunciation of one's own soul, demonstrated, however, by actions. More exactly, it is the death of the senses in a living soul.

Obedience is a freely-chosen death, a life without cares, danger without fears, unshakeable trust in God, no fear of death. It is a voyage without perils, a journey in your sleep.

Obedience is the burial of the will and the resurrection of humility.

Obedience is to give up one's own judgment but to do it with wise consultation.

It is very costly, beginning to die to the will and the senses. To continue dying is hard but not indefinitely so. In the end all aversion stops and absolute peace takes command.

John Climacus
Stairway to Paradise, 4 (PG88, 680)

18th May

If You Think You are Humble that Means You are Not

A monk said: 'Every time you feel a sense of superiority or a touch of vanity, examine your conscience. Ask yourself if you are keeping all the commandments, if you are loving your enemies and weeping for their faults, if you consider yourself an unprofitable servant and the worst sinner in the world. But even after this examination of conscience, do not take too high an opinion of yourself as if you were perfect: such an idea would wreck everything!'

Another monk said: 'Whoever is praised and honoured more than is deserved suffers a great loss, while the one who does not receive honours from others will be glorified in heaven.'

People asked a monk: 'What is humility?' He replied: 'Humility is if a brother or sister sins against you and you forgive them before they come to ask you to.'

A brother asked a monk: 'What is humility?' The

monk said: 'To do good to whoever does evil to us.'
The brother insisted: 'And if one does not achieve as
much?' The monk's reply was: 'Then go away and
try to keep your mouth shut.'

Sayings of the Desert Fathers, nos. 165ff. (PG65)

19th May

To Rise You Must Go Downward

Origen said:
    'If you are not humble and serene, it is impossible
for the grace of the Holy Spirit to dwell in you.'
    Augustine said:
    'God humbled himself: human beings should blush
to be proud.'
    Gregory the Great said:
    'The more humility aims at the depths, the higher it
climbs on the path to the summit.
    'Humility in listening to the Word of God makes the
path ready for the Lord to enter our heart.'
    Isidore said:
    'Whoever acquires virtue without humility is throw-
ing dust into the wind.'

Defensor Grammaticus
Book of Sparkling Sayings, 4 (SC77 pp.102ff.)

20th May

Have You Ever Seen the Snow Catch Fire?

Just as certain winged creatures are too fat to fly, so are people who over-feed their bodies.

Just as pigs do not feel attracted to dry mud, so do the devils find no pleasure in a body desiccated by penance.

Just as oil calms the rage of the sea even it seems to resist the pacifying effect, so is the heat of the body's passions cooled by fasting even if they object.

Just as water when it is squeezed on all sides shoots up above, so does the soul when it is pressed hard by dangers often rise to God and be saved.

Just as fire is not born from snow, so is the seeker after worldly honours not seeking heavenly ones.

Just as people who spend hours in bed are easily burgled, so are those who wish to practise virtue without withdrawing from the world.

Just as anyone fighting a lion is lost as soon as he takes his eyes off him, so is the one fighting the flesh if he takes a break for a moment.

John Climacus
Stairway to Paradise, 26, Appendix (PG88, 1084)

21st May

Sobriety, the Guardian of the Spirit

Sobriety is a guardian of the spirit. It stands on guard day and night at the gates of the heart, to sort out the thoughts that present themselves, to listen to their suggestions and to observe their intrigues.

In the first place, control the imagination strictly: it is the only route by which Satan can slip thoughts into the mind to deceive it.

Then preserve in your heart a deep silence, an undisturbed tranquillity.

Next, invoke the help of Jesus unceasingly and humbly.

Finally, keep the thought of death alive in your soul.

This is the way for that guardian, sobriety, to stop evil thoughts from approaching.

Hesychius of Sinai
Philocalia, 1 (Athens 1957, p.142)

22nd May

Let your Soul keep a Good Look-Out

An old desert father once said: 'Every morning and every evening a monk ought to make a reckoning with himself over his actions and ask himself: "Have I perhaps done what God does not want me to do? Or have I not done what God wants me to do?" '

A second ancient father said: 'If you waste gold or silver, you can find some more gold or silver, but if you waste time, you will never find any more.'

And a third then said: 'In the morning when you get up you ought to issue this command: "Body, work for your living; soul, keep awake so as to win your heavenly inheritance!" '

A brother said to an older monk: 'There does not seem to be any conflict in my heart.' He received this reply: 'You are like a house that is open to the four winds, so that anyone who likes can go in or out without your noticing. If you only had one door to it, and chose to shut it in the face of wicked thoughts, then you would notice them and you would have to fight against them.'

It is told that a thought came to a monk: 'Rest today and you can do penance tomorrow.' He replied: 'No, I will do penance today and rest tomorrow.'

A venerable saint said: 'If the inner person is not watchful, the outer person cannot be watched.'

Sayings of the Desert Fathers nos. 132ff. (PG65)

23rd May

Wisdom is not only Knowledge

Augustine said:
'The wise will shine like stars and those who can make others wise will be bright with eternal splendour.

'Feed your soul on divine readings; they will prepare for you a spiritual feast.'

Jerome said:
'It is much better to speak the truth clumsily than to wax eloquent with a lie.'

Gregory said:
'Wisdom is to fear God and keep far from evil.

'The beginning of wisdom is to avoid evil: the second stage is to do good.

'Whoever wants to understand what he is hearing must hasten to translate what he has already heard into action.'

Isidore said:

'Simplicity joined with ignorance is called stupidity: simplicity joined with prudence is called wisdom.'

Defensor Grammaticus
Book of Sparkling Sayings, 18 (SC77, pp.28off.)

24th May

Contemplation of God Acquired by Means of his Word

The Lord says: 'Martha, Martha, you are anxious and troubled about many things; one thing is necessary. Mary has chosen the better part which shall not be taken away from her.' [Luke 10:41-42]

We too ought to be eager to possess what no one can take away from us, namely the gift of earnest, attentive listening to the Word of God. We know from the parable of the Sower that the seeds even of the heavenly Word are taken away if they are sown along the path. So let the longing for wisdom inspire you as it did Mary, and never think those people idle who are seeking it.

Certainly, the Lord did not rebuke Martha for her devoted service. He is rich in many gifts and distributes them severally among human beings. Mary is judged the wiser of the two sisters because she chose what she saw to be the most important thing.

The Apostles, you remember, reckoned that it was not good to leave the Word of God to serve tables. [Acts 6:2] Yet each kind of service is a work of wisdom. Stephen who was chosen to serve tables was full of wisdom. [Acts 6:5-10] But the server should obey the teacher, and the teacher should encourage the server.

The Church is one body, although it has many different members, and each needs the other. 'The eye cannot say to the hand, "I have no need of you," nor again the head to the feet, "I have no need of you." ' [cf. 1 Cor. 12:12-21] For although some members are of chief importance, all are necessary. Wisdom, however, has its seat in the head whereas action relies on the hands. The truly wise are those whose souls are in Christ.

Ambrose
On the Gospel of St Luke, 7, 85 (PL15, 1808)

25th May

Persevering is More Important than Beginning

Jerome said:

'Christians will not be asked how they began but rather how they finished. St Paul began badly but finished well. Judas's beginning was praiseworthy but his end was despicable.

'Many start the climb but few reach the summit.'

Gregory said:

'The value of good work depends on perseverance.

'You live a good life in vain if you do not continue it until you die.'

Isidore said:

'Our behaviour is only acceptable to God if we have the strength of purpose to complete any work we have undertaken.

'Virtue is not a matter of starting well but of carrying on to the very end.

'The reward is not promised to the one who begins, but rather to the one who perseveres.'

Defensor Grammaticus
Book of Sparkling Sayings, 22 (SC77, pp.318ff.)

26th May

Hunger for Righteousness

Many say that righteousness consists in always giving to each what is right, what each deserves. I believe, however, taking account of the depth of the divine dispensation, that the word 'righteousness' ought to include something more.

'Blessed are they that hunger . . . after righteousness, for they shall be satisfied.' [Matt. 5:6]

When certain things are offered us as food, all of different sorts and very desirable, we need a great deal of patience to discover what is good nourishment and what is harmful. There is a danger that we will want to eat something that may lead to illness or death. Well then, only the person who is hungry for God's righteousness finds what everyone ought to be looking for.

In this passage, the Word says that righteousness is offered to all those who are hungry for it. It is clear that the word 'righteousness' means the sum total of the virtues. It means that the person is blessed who possesses prudence, courage, moderation, temperance, self-control, who is hungry, in short, for all included in the definition of virtue.

I insist on 'all'. It is not possible for one particular virtue to be isolated from the others and to remain a perfect virtue. For this reason, people in whom we do not find what we reckon as good, undoubtedly have in them the opposite of good. So it is absurd to speak of righteousness as applied to a person who is unwise, foolhardy, uncontrolled or dissolute in some way.

Righteousness includes all the virtues and none is left out.

Gregory of Nyssa
On the Beatitudes, 4 (PG44, 1232ff.)

27th May

We are all Begging to have God

It is natural to look for beauty and to love it, even though the idea of what is beautiful varies between one person and another.

Now, what is more marvellous than the divine beauty? What can you think of that is more likely to give pleasure than the magnificence of God? What desire could be more ardent, more irresistible than the thirst which God inspires in the soul when once it has been purified of every vice and cries out: 'I am sick with love.' [S. of S. 2:5]

The divine beauty is beyond description in words. We could compare its brilliance to the light of the morning star or the moon or the sun. But we should be as far from a true description as midday is from the dead of night.

This beauty is invisible to the eyes of the body; only the soul and the mind can perceive it. Every time it illumines the saints, it leaves in them a sting, a nostalgia so strong as to wring from them the cry: 'Woe is me, that I am in exile still.' [cf. Ps. 120:5]

By our nature we human beings aspire to what is beautiful and love it. But what is beautiful is also good. God is good. Everyone looks for the good, therefore everyone looks for God.

Basil the Great
The Greater Rules, 2 (PG31, 909)

173

28th May

We Cannot but Love God

The love of God is not taught. No one has taught us to enjoy the light or to be attached to life more than anything else. And no one has taught us to love the two people who brought us into the world and educated us. Which is all the more reason to believe that we did not learn to love God as a result of outside instruction.

In the very nature of every human being has been sown the seed of the ability to love. You and I ought to welcome this seed, cultivate it carefully, nourish it attentively and foster its growth by going to the school of God's commandments with the help of his grace.

In fact, the virtue of love despite being only a single quality embraces with its power all the commandments. The Lord says: 'If anyone loves me, he will keep my word.' [John 14:23] And again: 'You shall love the Lord your God . . . and you shall love your neighbour as yourself. On these two commandments depend all the law and the prophets.' [Matt. 22:40]

You and I have received from God the natural tendency to follow his commandments. In consequence, on the one hand, we cannot raise objections as if he were demanding something extraordinary from us, and, on the other hand, we cannot boast as if we had done something greater than the powers given to us.

If that is how things stand, we ought to say the same about love. God would not have given us the commandment to love him without also giving us the natural faculty for loving him.

Basil the Great
The Greater Rules, 2 (PG31, 908ff.)

174

29th May

Loving your Neighbour in Need

A brother asked an aged monk: 'There are two brothers: one of them leads a life of solitude six days a week and does much penance, while the other is dedicated to the service of the sick. Which of the two is behaving in the way that is more acceptable to God?'

The old man answered him: 'The brother who is always making a retreat would never attain the heights that the one who serves the sick has reached, not even if you hoisted him with a hook in his nose.'

A brother was looking after one of the Fathers who was sick. The Father's body was covered in running sores and gave off a foul smell.

The brother therefore thought to himself: 'I'm leaving; I can't stand the stench.' But he took a container and filled it with pus from the sores, telling himself: 'Yes, I'll leave, but first I want to drink this stuff.'

In that very moment he had another reaction: 'I will neither run away nor drink this liquid.' Thus the brother continued to serve the sick man.

Two monks were sitting having a heart-to-heart talk. One of them, who was ill, began to cough and to spit. His spittle, without his wanting it to, fell on the other.

The other immediately thought of protesting: 'Stop spitting over me!'

But in struggling against this thought he took a wager with himself: 'Only if you are ready to swallow his spittle yourself can you make such a protest.' And the conclusion was: 'I shall not swallow it and I shall say nothing.'

Desert Sayings of the Fathers nos. 224ff. (PG65)

30th May

Make your Love as Big as the World

Augustine said:

'It is by running along the road of true love that we can reach our heavenly homeland.

'Without love, everything we do is useless. We are wasting our energies if we do not have love, which is God.

'Human beings only become perfect when they are overflowing with love.

'One can believe in the right way, but without love one cannot attain eternal happiness.

'Love is so strong that without it neither prophecy nor martyrdom avail.

'Love is the sweet and saving food without which the rich are poor, thanks to which the poor become rich.

'Enlarge your love to the size of the world if you want to love Christ, since the members of Christ are to be found all over the world.

'Only those who have the perfection of Christ's love are able to live together. Those who are without it continually upset one another and their anxiety is a misery to the others.'

Defensor Grammaticus
Book of Sparkling Sayings, 1, 5ff. (SC77 pp.58ff.)

31st May

Light, Fire and Flame

Love in its nature makes a human being like God, as far as is possible for a human being. The soul is intoxicated by the effects of it. Its characteristics are a fountain of faith, an abyss of patience, an ocean of humility.

Love is the complete repudiation of any unkind thought about one's neighbour, since, 'Love thinks no evil.' [1 Cor. 13:5]

Love, unchangeable tranquillity and our adoption as children of God are different from each other only in name. As light, fire and flame are present in the selfsame operation, so are these three manifestations of the Spirit.

When someone is completely permeated with the love of God, the brightness of his soul is reflected by his whole personality as if in a mirror.

Therefore the one who loves God also loves his brother or sister. Indeed, the second love is the proof of the first.

John Climacus
Stairway to Paradise, 30 (PG88, 1156)

June

My house, O God,
is your church

1st June

Make your Spouse Beautiful

'Wives, be subject to your husbands, as to the Lord.'[1] From these words of Paul you sense how open-hearted should be your wife's subjection. But now listen to what Paul requires of you. Follow the same example. 'Husbands, love your wives as Christ loved the Church.' You see how much obedience is asked of you. Now hear how much love is required.

You want your wife to obey you as the Church obeys Christ? Then you must care for her as much as Christ cares for the Church. Should it be necessary to die for her, to be cut into a thousand pieces, to bear any sort of suffering, you should not say no; and if you have indeed suffered like that, you still have done nothing compared with what Christ has done. In point of fact, you would be doing these things for one to whom you are already united, while he has done them for one who opposed him and hated him, despised him, spat on him, rejected him. With all the tenderness of his soul he prevailed upon her to kneel at his feet without insulting her, without humiliating her, without making her afraid.

You, too, must behave in the same way with your wife. Even if you see that she despises you, even if she rejects and humiliates you, you can bring her back to you if you take trouble over her, if you care for her, if you are fond of her, if you love her.

Nothing is stronger than these bonds, particularly between husband and wife. By resorting to intimidation you might be able to keep a domestic servant attached to you – but not even him, for probably the servant will

---

[1] All this passage is a commentary on Eph. 5:21-33. All quotations are taken from there, unless otherwise noted.

leave you and escape. The companion of your life, the mother of your children, the basis of all your joy, ought not to be tied to you by threats and fear, rather by love and the warmth of emotion. What sort of union would that be in which the wife is afraid of her husband? And what pleasure could her husband find in staying with her as if she were a servant?

Whatever kind of woman you have chosen, you cannot have chosen anyone like the spouse Christ has chosen in marrying the Church. And if she is different from you, it is not so different as the Church is from Christ. Even so, he has not hated her, or loathed her for her terrible deformity. You want to know the extent of her deformity? Then listen to Paul: 'You were one time darkness.' [Eph. 5:8] Do you see how obscure she was? What is more obscure than darkness?

See too how brazen-faced she was. 'We were passing our days in malice and iniquity.' [Titus 3:3] And how unclean: 'We were foolish and disobedient.' [ibid.] What I mean to say is, she was a fool and a blasphemer, and yet, despite that, he sacrificed himself for that deformed spouse as if she had been beautiful, most deserving of love, marvellous. Full of admiration, Paul exclaims: 'One will hardly die for a righteous man, yet Christ died for us while we were still sinners.' [Rom. 5:7-8]

After taking a spouse like that, he made her beautiful and he washed her. He did not shrink even from that. He did it 'that he might sanctify her, having cleansed her by the washing of water with the word, that he might present her to himself in splendour.' With water he washed her uncleanliness away, water accompanied with a word. What word was it? 'In the name of the Father, the Son, and the Holy Spirit.' He not only adorned her, he made her resplendent 'without spot or wrinkle or any such thing.'

We too, in our spouse, seek this beauty. It could

be that we are in a position to create this beauty ourselves. Do not ask of your wife what is not in her power. Note carefully that the Church received everything from the Lord. It was he who made her resplendent without spot or wrinkle.

John Chrysostom
On the Letter to the Ephesians, 20, 1ff. (PG62, 135)

2nd June

Lifelong and Irrevocable Union

Marriage is rightly recommended to the faithful for its fruits, the gift of children, and for the conjugal modesty of which the mutual fidelity of the spouses is the guarantee and bond.

But there is another reason too. In this union there is also a mystery which makes it sacred and causes the Apostle to say: 'Husbands, love your wives as Christ has loved the Church.'

The effect of such a marriage is that man and woman once they are committed and bound to one another remain irrevocably united for their whole lives without being permitted to separate, except for the reason of adultery.

Is it not perhaps the same as with the union of Christ and his Church? They are alive together eternally; no divorce can ever separate them.

Augustine
On Marriage and Concupiscence, 1, 10 (PL44, 420)

3rd June

'Be Fruitful and Multiply, Fill the Earth and Subdue it'

Lord our God, Creator of all things, you have created man from the dust, have given him a helpmeet fashioned from a rib taken from him himself and then have joined them together in the intimacy of marriage that they may live together and increase the human race. You have said to them: 'Be fruitful and multiply, fill the earth and subdue it.'

You who are good, who are the friend of humanity, bless the union of these two servants of yours who are married in accordance with your will.

Bless them! Make them to be multiplied like our first fathers, Abraham, Isaac and Jacob whom you blessed. Bless them like Abraham and Sarah. Raise them up like Isaac and Rebecca. Multiply their descendants as you multiplied the stock of Jacob. Glorify them as you glorified Jacob in Egypt. Make them fruitful, as you made fruitful Hannah and Elkanah by giving them a son, the faithful Samuel, your prophet. Make them worthy of the visit of the holy archangel, as you made worthy Zachariah and Elizabeth to whom you gave the privilege of conceiving the greatest among those born of woman, John, the fore-runner of your only Son.

Lord, you blessed also Joachim and Anna, for you caused to be born of them the spiritual ark, Mary the Mother of God. In her was your Son made flesh. He came into the world. He blessed the wedding at Cana in Galilee.

Bless also these your servants who are now made one. Grant them the abundance of your blessing, grant them wisdom, grant them health. May they be united in body and spirit, religion and piety. May they become worthy of your blessing. May they glorify your holy Name, your only Son and the Holy Spirit, now and for ever.

> *Marriage Blessing in the Coptic Rite* (cf. A. Raes, *Le mariage dans des Eglises d'Orient*, Chevetogne 1958, pp.36ff.)

4th June

With the Strength of the Cross

Lord, Eternal God, you unite two unlike and separate beings and make them one, binding them together in an indissoluble fusion. You have blessed Isaac and Rebecca and shown that they were the heirs of your promises by multiplying, as the sand on the sea-shore, the people born from them.

So now also, kind and merciful God, bless this your servant and your handmaid whom you have redeemed. Through your holiness be their guide; may they walk in the ways of righteousness, fulfilling that which is pleasing in your sight; may they live in this world in obedience to your commandment, till they see their children and their children's children; and in the world to come may they inherit those good things that do not pass away and crowns that do not fade.

Lord God, you have chosen in the midst of the nations your holy Church to make of her your spouse and you have given to her as a crown the holy cross which is ever victorious. You gather together in unity all those who were scattered abroad and unite them with the indissoluble bonds of the covenant. You have blessed the patriarchs and shown in them the heirs of your promises.

Bless now this your servant and your handmaid with the strength of your cross, you who are merciful, you who love all the human race, you to whom belong glory and power and honour now and for ever.

Blessing of Newly-weds with the Cross in the Armenian Rite (cf. A. Raes, op.cit., pp.84ff.)

5th June

Find your Joy in your Spouse

(*During the nuptial rite wine is brought in the chalice and the priest blesses it.*)

O God, by your power you have made all things, you have created the universe and adorned it with the crown of all your works. As we offer this your chalice to be shared by these two who come to be united in one life together in marriage, we ask you to bless it with your spiritual benediction.

(*The priest offers the chalice to the spouses three times and leads them round the altar three times while the master of ceremonies holds crowns over them.*)

Isaiah rejoices because the Virgin has conceived and brought into the world a son, Emmanuel, God and man. Orient is his name. In glorifying him we glorify the Virgin. O holy martyrs who have fought and conquered and won your crowns, intercede with the Lord that he may have mercy on our souls.

(*The priest takes the crown from the husband.*)

O man, may you be glorified like Abraham, may you be blessed like Isaac, may you be fruitful like Jacob. Walk along your way in peace and fulfil the commandments of God in righteousness.

(*Then he takes the crown from the wife.*)

You also, O bride, may you be like Sarah, may you be joyful like Rebecca, may you be fruitful like Rachel. Find your joy in him who is your husband. Keep the precepts of the Law for this is pleasing to God.

O God, O our God, who went to Cana in Galilee to bless a wedding, bless also these your servants who are united in accordance with your providence to lead their life together in marriage. Bless what they do, and what they undertake. Preserve their crowns in your kingdom and keep them free from blemishes, from filth and falsity, throughout all ages, world without end.

Blessing of the Nuptial Chalice in the Byzantine Rite
(cf. A. Raes, op.cit., pp.66ff.)

6th June

God's Crown is Over You

God has crowned the earth with flowers of every kind. The Lord has crowned the heavens with shining stars: the sun, the moon, and a multitude of stars. God has crowned kings, priests, prophets, apostles and holy martyrs. The Lord has crowned the earth with the sea. May he also bless these crowns with his heavenly blessing, in answer to the prayers of Mary, mother of God, and all the saints.

(*Putting the crown on the head of the husband.*)

The Lord God, who has crowned the holy fathers with the crown of righteousness and has crowned and exalted kings, look on your life with mercy; and may his right hand, full of pity, crown you as he crowned Abraham, Isaac and Jacob. And since you have come to the Church to beg from her reconciliation and succour, may the Lord grant you his merciful grace, pardon you all sins and shortcomings, guard you and come to your aid now and for ever.

(*Putting the crown on the head of the wife.*)

God, who crowns all holy women, and has blessed Sarah, Rebecca and Rachel, bless you with the right hand of his divinity, pour his pity over your limbs and adorn you with the crown of glory. May you be in the Church as a vine that has been blessed and that brings forth spiritual fruit. May the Lord grant you and your husband joy in the discovery of peace and of mutual love, and may he give you children, in answer to the prayers of the mother of God and of all the saints.

May the Church which has crowned you both, the priests, the assembly which has prayed for you both, old and young, youths and maidens, married people and your attendants, all the assembly which is here with you raise their voices to the Lord to give him glory.

The Blessing of Nuptial Crowns in the Maronite Rite
(cf. A. Raes, op.cit., pp.148ff.)

7th June

Maker of Images of God

Holy marriage, chosen gift exalted above all earthly gifts!

Tree laden with fruit, noble scion sprung from virgin

life, abode of the burgeoning soul, bond of blessing for the increase of the human race!

Sweet comfort of our race, creator of humanity and maker of images of God!

Marriage receives the blessing of the Lord.

Like a mother, it carries the whole world in itself.

Marriage can hold its head high and say freely to everyone, all who have life because of it:

'Here am I with the children God has given me.'

Amphilochius
Orations, 2, 1 (PG39, 45)

8th June

Do not Despise Marriage

When you treat marriage with such disdain, you outrage the divine wisdom, you slander creation itself. If marriage is something impure, then all the beings which have been created from such a union are impure, then you too are impure, then the whole human race is impure. How then could there by any virgin if there is no longer any purity?

You shun marriage because you think of it as something shameful. But in rejecting it for this reason, you yourself become the most shameful creature in the world. You are debasing virginity, putting it lower than fornication.

You are unmarried? That does not of itself make you a virgin. I only call people virgins if they have renounced marriage when they were entirely free to marry. If you regard marriage as a prohibited state, you are making it no longer a free choice but blind submission to a

189

principle. By numbering marriage among the gravest sins, you cannot pretend that your continence is thereby made laudable. To abstain from what is prohibited cannot be a sign of generosity or love.

If you condemn marriage, at the same time you are diminishing the glory of virginity. If, on the other hand, you recognize the beauty of marriage, you are making virginity more beautiful, more splendid. For a good thing which only appears such if compared with an evil one is not in fact a perfectly good thing.

Marriage is a beautiful state and just because of that, virginity deserves our admiration because it surpasses something which is already regarded as beautiful.

John Chrysostom
On Virginity, 8, 1ff. (SC125, pp.115ff.)

9th June

Three Persons, One Flesh

Marriage is the representation of an important reality. It is a representation of Jesus Christ and the Church. It is a mystery, and the mystery consists in this, the fact that the spouses are united and the two become one. In great silence, while all around them there is complete tranquillity, the two are united and together form the image of God. One meets the other to make one body.

Every father is happy at the marriage of a daughter or a son, because he sees that two persons are about to form a single body. He has spent a lot of money on his children, they have cost him a great deal, and to see them not marrying does not help to support him: one body divided into two, that is what they are.

But when they marry how do they become one flesh? It is as if you were to take gold purer than any that exists and mix it with more gold. The wife receives the seed – fused as though in a crucible of pleasure – nourishes it, protects it, and adding her own contribution delivers it to her husband as a baby, a third person to make a bridge between the two parents. The three are one flesh, counting the baby who binds the father and mother together.

But then, if they do not have children, will they in that case not be two forming one flesh? They will be one flesh just the same, because it is the conjugal union that creates this unity by mingling together the bodies of the two spouses. Add a little seasoning to the oil and the mixture is complete. The same thing happens in marriage.

John Chrysostom
On the Letter to the Colossians, 12, 5ff. (PG62, 387)

10th June

Where the Two are, There also is Christ

Where shall I find the strength to describe adequately the joy of a marriage contracted in Church, confirmed at the altar, sealed by the blessing which the angels announce and God the Father ratifies?

What a beautiful pair two believers make when they put in common their hopes, their ideals, their way of living, their attitude of service! Both of them are servants of the same Lord, without the slightest difference of body or soul. So they pray together, they kneel together, they fast together. They teach one another, they encourage one another, they support one another. In the congregation they stand together, they are together at the table of the Lord, together in trials, in persecution, and in joys. There is no danger of their hiding something from one another nor of their avoiding or annoying each other.

They are happy to visit the sick and help the needy. They give alms with no ulterior motive, they share in the eucharistic sacrifice unhurriedly, they carry out their duties every day without wearying. They make the sign of the cross openly, they give God thanks without any reserve, they bless themselves without any shyness in their voices. They recite the psalms and hymns in alternate verses and compete to see which of them sings the praises of God best.

Seeing and hearing this, Christ rejoices and gives his peace to the couple. Where the two are, there also is Christ.

Tertullian
To his Wife, 2, 9 (PL1, 1385ff.)

11th June

Tell the Sisters . . .

Tell the sisters to love the Lord and to be happy with their husbands, whether in the flesh or the spirit.

Equally recommend the brothers, in the name of Jesus Christ, to love their wives as Christ loves the Church.

If anyone is able to remain a virgin in honour of the

192

Lord's human nature, let that person be humble: anyone who boasts of virginity is lost in eternity.

It will be well, furthermore, that men and women who marry should contract their union with the consent of the bishop, so that their marriage may be according to the Lord.

Let everything be done in honour of God.

Ignatius of Antioch
Letter to Polycarp, 5, 1ff. (SC10, pp.175ff.)

12th June

Say your Prayers Together

Say your prayers together. And let the husband teach his wife that in this life there is nothing to fear, except offending God.

Anyone who marries with this intention, and who puts this way of living above all else, will not be inferior to a monk.

He who has taken a wife will be no less worthy of esteem than the man who has not.

John Chrysostom
Letter to the Ephesians, 20:9 (PG62, 147)

13th June

We are One Another's Hands

In the consummation of the union of love we help one another, and because we are sprung from the earth we are following the primordial law of the earth, which is also God's law.

Look at the benefits good marriages bring to humanity. Who are the teachers of wisdom, the discoverers of the deepest knowledge, the explorers of everything on the earth, in the sea, or in the sky? Who are the lawgivers in the cities, and before them, the founders of the cities themselves? Who founded the arts? Who populated the squares, and the houses, the tables of banqueters? Who brought together the choirs that sing in the churches? Who tamed the ferocity of primitive life, first tilled the soil, and crossed the seas? What, if not marriage, could unite what was divided?

Here is a better point still. We are each other's hand and ear and foot, because marriage doubles our energy, cheers our friends, and depresses our enemies.

Sharing our troubles lessens the pain; joys put in common are sweeter; harmony makes riches more precious. And marriage is more precious than the riches themselves.

Marriage is the key to the control of the desires; it is the seal of an unshakeable friendship; it is drink from a hidden spring; strangers cannot taste it; it bubbles up yet cannot be drawn from outside.

Those who are united in the flesh form one soul and purify their religion by their reciprocal love.

Gregory Nazianzen
First Poem, 2, 189-562 (PG37)

14th June

Above All Else Harmony

The two spouses try to eradicate every cause for sorrow, to reinforce the harmony of the family and make it grow.

The wife should abandon herself to her husband; and the husband, when he is free from the anxieties and troubles of public life, should find in the heart of his wife a safe haven where he can enjoy help and comfort.

The wife in fact is the one who can help her husband. She has been given to him precisely for this purpose – to be his consolation and strength.

Her virtue and her sweetness are the joy of her husband; she is not only his companion but his helper in all sorts of circumstances. She makes everything easy and trouble-free for him; she does not weary him further by telling him the innumerable little complications that arise every day in the home. Like a capable pilot she succeeds in steering her husband's storm-tossed mind towards perfect serenity. Her steadiness is a source of great relaxation for him.

Two souls united thus have nothing to fear either from present circumstances or future events. When there is harmony, peace and mutual love, the man and his wife already possess everything good. No preoccupation vexes them and they can live serene behind the impregnable fortifications which protect them, namely harmony in conformity with God.

For that reason they are harder than diamonds and tougher than steel. They walk with a firm step on the road to eternal life, enjoying the continual increase of divine grace.

I urge you; let us place harmony above all good things,

and undertake with all our strength to maintain peace and tranquillity in our homes.

John Chrysostom
On Genesis, 38, 7 (PG53, 359)

15th June

Distance does not Count with Love

Let us be prudent in the maintenance of marital fidelity.

When a couple are united, even if the husband is abroad on a journey, distance ought not to diminish the joy of their love. Near or far, it is always the same law that unites them. Together or apart, it is always the same bond that guarantees the privileges of conjugal love. Even if one of the two is travelling a long way away, the same yoke of shared blessings unites them closely one to the other, because they have accepted the yoke of grace not only on their bodies but also on their souls.

You, husband, set aside your pride and rough manners when your wife approaches you with solicitude; stifle all irritation when she, full of tenderness, invites you to love. You are not her owner, but her spouse. You have not found a slave, but a wife. God has willed that you should be not a master, but a guide to the weaker sex. Copy her tenderness, respond eagerly to her love. Marriage requires you to soften the spikiness of your character; union with your wife obliges you to remove all hardness from your heart.

Never seek another woman's couch; never yearn for physical union with anyone else. Adultery is a grave matter: it is an outrage against nature. In the beginning

God made Adam and Eve, masculine and feminine, and he made the woman by taking her from the man, by removing a rib from Adam. And he ordered the two to become one body and to live in one spirit.

Why then should you want to tear apart what is a single body, to divide what is a single soul? Adultery is a violation of nature.

Ambrose
Hexaemeron, 5, 7 (PL14, 134ff.)

16th June

My Body is no Longer Mine; It is my Wife's

St Paul says: 'The husband should give to his wife her conjugal rights, and likewise the wife to her husband.'[1] What 'rights' is Paul speaking of?

He wants to make us understand that the wife is no longer the owner of her own body: she is the slave, and at the same time the owner, of her husband. If you try to escape from this slavery, says Paul, you offend the Lord. The Apostle speaks here of 'rights' because he wants it to be clear that neither spouse can freely do as he or she chooses but one is slave of the other.

If a harlot tries to seduce you, you ought to think: 'I am not the owner of my body; it belongs to another.' And the wife should think the same if anyone assails her chastity: 'My body is no longer mine, it is my husband's.' So that applies to both. Both of them have the same 'rights'. There are no special privileges for the

[1] All this passage is a commentary on 1 Cor. 7:3-5

197

man. 'The husband does not rule over his own body, but the wife does.' Perfect equality, no privilege.

Paul adds: 'Do not refuse one another except by agreement.' What does he mean? The wife is not to claim to practise continence against the husband's will, nor the husband against the will of his wife. Why so? Because serious evils could result. Adultery, fornication, family disasters are often caused by this.

Take a married couple and suppose she wants to observe continence against his wishes. What can she say if he then gives himself over to evil, or at the very least feels aggrieved, hurt, angry, goes to law and makes her life intolerable? What will she have gained by her continence if love has been destroyed?

John Chrysostom
On the First Letter to the Corinthians, 19, 1 (PG61)

17th June

How to Show your Spouse the Way of Salvation

Paul puts the question: 'Wife, how do you know whether you will save your husband?' [1 Cor. 7:16] What is our answer?

For my part I should answer that she will be able to save her husband if, while remaining a woman, she rises above her nature and attains the virtues of the saints.

She certainly will not save her husband by treating her skin with cosmetics, by living in pleasure, by always asking for more money, by spending extravagantly.

On the contrary, she will achieve it by showing herself in command of every situation, by demonstrating great moderation and great simplicity, by avoiding giving importance to money. If she does this, she will be convincing when she says to her husband: 'We have enough to eat, we have clothes to wear. Let us be content with that.'

She will be able to save her husband by openly putting the Gospel into practice.

John Chrysostom
On Virginity, 47, 1ff. (SC125, pp.263ff.)

18th June

Jealousy like a Whirlwind

Think of a jealous husband, or worse, of a husband who is jealous for no tangible reason.

A war or a whirlwind descending on a house, what other metaphor could we use?

Anguish, suspicions, lawsuits. A man who is devoured by jealousy is more restless than a madman. He does not stop gesticulating, rushing about, dumping his ill humour on everyone. He vents his anger on anyone he meets, even if there is no reason for it.

His happiness is gone, only sorrow and bitterness are left.

Whether he stays at home, or goes out in the street or travels, whatever he does makes his trouble more acute, more dreadful than death; his jealousy is a thorn in the flesh, a wound in his soul, and it gives him no rest.

In bed, he tosses and turns about as if he were on hot coals. Nothing can distract him from the whirlwind of his jealousy, not the companionship of friends nor the concerns of work, nor the fear of danger, nor the merry-go-round of amusements.

The storm which is raging in his soul has a force more violent than any joy, or any other grief.

John Chrysostom
On Virginity, 52, 1ff. (SC125, pp.289ff.)

19th June

A Mother Dies many Deaths

It is difficult to avoid sufferings in married life.

The wife, even though she will only have to die once herself, is still afraid of many deaths. Though she has only one soul of her own, she is deeply concerned for many souls.

She is afraid for her husband; she is afraid for her children. The more the family tree has blossomed, the more the fears increase. If one of her family suffers misfortune, such as the loss of money or an illness, she is desolated, and more agonized than the victim himself.

If all the rest of the family leave this life before she does, this is an intolerable suffering for her.

If death has not taken its toll of them all, the fact that any one of them is left is certainly a consolation to her, but a consolation imbued with anxiety. The fear that troubles her for those still alive is no less than her grief for those who have departed this life.

Indeed, although it may surprise you, her case is even more desperate. For time softens the grief caused by the death of her loved ones, but anxiety for the living never ceases.

John Chrysostom
On Virginity, 56, 1ff. (SC125, pp.305ff.)

20th June

Men have Found many Ways of Torturing their Wives

If the husband is a man who knows how to control himself but his wife is bad, a backbiter, a gossip and a spendthrift, how will the poor man put up with such a proud, impudent and brutal character all his life?

And if it happens the other way round? If the wife is modest and gentle, while he is a brute, spiteful and choleric, ambitious for money or power, and treats her like a slave, how will she be able to bear such slavery? And if he actually reaches the point of ignoring her completely with no touch of remorse? The wife has two solutions: either to commit herself with all her energies to making him a better man, or, if that is not possible, to endure bravely this ruthless struggle, this war without a truce.

Perhaps the husband will separate from her against her will. In that case St Paul invites her to maintain continence: 'The wife should not separate from her husband; but if she does, let her remain single.' [1 Cor. 7:11]

Men have discovered so many ways of torturing their wives. When the situation becomes intolerable, there is no alternative for the wife but to keep continence.

John Chrysostom
On Virginity, 40, 1ff. (SC125, pp.233ff.)

21st June

The Danger of Marrying a Rich Wife

A poor man who is simple and of humble origins marries a girl belonging to a family that is important and influential and very rich. An enviable situation, you say? Nothing of the sort.

When women have enough food for their pride, there is no stopping them. Like a flame fastening onto dry wood, they raise their heads and break all bounds. The husband becomes a doormat, not to mention the butt of scolding, humiliation, bullying.

I have often heard it said by a man who is about to marry: 'The important thing is that she's rich. I'll think about making her draw in her horns later.'

Such reasoning takes no account of the difficulties of the job. And, even if it were possible, it would lead to serious problems.

For when a woman is kept under by force or the fear of violence, the situation becomes more painful than if she were in command, because violence destroys both love and joy. If there is no longer any affection, no longer any impulse to love, if there is only fear and force, what value can there be in that marriage?

John Chrysostom
On Virginity, 53ff. (SC125, pp.299ff.)

22nd June

Speak to Your Wife like This

Tell your wife with great tenderness: 'I have taken you, my love, to be the companion of my life. I have asked you to share with me in a very high mission together: to have children and make a home. And now I would ask something else of you.'

Before explaining to her what this something else is, tell her how much you love her. Nothing prepares the ground so well in those who we talk to than knowing that we speak from overflowing love.

How will you show this love to her? Tell her: 'I could have married plenty of other women, rich or of a different social class, but I did not choose any of them. It is you that I am in love with, the way you behave, your modesty, your good sense. I could have married a rich woman, a super-rich one. But I was not attracted to them; I wanted to marry you: because I prefer the virtue of your soul to all the gold on earth.

'I value your love above everything, and there could not be any greater misfortune for me than to fall out with you. I could lose all my possessions; I could become the poorest of men and face worse risks and suffer no matter what; but I can put up with anything just so long as you are by my side and love me. I want, too, to have children very much, but only if you love me. And I think you have the same feelings.'

Include in what you say, also, the Apostle's words that God himself wills this bond of tenderness. Make her see that for you it is a joy to be with her, and that thanks to her you would rather be at home than out of doors. Give her preference over your friends and even over the children she gives you, and love them because of your love for her.

Praise and admire her if she does something well. If she chances to make a mistake, one of those slips that can happen to very young women, give her your advice and remind her of previous suggestions.

Only then, only after making her understand all this, tell her there need be neither richness nor luxury in your home, and help her to dress with modesty and decorum.

John Chrysostom
On the Letter to the Ephesians, 20, 8 (PG62, 146)

23rd June

Jesus did not Bring a Silver Bowl from Heaven with Him

A farmworker needs a shovel, a plough, various tools. But no one would make a mattock out of silver or a scythe of gold. In agriculture it is the usefulness of the tools we look at, not their money value.

So why don't we think in the same way about the furnishings of our homes? Why don't we argue the same way in their case?

Let our furnishings, also, be limited to what is strictly necessary. Our criterion in choosing them should not be their magnificence. Tell me this: doesn't a table knife cut just as well even if it is not made of silver, if it doesn't have an ivory handle?

Our Lord ate from ordinary plates. He made his disciples sit on the grass, on the ground. He washed their feet after girding himself with a towel, our humble Lord who is Lord of the universe. And he did not bring with him from heaven a silver bowl . . .

All Christians who are servants of the one God ought to show signs of the same holiness in the belongings and the furniture they use. Let us acquire things that we are not going to throw away. Let us use them and keep them carefully and offer them readily to others. The most useful things are the best. Things that cost only a little are preferable to expensive ones.

If we don't do this, we should be managing our money badly. And money badly managed is a den of iniquity.

Clement of Alexandria
The Teacher, 2, 3 (PG8, 432ff.)

24th June

Let us Prepare Two Tables

When we return home, let us prepare two tables, one for bodily food, the other for that spiritual food which is the Holy Scripture.

Let the husband repeat what has been said in the holy assembly; let the wife learn it and the children listen to it.

Let each of you make your home a church.

Are you not responsible for the salvation of your children? Are you not likely to have to give an account of their upbringing?

Just as we, the shepherds of the flock, will give an account of what we have done for your souls, so fathers of families will have to answer before God for all the people in their home.

John Chrysostom
On Genesis, 6, 2 (PG53)

25th June

'Respectable' Adultery

The Lord says this: 'Every one who divorces his wife and marries another commits adultery, and he who marries a woman divorced from her husband commits adultery.' [Luke 16:18]

You, however, divorce your wife as if you had every right to do so and you are not afraid of doing her an injury. You believe it is permissible because the natural law does not forbid it.

But the law of God does forbid it! And you, without being disobedient to human law, ought also to fear God. Listen to his law: 'What God has joined together, let no man put asunder.' [Matt. 19:6]

It is not of any great importance whether you commit adultery openly or under the guise of 'marriage'. There is one difference only: the fault committed on the pretext of principle is more serious than that which is committed secretly.

Ambrose
On the Gospel of St Luke, 8, 2 (PL15, 1765)

26th June

The Word that Hurts but Heals

The word of Wisdom exhorts us thus: 'Have you sons? Discipline them and break them in from their earliest years. Have you daughters? See that they are chaste, and do not be too lenient with them.' [Ecclus. 7:23-24]

It is true that we love our own children very much,

more than anything else. But those who speak only gentle words to them are in fact loving the children they are afraid of hurting only a little. On the other hand, those who correct them strictly are hurting them today but doing them good for the future.

Our Lord did not seek what is comfortable today for us. Rather he sought for us a good future. So let us follow his educational method inspired by love.

This admonition is a loving reproof that enlightens the mind. Christ our teacher had recourse to it when, for example, he said: 'O Jerusalem, Jerusalem, killing the prophets and stoning those who are sent to you! How often would I have gathered your children together as a hen gathers her brood under her wings, and you would not!' [Matt. 23:37]

Reproof may be made with contempt. Reproof may be made with vehemence, as a violent censure. But reproof may be made to lay bare sins. This is the kind of correction the Lord is constrained to use because in so many people faith has evaporated.

Reproof and correction hurt the soul that they heal of its faults. But they keep the death of the soul at bay.

Clement of Alexandria
The Teacher, I, 9 (PG8, 340)

27th June

Obedience is not Weakness

'Jesus was obedient to his parents.' [Luke 2:51] Master of virtue though he was, he still obeyed the duties of family love. Why do you marvel that, in addition to showing obedience to the Father, he also obeyed his mother? In this submission is revealed not weakness, but love.

Take some useful teaching from his example. Learn how much you owe to your parents. You cost your mother the perils of pregnancy, a long period of weariness and pain. Your birth, the fruit that she longed for so much, freed her from the pains of childbirth but not from anxieties on your account.

And what shall we say about the worries of fathers? They work hard to provide the necessities of life for their children. They are like a farmer who sows seed for future generations to reap. This in itself is enough to command at least respect in return.

Why, for an evil person, does his father's life seem too long or the time to enjoy his inheritance too short, while Christ does not disdain to have us as his co-heirs?

Ambrose
On the Gospel of St Luke, 2, 65 (PL15, 1575)

28th June

When Parents are Elderly

After having said: 'You shall love the Lord your God,' and 'You shall love your neighbour,' the Law quite rightly goes on to say: 'Honour your father and your mother.'

This is the first step in love. God in fact willed that you should be born of them. Avoid hurting them. Love for your parents should be such as to spare them pain, or even the appearance of it.

But to spare them pain is not enough. You must honour them, as the Son of God honoured his parents.

You have read in the Gospel; 'Jesus was obedient to them.' [Luke 2:51] If God was obedient to those who were his servants, what should you not do for your father and mother? Jesus, moreover, honoured his heavenly Father as no one else has ever known how to honour him: to the point of making himself 'obedient unto death.' [Phil. 2:8]

If your parents are elderly, provide for their keep. Do not let them go hungry on the grounds that other mouths, however poor, need the food that you could give them.

You should be heartily ashamed if your aged mother is holding out her hands to ask alms of strangers at the door of the church and you pass her by with your head in the air, making a show of fine clothes and bracelets and rings.

What answer would you give her if she asked you for payment of the debt that you owe her by nature, the reward to which she is entitled for the time that she fed you?

Ambrose
On the Gospel of St Luke, 8, 74 (PL15, 1788ff.)

29th June

Two Loves Conflicting?

'Do you think that I have come to bring peace on earth? No, I tell you, but rather division; for henceforth in one house there will be five divided, three against two and two against three; they will be divided, father against son and son against father, mother against daughter and daughter against her mother, mother-in-law against her daughter-in-law and daughter-in-law against her mother-in-law.' [Luke 12:51-53]

The Lord has put together in a single precept surrender to God and family affection. He has said: 'You shall love the Lord your God,' and also, 'You shall love your neighbour.'

Should we be right in thinking that he has changed the idea of loving to such an extent as to put in opposition to one another the two loves by ordering division between people of the same blood? If that were so, how could the Lord be 'Our peace, who has made us both one' [Eph. 2:14] and why should he himself say: 'Peace I leave you, my peace I give to you' [John 14:27], if he came to separate parents from their children and children from their parents? How can anyone who leaves his father be faithful to God if at the same time 'Cursed is he who does not honour his father'? [Deut. 27:16]

Let us remember that religion comes first and family affection only in second place. Then everything becomes clear. You should put human affairs second to divine imperatives.

If we have a duty to love our parents, we also have one paramount duty of love to the Father of our parents.

Ambrose
On the Gospel of St Luke, 7, 134ff. (PL15, 1734)

30th June

The Family Above the Family

'My mother and my brothers are those who hear the word of God and do it.' [Luke 8:21] As is to be expected of a Master, Jesus gives an example to others by his behaviour. Because it is he who commands, he also follows his own precepts himself.

He teaches us that it is not possible to be disciples without leaving father and mother. We must obey this teaching first.

He is not condemning respect for one's mother by this teaching, since this other precept also comes from him: 'Whoever curses his father or mother shall be put to death.' [Exod. 21:17; Matt. 15:14; Mark 7:10] But he knows that he ought to be more faithful to the mystery of the Father than to his affection for his mother.

He is not rejecting his parents unjustly, but he is making us understand that the bonds of the spirit are more sacred than those of the flesh.

No one should think that someone is lacking in filial affection if he fulfils the precept of the Law: 'Therefore a man leaves his father and mother and cleaves to his wife, and they become one flesh.' [Gen. 2:24]

This mystery is also illustrated by the mystery of the Church. Christ was not able to prefer his parents to the one who formed with him a single body. [cf. Eph. 5:25-32]

Ambrose
On the Gospel of St Luke, 6, 36ff. (PL15, 1678)

July

Many, but one heart,

one soul

1st July

If You Think You can Go it Alone

If anyone claims to be able to be completely self-sufficient, to be capable of reaching perfection without anyone else's help, to succeed in plumbing the depths of Scripture entirely unaided, he is behaving just like someone trying to practise the trade of a carpenter without touching wood. The Apostle would say to such: 'It is not the hearers of the Law who are righteous before God, but the doers of the Law who will be justified.' [Rom. 2:13]

Our Lord, in loving each human being right to the end, did not limit himself to teaching us in words. In order to give us an exact and telling example of humility in the perfection of love, he put on an apron and washed the disciples' feet.

So what about you, living entirely on your own? Whose feet will you wash? Whom will you follow to take the lowest place in humility? To whom will you offer brotherly service? How, in the home of a solitary, can you taste the joy that is evident where many live together?

The spiritual field of battle, the sure way of inner advancement, continual practice in the keeping of the commandments, this is what you will find in a community. It has the glory of God as its aim, in accordance with the word of the Lord Jesus: 'Let your light so shine before your fellows that they may see your good works and give glory to your Father who is in heaven.' [Matt. 5:16]

What is more, community preserves that particular characteristic of the saints which is referred to in the Scriptures thus: 'All who believed were together and had all things in common.' [Acts 2:44] 'The company of those who believed were of one heart and soul and no one said that any of the things which he possessed was his own, but they had everything in common.' [Acts 4:32]

Basil the Great
The Greater Rules, 7 (PG31, 933)

2nd July

You Cannot Live with Feet Only

Those who are pursuing the same objective, if they live together, will find many advantages in this sharing of their life.

In the first place, none of us is self-sufficient when it is a question of material needs. We all need one another to procure the necessities of life.

The foot, for example, is capable of doing certain things on its own. If the absurd could happen and it was cut off from the other limbs, the owner would realize that the foot's capabilities are not enough to preserve its existence and acquire the things it must have.

This is what happens in the solitary life: what we have is no use to us and what we are lacking we cannot procure. Yes, it is God's will that we should be indispensable to one another so that we can be in unity with one another.

Besides this, Christ's commandment to love does not allow us to be solely concerned with ourselves. 'Love does not seek its own interest.' [1 Cor. 13:5]

The solitary life, by contrast, seeks exactly that, namely the advantage of the individual – an objective which is evidently the opposite of the law of love. Suffice it to consider how Paul kept this law: 'Not seeking my own advantage, but that of many, that they may be saved.' [1 Cor. 10:33]

In the second place, it is difficult for solitaries to discover their faults. They do not have anyone to point them out. They have no one to correct them.

A reproof, even if it comes from an opponent, stirs up the desire for improvement if the soul is well disposed. But the person who is not living in community will find neither reproof nor improvement.

Basil the Great
The Greater Rules, 7 (PG31, 928)

3rd July

If You Love God You will Love your Neighbour, If You Love your Neighbour You will Love God

Surely everyone knows that human beings are social creatures and for that reason are not made for a solitary and uncivilized life. Nothing is better suited to our nature than to have continual relationships to seek one another out and to love one's own kind.

The Lord asks no more than the fruit of the seed he has implanted in us, when he says: 'A new commandment I give to you, that you love one another.' [John 13:34]

To lead us to obey this precept he does not want the badge of recognition of disciples to consist in miracles. Rather he asserts: 'By this all will know that you are my disciples, if you love one another.' [John 13:35]

And between the commandment to love God and the

commandment to love your neighbour, he has established so close a bond that he takes as done to himself anything done to our brothers or sisters. He says: 'I was thirsty and you gave me drink.' [Matt. 25:35] And he adds: 'As you did it to one of the least of these my brethren, you did it to me.' [Matt. 25:40]

The keeping of the first commandment includes the keeping of the second, and in the fulfilment of the second the first is fulfilled.

Whoever loves God loves his neighbour. The Lord says: 'Anyone who loves me will keep my word' [John 14:23] and 'This is my commandment, that you love one another as I have loved you.' [John 15:12]

So then, whoever loves his neighbour loves God, and God reckons our unity with our brothers and sisters is unity with him.

One is reminded of Moses. He loved his brothers and sisters so much that he asked to be blotted out of the book of the living if the people did not receive forgiveness of their sins. [Exod. 32:32]

Basil the Great
The Greater Rules, 3 (PG31, 917)

4th July

Shut No One out from Your Love

Do all you can to love everyone. If you are not yet able to, at the very least don't hate anyone. Yet you won't even manage this if you have not reached detachment from the things of this world.

You must love everyone with all your soul, hoping,

however, only in God and honouring him with all your heart.

Christ's friends are not loved by all, but they sincerely love all. The friends of this world are not loved by all, but neither do they love all.

Christ's friends persevere in their love right to the end. The friends of this world persevere only so long as they do not find themselves in disagreement over worldly matters.

A faithful friend is an effective protector. When things are going well, he gives you good advice and shows you his sympathy in practical ways. When things are going badly, he defends you unselfishly and he is a deeply committed ally.

Many people have said many things about love. But if you are looking for it, you will only find it in the followers of Christ. Only they have true Love as their teacher in love.

This is the Love about which it is written: 'If I have prophetic powers, and understand all mysteries and all knowledge, but have not love, I am nothing.' [1 Cor. 13:2]

Whoever has love has God, because God is Love. [1 John 4:16]

> **Maximus the Confessor**
> *Centuries on Charity*, 4, 82ff. (SC9, pp.170ff.)

5th July

Many Languages but One Human Nature

The common nature of humanity is not spoiled by differences of language. Among both the Greeks and among other nations it is possible to find those who ponder on goodness and those who practise evil.

This opinion is shared also by the pagans. The Greeks themselves recognize that among people of other races can be found a care for virtue, and that they are not prevented from attaining it by having different languages.

Moreover, the heralds of truth, the prophets and the apostles, did not possess the fluency of the Greek tongue, but they were nonetheless overflowing with true wisdom. They brought the divine teaching of God to all the nations, and with their writings about virtue and religion they crossed land and sea.

Theodoret
The Cure of Pagan Diseases, 5, 58ff. (SC57 pp.245ff.)

6th July

Two Sexes but Only One Human Nature

The author of the story of our creation teaches us that the Creator formed from the clay a man, formed from the man's rib a woman and then, starting from the union of the two, filled the earth with their descendants.

God did not create the woman from just any kind of material. He took from the man what he needed to create her. The reason? To prevent the possibility of the woman thinking she had a different nature and taking for that reason a direction opposed to the man's.

Moreover, God lays down the same rules for the male as for the female, because the difference between them lies in the structure of their bodies, not of their souls.

Woman is endowed with reason on a par with man.

She has the ability to think, she knows what she ought to do, she knows as he does what to avoid and what to look for. More than that, sometimes she is better than man at seeing what is useful, and she is a wise adviser.

Finally, because the struggle for sanctity is common to the man and the woman, God offers the same prize to one as he does to the other.

Theodoret
The Cure of Pagan Diseases, 5, 55ff. (SC57, pp.244ff.)

7th July

Helps and Hindrances in Human Relations

Ambrose said:

'To be good in the company of sinners is more praiseworthy than to be good among the good. Not to be good in the company of the good is a grave fault whereas to remain good in the midst of sinners merits great praise.

'The lives of the saints are the rule of life for others.

'If we make friends with someone who is holy, then thanks to our contact with him, thanks to his words and example, love for the truth is kindled in us.'

Isidore said:

'If you keep company with the good, you will share their virtues, since usually like seeks like. Contrariwise, it is risky to resort to the company of the bad whose will is bent towards evil. It is better to earn their hatred than their friendship. Just as sharing the life of the saints brings many advantages, so consorting with evil people produces many miseries.

'While it is desirable that the good should always live in peace among themselves, it is desirable that evil people should never be in agreement.'

Defensor Grammaticus
Book of Sparkling Sayings, 63 (SC86, pp.194ff.)

8th July

Can a Parrot be Worth More than an Orphan?

Some men, instead of learning how to keep house and look after themselves, have recourse to domestic servants, and get themselves cooks and housemaids.

Others, womanisers, spend whole days with their lady loves, telling lewd stories and corrupting them with their remarks and their deceitful actions.

Others still, become slaves to lust through the influence of high-ranking prostitutes and behave like pigs in the trough.

Some of our women are happy to spend their lives in the company of effeminate men.

Other women, more sophisticated, amuse themselves bringing up as pets such creatures as birds or peacocks. They play with them and find their pleasure in them.

But they neglect the widow, who is obviously worth much more than a thoroughbred lapdog and they despise the elderly who in my opinion are more deserving of love than an animal is. They do not entertain orphans, but they do bring up parrots. Or they completely abandon their offspring out of doors while they coddle their pet birds in the house.

And they do not give any food to the hungry even though they are more beautiful than a monkey and know how to say something more interesting than the song of the nightingale.

Clement of Alexandria
The Teacher, 3, 4 (PG8, 592)

9th July

From Egoism to Pride is Not Far

Egoism is the source of the passions.

From egoism spring gluttony, avarice, conceit. From gluttony springs lust, from avarice greed, from conceit springs pride.

All the other vices, without exception, are merely consequences of this one thing: anger, melancholy, rancour, sloth, envy, slander and so on.

At the beginning of all the passions there is egoism, just as at the end there is pride.

Egoism is an irrational attachment to self. If anyone succeeds in destroying it, he is destroying all the passions which derive from it at one stroke.

Parents are unhealthily attached to the children they have produced: so is the intelligence to the arguments it has thought up.

Passion pure and simple! The wise are not dogmatic in their reasonings. If they are persuaded that they are true, they find in this a reason to be more distrustful of their own judgment and to submit their considerations to the judgment of other wise people.

Maximus the Confessor
Centuries on Charity, 3, 56 (SC9, pp.140ff.)

10th July

Do not Judge

The Fathers teach us that nothing is more serious than judging your neighbour. Despite this, such a serious evil is committed even for things, let's say, of little seriousness.

It all begins with vague suspicions and thoughts like this: 'What does it matter if I hear what so-and-so is saying? What harm is there in going to see what that person is up to?' The mind quickly forgets its own sins and becomes all the time more interested in the actions of others. This results in rash judgments, slander, contempt. In the end the mind falls into the same sins that it condemns in others.

When someone ceases to worry about his own sins and, as the Fathers say, 'is not concerned about his death,' it is absolutely impossible for him to be corrected. Such a person does nothing but stick his nose into his neighbour's affairs. And nothing annoys God so much or makes people so miserable as speaking evil of one's neighbour and judging him.

There is a difference between speaking evil of one's neighbour and judging him.

Speaking evil means saying, for instance, 'So-and-so has told a lie; he has lost his temper; he has committed fornication,' or something of the sort. The neighbour's sin is exposed on the spur of the moment.

Judging, on the other hand, means saying: 'So-and-so is a liar; he is bad-tempered; he is a fornicator.' The permanent disposition of his soul is under judgment, his whole life is being judged, and this is indeed serious.

Dorotheus of Gaza
Teachings, 6 (SC92, pp.269ff.)

11th July

Pure like Susanna

Has so-and-so slandered you? Don't give in to hatred. If you hate the slanderer, you are hating a person and therefore breaking the commandment to love. The evil done with words you are now doing by your deeds. On the other hand, if you keep the commandments, you are helping the other as much as you can to become free from this sin.

Nothing causes as much suffering as to be slandered in regard to one's faith or one's behaviour. It is impossible to remain indifferent, unless you are like Susanna who in her purity turned her gaze on God, who alone can free us from slander, demonstrate our innocence and cheer the soul with hope.

The more you pray with all your heart for the one who has slandered you, the more readily God reveals the truth to those whom the slander has scandalized.

But you, in your turn, take good care not to compromise the good reputation of a brother or sister by letting slip hurtful comparisons in your conversation. The result of those unkind words is bound to be an unconscious but unyielding grudge against them.

Praise that brother or sister, praise them in public. And pray sincerely for them as for yourself. Very soon then you will be free of this dislike.

Maximus the Confessor
Centuries on Charity, 4, 83ff. (SC9, pp.158ff.)

12th July

Hypocrisy and Lies, Mother and Daughter

Fire is produced from stone and steel; lying comes from loquacity and gossip. And the lie destroys love.

No one who has any sense would say that telling lies is not an important sin. The Holy Spirit has severely condemned it. 'You destroy those that speak lies,' says David to God. [Ps 5:7]

The mother of lying is hypocrisy, mother and also, often, its substance as well. Hypocrisy in fact works out the lie beforehand and then puts it into practice.

Those who possess the fear of God are the furthest from telling lies, because they have an honest judge, their own conscience.

As with all the passions, we ought to recognize various types of lying according to the damage done. One person tells lies from fear of punishment; another when no danger is threatening; another because of conceit; another for enjoyment; another to raise a laugh; and yet another to do harm to his neighbour.

A child does not know what a lie is, so his soul is free of malice.

Someone who is elated with wine speaks the truth on all subjects, even without meaning to. In the same way, anyone who is inebriated with the spirit of penitence will never be able to tell lies.

John Climacus
Stairway to Paradise, 12 (PG88, 853)

13th July

Are You Demanding Justice?

How can you raise your hands to heaven and move your lips to ask forgiveness for yourselves? God would be ready to forgive your sins, but you are preventing him by not forgiving your brothers and sisters their sins.

You say to me: 'They are brutal, they are violent, they behave in a way we simply must punish.'

But it is precisely for that reason that you ought to forgive them. Maybe you are suffering a thousand wrongs at this moment. You have been robbed? You have been slandered? You want to see them punished. Then give your forgiveness instead. If you take the law into your own hands either in word or deed, God will not be concerned to give you your rights. You have already taken them for yourselves. Not only will God not give you your rights. He will punish you for having offended him.

So it is rash to demand your rights on your own account, especially when the judge is God.

Go down on your knees before him. He will solve your problem better than you could. He has bidden you only to pray for the one who has done you wrong. As far as the treatment of this fellow is concerned, he has told you to leave all action to him, and to him alone.

John Chrysostom
Sermon to the People of Antioch, 20, 3ff. (PG49, 202)

14th July

How to Eradicate Ill-Feeling

Do you maintain that you are keeping the commandment of love towards your neighbour? If so, why is there so much bitter ill-feeling in you against this or that person? Is that not perhaps a sign that you are preferring transient goods to loving, and that just to possess them you are struggling even to the point of hostility to your brothers and sisters?

Sadness and ill-feeling go hand in hand. So if you are sad when you see your brother or sister's face, that probably means that you are harbouring ill-feeling.

If it does, then pray for that brother or sister and you will weaken the drive of your passion, because prayer will purge of all bitterness the memory of the evil the other has done to you. After that, by acquiring love for your neighbour, you will eradicate any trace of that passion from your soul.

If someone else is harbouring ill-feeling against you, show yourself friendly towards him and also humble. Treat him well and you will set him free from his passion.

It is essential to eradicate envy, anger and ill-feeling against people who have offended us. But this in itself does not mean you are loving them. One can avoid returning evil for evil simply because the Law commands it, without experiencing a scrap of love. In this way you will make no progress to repaying evil with good.

Yet readiness to do good to someone who hates us is a characteristic of perfect love alone.

Maximus the Confessor
Centuries on Charity, 3, 15ff. (SC9, pp.127ff.)

15th July

If Someone Causes You Trouble

'Love is patient and kind.' [1 Cor. 13:4] Consequently, to be discouraged by the misfortunes that happen, to fly into a rage with those who are the cause of them, to stop loving them, isn't that perhaps dodging the will of a wise God?

Watch yourself, for fear lest the evil that is setting you at odds with your neighbour derives, not from your neighbour but from your own heart. Hurry to be reconciled with him in case you are breaking the commandment of brotherly love.

Be on your guard against neglecting this commandment. It can make you a child of God. But if you break it, you become a child of hell.

To envy or to be envied, to cause hurt or to receive it, to offend or to be offended, to persist in a suspicion – all this is an obstacle to love between friends. A neighbour of yours perhaps has been a trial to you and you have been so cross about it as to begin to hate him. Don't let yourself be overcome with hatred, but overcome hatred with love.

In practical terms, pray sincerely for him, accept his apologies, make yourself his champion, take on yourself the responsibility for your trials, and bear the situation with courage until the clouds disperse.

Maximus the Confessor
Centuries on Charity, 4, 18 (SC9, pp.156ff.)

16th July

Poison in your Heart: the Memory of Insults

The memory of insults is the residue of anger. It keeps sins alive, hates justice, ruins virtue, poisons the heart, rots the mind, defeats concentration, paralyses prayer, puts love at a distance, and is a nail driven into the soul.

If anyone has appeased his anger, he has already suppressed the memory of insults, while as long as the mother is alive the son persists. In order to appease the anger, love is necessary.

Remembrance of Jesus' passion will heal your soul of resentment, by making it ashamed of itself when it remembers the patience of the Lord.

Some people have wearied themselves and suffered for a long time in order to extract forgiveness. By far the best course, however, is to forget the offences, since the Lord says: 'Forgive at once and you will be forgiven in generous measure.' [cf. Luke 6:37-38]

Forgetting offences is a sign of sincere repentance. If you keep the memory of them, you may believe you have repented but you are like someone running in his sleep.

Let no one consider it a minor defect, this darkness that often clouds the eyes even of spiritual people.

John Climacus
Stairway to Paradise, 9 (PG88, 841)

17th July

Reconciliation with our Neighbours

Augustine said:

'Every individual will receive from God the amount of indulgence he has himself given to his neighbour.'

Jerome said:

'As God in Christ has forgiven us our sins, so let us also forgive those who sin against us.'

Gregory said:

'Only the one who has forgiven can seek forgiveness.'

Isidore said:

'In vain do they who neglect being reconciled with their neighbours seek to be reconciled with God.'

Caesarius said:

'There is no trace of sin remaining in the soul that generously forgives the one who sins against it.'

Defensor Grammaticus
Book of Sparkling Sayings, 5 (SC77, pp.114ff.)

18th July

How to Love a Friend . . . and Persecute an Enemy

Augustine said:

'The evil-doer is sad when he sees that his enemy has taken a warning and avoided punishment.'

Gregory said:

'We are only faithful to our friends when our actions match our promises.

'People have no right to persecute their enemies with

the sword, but they should persecute them with prayer.'

Jerome said:

'Often our friends are only so-called friends: not being able to tempt us openly, they try to do it secretly.

'No violence destroys a firm friendship nor does time break it up: it remains strong wherever destiny takes it.

'True friendship is that in which you do not demand anything of your friend except his good will: friendship seeks no reward from its friend.

'You cannot be superficial when it is a question of friendship: it is a bond that requires constancy.

'It is better to put up with continual hostility from those in bad faith than to hurt your neighbour with friendship that offends God.'

Defensor Grammaticus
Book of Sparkling Sayings, 64 (SC86, pp.200ff.)

19th July

Our Enemies do not Know the Gratitude We Owe Them

An enemy is by definition one who obstructs, ensnares and injures others. He is therefore a sinner. We ought to love his soul by correcting him and doing everything possible to bring him to conversion. We ought to love his body too by coming to his aid with the necessities of life.

That love for our enemies is possible has been shown us by the Lord himself. He revealed the Father's love and his own by making himself 'obedient unto death',

[Phil. 2:8] as the Apostle says, not for his friends' sake so much as for his enemies. 'God shows his love for us in that while we were yet sinners Christ died for us.' [Rom. 5:8]

And God exhorts us to do the same. 'Be imitators of God, as beloved children. And walk in love, as Christ loved us and gave himself for us.' [Eph. 5:1-2]

God would not ask this of us as a right and proper thing to do, if it were not possible.

On the other hand, is it not perhaps true that an enemy can be as much of a help to us as a friend can?

Enemies earn for us the beatitude of which the Lord speaks when he says: 'Blessed are you when others revile you and persecute you and utter all kinds of evil against you falsely on my account. Rejoice and be glad, for your reward is great in heaven.' [Matt. 5:11-12]

Basil the Great
The Lesser Rules, 176 (PG31, 1200)

20th July

Open the Route to God for your Opponents

Don't ever hurt one of your neighbours by using words in two senses. He could reply in the same way and you would both be wandering off the path of love.

Go to him and warn him with affectionate sincerity. When you have between you removed the cause of your unhappiness, you will both of you be free from anxiety and bitterness.

Don't recall to your memory anything your neighbour

may have said in a moment of acrimony, whether he insulted you to your face, or spoke evil of you to another and that person has come and reported it to you. If you let yourself become angry, it is but a short step from anger to hatred.

Christ wants you never, in any way, for any reason, to cultivate a spirit of hatred, bitterness, anger or ill-feeling. The four gospels proclaim that on every page.

Only God is good by nature. The imitator of God is only good by intention, insofar as he wants to reconcile sinners with him who is good by nature. Therefore when they offend the imitator of God, he blesses them, and when they slander him, he prays for them. In short, he does everything possible not to stray far from the path of real love.

Maximus the Confessor
Centuries on Charity, 4, 32 (SC9, pp.159ff.)

21st July

I Suggest a Different Kind of Envy

Nothing is so divisive as envy, which is a deadly evil, in a certain sense more deadly than greed.

A greedy person is happy when he gets something. An envious one is happy, not when he himself gets something, but when someone else does not. He sees his own personal profit, not in the good that comes his way, but in the evil that happens to someone else.

You are like that. What right have you to expect forgiveness, what justification can you claim for your actions, when the success of a brother or sister of yours causes you to fret and turn pale, when you ought to be rejoicing?

You want to be jealous? By all means be so. But be jealous in the sense that you imitate others in what is praiseworthy, seeking their aggrandizement, not their diminishment.

This is a jealousy worthy of praise: to imitate, not to despise; not to disparage other people's good deeds, but to realize your own faults.

Someone who is envious does the opposite. His own faults make no impression on him, but other people's good deeds upset him. He chafes at the sight of success that is not his own, and, like a worm, spoils the fruit of a neighbour's work.

He takes no trouble to improve himself, but if another person makes improvement, he does all he can to ruin him.

John Chrysostom
Homily on the First Letter to the Corinthians, 31, 4
(PG61, 262)

22nd July

Learn to Laugh in a Relaxed Way

Laughter is a sign of friendliness so long as it is not coarse.

In general, a person can do whatever is natural, but it must be in due measure and at the right time. Therefore you ought not to laugh always simply because you have the capacity, any more than a horse is always neighing because it is capable of neighing.

We ought to control our laughter, to learn to laugh in

moderation, being very careful not to let go of ourselves. Only then shall we be relaxed by it after wearisome toil or after a time of mental stress.

Clement of Alexandria
The Teacher, 2, 5 (PG8, 445)

23rd July

High Life

When we are having a party we must be sensible. We must avoid licentious music and an excess of drink. Otherwise we will be prone to drunkenness and erotic exhibitions.

The Apostle warns us: 'Let us then cast off the works of darkness and put on the armour of light; let us conduct ourselves becomingly as in the day, not in revelling and drunkenness, not in debauchery and licentiousness and other forms of unchastity.' [Rom. 13:12-13]

Let us keep well away from all that excites shameful and extravagant sensations and makes us deaf to the voice of God.

Clement of Alexandria
The Teacher, 2, 4 (PG8, 440)

24th July

A Chatterer is like an Old Boot

If two people are engaged in conversation they should speak in measured tones. Yelling and shouting is what idiots do. Talking in a whisper so that the person cannot hear is the mark of a fool.

In conversation we must not let ourselves be seized with the desire always to interrupt in order to show off our fatuous superiority. Everything ought to lead to tranquillity, as in the words of the greeting 'Peace be with you'. And, 'Do not answer before first listening.' [Eccles. 1:8]

Let us avoid being pompous or long-winded, or too hasty or too slow. Let us not talk for too long nor use too many words.

A chatterer is like an old boot. When all the rest has been used up, there is only the tongue left and that hurts the chatterer more than anyone else.

Clement of Alexandria
The Teacher, 2, 7 (PG8, 456)

25th July

The Powerful have a Thousand Masters

Those who live in what others consider splendour lose their liberty. They do not have one or two masters: they have a thousand.

Here we have a great man. He enjoys considerable wealth, enormous authority, illustrious ancestors, universal admiration. Yet he finds himself subjected to the yoke of a hard slavery.

He has a crowd of exacting masters. His first concern is to please the Emperor. Then there is such and such a prince who lends an ear to all the gossip and favours Tom today and Dick tomorrow. And then there are people of equal rank and his dependants, both friendly and hostile, to tyrannize over him.

The great, even if they have nothing with which to reproach themselves, yet have to be suspicious of each and every person they meet.

The truth is that those behind them are trying to get past them, while the others who are in front of them are doing all they can to keep that distance between them.

John Chrysostom
On the Gospel of St Matthew, 18, 4ff.
(PG57, 269)

26th July

The Ruler's Responsibility

The Superior who has the task of looking after everyone must act as if he had to give an account of each individual.

He must realize that he will answer personally for a brother who has fallen into sin, because he has not shown him the Law of God. He will also have to answer for the brother who remains still in his sin, because he has not pointed out to him the means of correction.

The Superior must not let himself be ruled by human

considerations, either by fear of offending one who is going wrong, or by the desire to make himself popular. Only love must be his inspiration, and he must say sincerely everything he thinks, determined not to tamper with the truth.

Otherwise, he is no better than a blind guide advancing towards an abyss and leading his brothers there too.

Basil the Great
The Greater Rules, 25 (PG31, 984)

27th July

The Most Efficient Ruler is the One who Serves with Love

Augustine said:

'Some people have the Law stamped on their memory but they do not stamp it on their deeds.

'You are not innocent if by your silence you let your brothers and sisters go to perdition while you could have corrected them.

'Let those in charge realize clearly what their task is: not to rule with force but to serve with love.

'The one who holds a position of authority ought to be more loved than feared.'

Defensor Grammaticus
Book of Sparkling Sayings, 32 (SC77, p.393)

28th July

Are You Over-Bearing?

The Superior must not reprove with anger. An angry or violent reproof does not set the brother free from his fault but it throws the Superior into a state of sin. That is why the Bible says: 'The Lord's servant must be . . . forbearing, correcting his opponents with gentleness.' [2 Tim. 2:24-25]

We ought not to be inflamed with anger when others have offended us, nor should we show ourselves too indulgent when they have offended someone else. It is in the second case that our displeasure should be more evident.

By such behaviour we avoid the suspicion that we are acting from self-love, and we make it clear – by the different way we treat each of them – that our aim is not to be furiously angry with the sinner but to root out his sin, should he have offended us or someone else.

If we are more indignant where we ourselves are concerned than when others are, the conclusion is obvious. It is not on God's account that we are angry, nor are we sorry for the danger in which the sinner has placed himself. The motive of our excitement is nothing but our self-love and our desire to dominate.

Basil the Great
The Greater Rules, 50 (PG31, 1040)

29th July

Knowing how to Teach

Jerome said:

'To teach others one must have learned over a long time the art of correct behaviour.

'Only stupid people teach what they do not themselves know.

'The pastor should also be master. In the Church, however saintly they may be, none should take the title of pastor unless they are capable of ruling those they feed.

'An effective orator reaches many listeners with few words.

'They lose the authority to teach if they undo their words by their deeds.'

Gregory said:

'Let no one take on him the office of preacher unless he loves his hearers.'

Augustine said:

'We should watch the hand of the actor, not the mouth of the speaker.'

Defensor Grammaticus
Book of Sparkling Sayings, 32 (SC77, pp.393ff.)

30th July

Knowing how to Learn

Jerome said:

'Take care not to seek to become a teacher first

and then a pupil, or an officer first and a soldier afterwards.

'Take care not to enter a street you have never been in before if you do not have someone to show you the way. You could get completely lost.

'No art can be learnt without an expert teacher.

'You will need a long time to learn what you ought to teach. If any applaud you, don't believe them.

'Those who are industrious and wise, even if they have something yet to learn, are already teachers because they ask questions with sagacity.'

Cyprian said:

'The one who learns what is better day by day is the one who will teach in the best way.'

Defensor Grammaticus
Book of Sparkling Sayings, 86 (SC77, pp.268ff.)

31st July

I Believe in Health, in Friendship and in Wisdom

Two things here on earth are essential: health and a friend. They are the two things most to be prayed for. Woe to the person who despises them.

Health and friendship are natural gifts. God has made human beings for living – hence health – and for not living alone – hence the search for friendship.

Friendship begins in the family, with your spouse and children and extends from there to strangers. But who, in fact, is a stranger? All human beings share a common parentage. Do you fail to recognize that person? There's a human being there! Are you dealing with an adversary? There's a human being there! With an enemy? There's a human being there too! Let a friend remain a friend and turn an enemy into a friend.

However, to these two things that we need to have in this world, health and friendship, we must add a third which is not of this world, namely wisdom.

Divine wisdom is on a different plane from human beings – stupid, sunk in error, attached to superfluities, ignorant of the eternal verities. Divine wisdom is no friend of the foolish and, because it is not their friend, it is to be found far removed from them.

Nevertheless, by taking to itself what was close to us, divine wisdom has come close to us. In this consists the mystery of Christ. Nothing is further from foolishness than divine wisdom and nothing is closer to human beings than their humanity: divine wisdom has assumed humanity and come close to human beings by means of what is close to them.

So we believe in three things: health, friendship and divine-human wisdom.

Augustine
Serm. Denis, 16, 1 (Miscellanea Agostiniania, 75-77)

August

The world: joy for humanity and
glory for God

1st August

God has Created Everything for Your Sake

The creation is beautiful and harmonious, and God has made it all just for your sake.

He has made it beautiful, grand, varied, rich. He has made it capable of satisfying all your needs, to nourish your body and also to develop the life of your soul by leading it towards the knowledge of himself – all this, for your sake.

For your sake he has made the sky beautiful with stars. He has embellished it with sun and moon for your sake, so that you can take pleasure in it and profit by it.

What could be more marvellous than the sky? By day it is bright with the sunshine and by night it illumines the earth with innumerable stars, twinkling like shining eyes. For seafarers and travellers the stars are like pilots to lead them by the hand. In the darkness of a moonless night the helmsman goes ahead confidently on the course pointed out to him by the stars. The stars are a long way off, yet they guide him with accuracy as if they were by his side. Without saying a word to him they bring him safely to harbour.

John Chrysostom
On Providence, 7, 2 (SC79, pp.109ff.)

2nd August

The Universe is Like a Human Being

The world is like our bodies. It, too, is formed of many limbs and directed by a single soul. Yes, the world is an immense being directed by the power and the word of God, who is, so to say, its soul.

It seems to me that Scripture, too, is hinting at this in the passage where we read: ' "Do I not fill heaven and earth?" says the Lord,' [Jer. 23:24] and 'Thus says the Lord: "Heaven is my throne and the earth is my footstool." ' [Isa. 66:1] The Saviour repeated the same thing when he taught: 'Do not swear at all, either by heaven, for it is the throne of God, or by the earth, for it is his footstool.' [Matt. 5:34-35] In his turn Paul, speaking to the Athenians, said: 'In him we live and move and have our being.' [Acts 17:28]

How could we live and move in God, if God did not contain and embrace the whole world with his strength? How could heaven be God's throne and the earth his footstool, as the Saviour affirms, if the power of God did not fill everything both in heaven and on earth?

Origen
Principles, 2, 1, 2-3 (PG11, 183)

3rd August

Everything was Created by the Word

We believe in one Lord, Jesus Christ, the Only-begotten Son of God, begotten of the Father before all worlds, by whom all things were made, and from whose power none of the things he has created is exempt.

Let every heretic be silenced who suggests another creator or maker of the world. Let the tongue be silenced that blasphemes the Christ, the Son of God. And let them be silenced who say that the sun is God: God is the maker of the sun that shines. So also let them be silenced who maintain that the world is a creation of the angels and so would belittle the glory of the Only-begotten.

All things came to be through Christ, things seen and unseen, thrones, principalities and powers and anything else that may be named: Christ reigns over the things he himself has made. He has not snatched anyone else's spoils, but reigns over his own creation, as the Apostle John has said: 'All things were made through him, and without him was not anything made that was made.' [John 1:3]

I would like to give you an illustration of this truth, though I realize it is an inadequate one. After all, what visible object could be an accurate illustration of God's invisible power? However, let me give it to you, as we are all equally inadequate.

It is as if a king wants to found a city and submits the project to his son and heir for his consideration. The son follows the pattern given him and brings the work to completion. In this way, the Father's will remains sovereign while the son is exercising his power over what is being made.

In similar fashion, the Only-begotten Son, begotten

before all worlds, has created all things in accordance
with the will of the Father.

Cyril of Jerusalem
Catecheses, 11, 21 (PG33, 717)

4th August

If There Were Not a Hand on High . . .

Everything on the earth was made by the Word of the
Master. No human being yet existed to till the fields, a
plough did not exist, there was not, as yet, the help of
oxen, no one cultivated the earth. But the Word spoke
on the earth and caused it to bring forth fruit. The Word
gave orders thus: 'Let the earth put forth vegetation,'
[Gen. 1:11] and this order sufficed.

Today human beings till the earth and know how to
make use of beasts of burden. But even if they paid
all possible attention to the earth, even if the weather
were always favourable, without God it would all be in
vain.

Sweat and toil would be no use at all if there were not
a Hand on high ready to help and to cause everything
to ripen.

John Chrysostom
On Genesis, 5, 4 (PG53, 51ff.)

5th August

The Harmony of Opposites

A pure and simple realization: beings of opposite natures can unite in a concord of harmony.

There is a harmony, for instance, among the seasons: spring follows winter, summer follows spring and autumn follows summer. The four seasons have contrasting characteristics. One brings cold, the next brings heat, one signals the beginning of life, another its end. Yet they all render equal service to the human race. They are all equally useful.

It is impossible not to realize that there must be a being superior to earthly objects, which is invisible but gives unity to their multiplicity, and orders their existence.

If such a being did not exist and did not function, in what way could there be a mutual harmonization of heavy and light bodies, of dry and wet, of round and square, of fire and frost, of sea and land, of sun and clouds? The nature of each of them is different from that of every other. A terrible discord would be inevitable! One is causing heat and the other, cold, a heavy body sinks while a light one goes up, the sun gives light and the clouds bring shadow . . .

But in the universe there is no disorder, only order; no disharmony, only concord. So we need to reflect: there has always been the Lord to unite so many different elements and to make of them a complete harmony.

Athanasius
Against the Pagans, 36ff. (PG25, 72)

251

6th August

From the Visible to the Invisible

If you observe the heavens, says Scripture, their order will be a guide for you towards faith. They do in fact reveal the Artist who made them. If you then observe the beauty of the earth, it will help you to increase your faith.

It is true that we have attained faith, not because we have succeeded in seeing God with our bodily eyes, but because we have seen him with our minds which perceive the Invisible by means of the visible.

Look at a stone and notice that even a stone carries some mark of the Creator. It is the same with an ant, a bee, a mosquito.

The wisdom of the Creator is revealed in the smallest creatures. It is he who has spread out the heavens and laid out the immensity of the seas. It is he also who has made the tiny hollow shaft of the bee's sting.

All the objects in the world are an invitation to faith, not unbelief.

Basil the Great
On Psalm 32, 3 (PG29, 329)

7th August

The Static Journey of Faith

For thousands and thousands of years the earth has been ploughed and sown, human beings have trampled it and excavated it for minerals, the rain has beaten on it, the snow has covered it, the sun has scorched it.

And yet the earth has remained such as it is, and its fruits have remained the same too.

Nor has the sea changed by growing either smaller or larger, despite its water evaporating and then falling again as rain, despite the rivers opening into it from every direction.

It is the same with the air. It is not used up, although so many human beings and animals are continually breathing it, despite all the light and heat that are always permeating it.

The fact is that God is at work in the world, the same God who infuses into creation the energy needed for it to continue stable throughout all time.

To God then let us raise a hymn of praise with all our strength. Let us glorify God who made the world and governs it without ceasing.

And through the things that are seen let us be led towards the things that are not seen. To do this there is no need to travel. Only faith is needed, because only through faith can we see him.

Theodoret
The Cure of Pagan Diseases, 4, 60ff. (SC57, p.221)

8th August

You Would Have to be a Half-Wit

God is the cause of the universe, a cause which does not depend on any other cause. This is the teaching of our eyes when we look at the ordering of nature.

Our eyes observe visible objects and note how they are perfectly stationary and at the same time on the move, if it were possible to call immobility mobile.

253

Through visible objects is made apparent the ordering of nature whereby reason is able to deduce the Author of the universe. How indeed could the universe have begun to exist, and how could it be still in existence, if God had not given it existence and were not sustaining it day by day now?

When we see a musical instrument that is well made and well-tuned, or when we hear the sounds it gives out, we think at once of the person who made it or of the person who is playing it. We do not perhaps know him personally, but we think of him.

That is how it is with the Being who has made the world, who gives it motion and sustains it. His existence is indisputably clear to us. We do not understand him perfectly, but we think about him.

You would have to be a half-wit not to arrive at these conclusions, not to accept what nature shows us, not to recognize God, that is, the Being of whom our spirit is an image and of whom reason gives us an idea.

Granted, we are speaking of partial knowledge. If we had complete knowledge there would be no need to continue the search. We should already be in possession of the object of our desires, the goal of our whole life, the aim of our whole soul.

Gregory Nazianzen
Oration 28, 6 (PG36)

9th August

Myriad Flowers in the Field of the Sky

Nothing gives as much joy as the sky which is like a pure transparent veil, like a meadow with a thousand flowers – the stars, like a crown for our heads.

Nothing is as delightful as the rising of the sun when the night is fleeing away. Its rays are not yet scorching hot. The sky is turning red. In a moment its light reaches the earth, the sea, the mountains, the valleys, the hills, the whole sky, removing from nature the cloak of darkness and revealing it naked to our eyes.

Nothing rouses more admiration than the course of the sun, the regularity of its route, the service it never denies us, its beauty, its brightness, its splendour, its purity.

And its usefulness is beyond description. Just think what the sun does for seeds, for plants, for the human race, for animals, for the earth, for the sea, for the air, for everything that exists!

John Chrysostom
On Providence, 7, 11 (SC79, pp.115ff.)

10th August

When the Sun Rises Triumphant and Lovely as a Bridegroom

It looks small, the sun, but it possesses enormous power. It appears in the east and scatters its rays as far as the west. Indeed, describing the dawn, the Psalmist says: 'The sun comes forth like a bridegroom leaving his chamber and like a strong man runs its course with joy.' [Ps. 19:6] Yes, triumphant, and yet lovely and gentle, exactly like a bridegroom, it shows itself to everyone. Then, at midday, we very often have to take shelter, because it is burning hot. But at its rising it is like a bridegroom and it fills us with joy.

255

Now study the order it observes, although this comes not from itself but from the One who originally fixed its course.

You see how it behaves in summer. By rising higher in the sky it makes the days longer and gives people more time to work. In winter on the other hand it shortens its course so that the cold season may pass quickly and the nights may lengthen out to give relief to human beings and equally to the earth which in this way can prepare an abundant harvest.

As a result you see how perfect is the order in which the days and nights alternate. In summer long days and short nights, in winter the reverse, while in spring and autumn the duration of the light and of the darkness is the same.

The Psalmist says: 'Day to day pours forth speech, and night to night declares knowledge.' [Ps. 19:3] You might say that through the song of their behaviour day and night are proclaiming that the one God is he who has created all things and keeps them in being.

Cyril of Jerusalem
Catecheses, 9, 6 (PG33, 644)

11th August

Use the Night to Regain the Rhythm of Life

If you are willing to reflect on the meaning of night, you will also discover the infinite providence of the Creator.

Night restores the tired body and relaxes limbs which are tense through the efforts of the day. By means of rest, night helps them to regain their rhythm.

And not only that. Night sets you free from sorrow and relieves your worries. It often reduces fever by making sleep a cure and by changing itself into a doctor's assistant.

That is the importance of night. It is so great that often if you cannot benefit from your rest you will not have the strength to face a new day.

At night, as in a time of truce, the exhausted soul and the worn out body regain their energy and are prepared to take up their daily activity again. On the other hand, if we prolong the day into night by staying awake to work or even to do nothing, we are condemning ourselves to being useless because gradually our strength is wasted.

John Chrysostom
On Providence, 7, 26 (SC79, pp.123ff.)

12th August

Aspects and Powers of Water

Who is the father of the rain? Who makes the drops of dew? Who holds the clouds together and prevents them pouring water on the earth?

Sometimes he brings golden-lined clouds scurrying from the south. In some cases he lets them take a firm shape, in others he makes their form vary with every moment. They hold great quantities of water yet they do not break and they roam peacefully over the sky until he unleashes the winds on the world.

Who crystallizes the water into ice? The ice seems hard as rock, yet it is water. On some occasions the water becomes snow and looks like wool. On other occasions again he uses it to scatter the fog like ashes. In spring the rock melts and runs down the slopes.

Water always remains water yet it has many different powers. In vineyards water becomes 'wine to gladden the hearts of the people.' In the olive groves it becomes 'oil to make their faces shine.' And it also changes into 'bread to strengthen people's hearts,' [Ps. 104:15] and into fruit of every kind.

In the face of all these marvels who can fail to adore their Creator?

Cyril of Jerusalem
Catecheses, 9, 9ff. (PG33, 648)

13th August

When the Swan Spreads its Wings

Study fish. In the water they fly, so to speak, and they find the air they need in the water. They would die in our atmosphere, just as we would die in the water. Watch their habits, their way of mating and procreating their kind, their beauty, their permanent homes and their wanderings.

Study the enormous number of different kinds of birds, the variety of their shapes and colours. Some are mute, others sing. Who gave them the gift of song?

Who placed a tiny lyre in the breast of the cicada? Who has arranged things in such a way that this little creature gets excited in hot weather and fills the woods with its music and accompanies passers-by with it? And who helps the swan to compose its song when it spreads its wings to the blowing of the breeze?

It gives me joy to speak of these things because they unfold to us the greatness of God.

Gregory Nazianzen
Oration 28, 23 (PG36, 57)

14th August

The Intelligence of Animals and the Beauty of Plants

Admire the instinctive intelligence of animals and explain it if you can. Look how the birds build their nests, between rocks, in trees, under roofs. They make them in such a way that they can be safe and have a nice, comfortable place in which to raise their young.

And look at the bees and the spiders. Where do their love of work and their ingenuity from from?

I am not speaking of the ants, which have stores where they pile up great quantities of provisions, nor of their continual comings and goings, nor of their leaders, nor of the order they keep while they are working.

Can you explain all that and arrive at an understanding of the wisdom they point to?

Look in addition at the different kinds of plants, at the elegance of their leaves. They are delightful to the eye, and useful for the fruits they produce.

No! We cannot understand the nature of these things. Much less are we likely to be able to understand the nature of the first Being, the unique Being who is the fullness of everything.

Gregory Nazianzen
Oration 28, 25 (PG36, 60)

15th August

Learn from the Ant, Imitate the Bee

God gave one command: 'Let the earth bring forth living creatures according to their kinds: cattle and creeping things and wild beasts.' [Gen. 1:24]

From that single command, as if from a single source, sprang so many kinds of animal: the gentle sheep, the man-eating lion, and all the creatures devoid of reason which parallel the passions of humankind.

The snake reminds us of people who hurt their friends with poisonous gibes. The whinneying horse is like the quarrelsome youth. The tireless ant was created as a spur to the indolent: yes indeed, for there are youngsters who live an idle life. They stand convicted by an animal devoid of reason, and are reprimanded by the Scripture which says: 'Go to the ant, O sluggard; consider its ways, and be wise.' [Prov. 6:6] Do you not see that the ant heaps up reserves of food against the day when she will be in need of them? Imitate her by collecting for yourself the fruits of good works; they will be your treasure for eternity.

And then, you sluggard, look how hard the bee works. She flies from flower to flower to make the honey ready for you. With a like dedication you should read page after page of the holy Scriptures in order to gather salvation for yourself.

In the end, you will exclaim to the Lord in amazement: 'How sweet are your words to my taste: sweeter than honey to my mouth!' [Ps. 119:103]

Cyril of Jerusalem
Catecheses, 9, 13 (PG33, 652)

16th August

Procreation is Collaboration with God

God's statement, the commandment to beget children, is just as valid today, because he is always an artist who is fashioning humankind. It is certainly true that God is working even now on the world like a painter on his picture. The Lord taught us this too by saying: 'My Father is working still.' [John 5:17]

When the rivers no longer flow and no longer pour on to the great sea-bed, when the light has been separated in a perfect way from the darkness (though for the present this has yet to happen), when the good earth has ceased to produce fruit, when reptiles and quadrupeds have stopped reproducing and when the pre-arranged number of men and women has been reached, only then will there be a need to refrain from begetting children.

As things are, it is necessary for humanity to collaborate in bringing into the world beings in the likeness of God, because the world is already in existence, or rather it is being created. 'Be fruitful and multiply,' [Gen. 1:28] is the word.

Methodius of Olympus
The Banquet of the Ten Virgins, 2, 1 (ed. Zeoli, Florence 1952, pp.47ff.)

17th August

Our Alarming Ability to Ruin Everything

Some things are intrinsically good, some are intrinsically bad, and some are in between.

261

Things good in themselves are wisdom, justice, temperance, courage.

Things intrinsically evil are the lack of these virtues.

In the middle are wealth and poverty, fame and obscurity, health and illness, knowledge and ignorance and so on. They are said to be in the middle because in themselves they are neither good nor bad: it depends on their use whether they are called good or bad.

For instance, wealth is good when given to charity, but bad when spent on pleasure. Similarly poverty is good in teaching us patience and unshakeable gratitude to God, but bad if it produces blasphemy and servility with lack of endurance. Fame and notoriety are good if they teach us to be humble and to strive for future glory, but bad when they induce a spirit of dependence, adopting 'what people may think' as the criterion of our actions.

In conclusion, we must not condemn things. Nothing that God has made is bad. It becomes bad only if we, of our own free will, make a bad choice because we are urged on by, for example, self-love or passion.

Niceta Stethatus
The Spiritual Paradise, 3 (SC8, pp.64ff.)

18th August

Our World a Second Paradise

The visible and perceivable world, heaven and earth and all that they contain, has been created as a kind of extensive paradise for all, even before the paradise set in Eden for Adam.

God knew in advance that Adam would disobey. He

foresaw that the divine paradise would be closed to human beings and that they would have to go into exile. So he prepared this visible world, this second paradise, beforehand as a gift earmarked for us.

As our nature is twofold, so is the nature of this gift. It is both visible and intelligible. It is visible if we are considering seeds, fruits, animals, birds. It is intelligible inasmuch as, thanks to visible reality, what is said in Scripture is true: 'The greatness and beauty of created things give us a corresponding idea of their Creator.' [Wisd. 13:5]

In this second paradise, also, the tree of life and another tree called the tree of the knowledge of good and evil have been planted. What are they? Listen carefully.

The tree of life is God in person, the Creator of the universe. The tree of knowledge is our nature and our human abilities. The human being is, in fact, the one that has the ability to know good and evil.

Niceta Stethatus
The Spiritual Paradise, 8 (SC81, pp.162ff.)

19th August

Last Came the King

When God had created the heavens and the earth, there still had not appeared in the visible world that great and important creature, the human being. It was not to be expected that the monarch should make an appearance in advance of his subjects. On the contrary, only when the kingdom had first been made ready was the king to appear who was to reign over it.

263

So there arose first the continents, the islands, the sea, and, spread like a roof over them, the vault of heaven.

Riches from every quarter were gathered into the royal palace. By riches I mean all created things, the trees, the plants, everything that has sight and breath and life. I should include in their number, also, the materials which have been counted valuable in people's eyes because of their beauty, namely gold, silver and the precious stones which people love. The abundance of all these God hid like royal treasure in the bowels of the earth.

Only after that did God make human beings appear on earth. He intended them to be able to admire the beauty of the creation and to be lords over it. They were to be able, through their enjoyment of created things, to comprehend the wisdom of their provider. By the size and the beauty of them, they were to fathom the greatness of their Creator, which is beyond description or understanding.

That is why humankind was introduced last, after the rest of creation, not as some unimportant afterthought, but as a suitable sovereign over all that God had made.

Gregory of Nyssa
The Creation of Man, 2 (PG44, 132)

20th August

The Children of the Gospel are the Light of the World

The Psalmist sings: 'Instead of your fathers shall be your children; you will make them princes in all the earth.' [Ps. 45:16]

Who are the children of the Church, the Bride of Christ? They are the children of the Gospel who have attained to dominion over the world. Scripture says of them: 'Their voice goes out through all the earth' and again: 'They shall sit on twelve thrones judging the twelve tribes.' [Matt. 19:28]

Thanks to Christ, children are born to his Bride. They take the place of their ancient 'fathers', the patriarchs who do the works of Abraham and are honoured equally with them because they do works identical with theirs.

So believers are princes over all the earth, through the family connexion they have with what is good. The very nature of the good has conferred this primacy on them.

The children of Christ's Bride have become equal in rank to their fathers. They have a achieved the first place thanks to their practice of the virtues. For that reason their Mother has appointed them princes over all the earth. See what power the Queen has on earth, the appointment of princes to reign in it.

Basil the Great
On Psalm 44, 12 (PG29, 413)

21st August

Is Authority in the World Good or Evil?

'The devil took Jesus up and showed him all the kingdoms of the world.' [Luke 4:5]

How do you explain the fact that the devil then promises Jesus to give him authority over the world, while elsewhere we read that 'There is no authority except from God'? [Rom. 13:1] Is there a contradiction here? Nothing of the sort. It is undeniable that all authority comes from God. Without God the world would not exist, because: 'The world was made through him.' [John 1:10] All the same, although the world was made by God, the works of the world are evil, because: 'The whole world is in the power of the evil one.' [1 John 5:19]

In short, the constitution of the world comes from God, whereas the works of the world come from the evil one. So the authority comes from God, but the ambition to wield authority comes from the evil one.

Authority is not evil in itself, but a certain use of authority is. Although it does not come from the devil, authority is subject to the snares of the devil.

Ambrose
On the Gospel of St Luke 4, 28ff. (PL15, 1620)

22nd August

Desire and Deceit

Some people in past centuries worshipped the sun, others worshipped the moon, others the great multitude of the stars to which they attributed power to rule the world.

Others again worshipped the earth, water, air, fire, because of their usefulness. Without them human beings would not be able to live.

Others again worshipped visible objects, beautiful ones in particular, considering them to be gods. Some even worshipped portraits and statues.

They did this because they did not know the Original Being.

There was, however, in this worship, the cunning

of the evil one, who made use of what was good to achieve his evil ends. Seeing in human beings a desire roaming in search of God, he wanted to secure his own authority over them by frustrating that tendency. And so he took them by the hand just as one leads a blind person along the street.

Gregory Nazianzen
Oration 26, 14 (PG35)

23rd August

The Same God who Acts in Nature Acts in Our Hearts

We read in the Psalm: 'The voice of the Lord is upon the waters. The God of glory thunders, the Lord, upon many waters. The voice of the Lord is powerful, the voice of the Lord is full of majesty.' [Ps. 29:3]

These words are concerned with the kingdom of nature.

What are clouds, if not water? No sooner does a clap of thunder burst from the clouds than we immediately think of God making his glory resound.

But if you wish, you can understand this 'thundering of God' also as the change that took place after Jesus' baptism in the water. From that moment the strong voice of the Gospel began to resound within people's souls to lead them to holiness.

The Gospel itself is a thunder clap. Not for nothing did the Lord change the name of two disciples and called them 'sons of thunder'. [Mark 3:17] In that case the waters are understood to be the saints, in the double sense that they receive 'a spring of water welling up to eternal life', [John 4:14] and 'out of their heart shall flow rivers of living water' [John 7:38], that is to say the spiritual teaching which refreshes other souls.

Above these waters is the Lord, and his voice is full of majesty.

Basil the Great
Homily on Psalm 28, 3 (PG29, 289)

24th August

Be Joyful in the Lord All You Lands

The Psalmist says: 'Be joyful in the Lord all you lands!' Have all the lands heard this invitation? Yes, all the lands have heard this invitation. Already all the lands are making a joyful noise to the Lord. If one part is not yet praising him, it soon will.

The Church going out from Jerusalem is spread out among all peoples. The good are mixed in with the wicked. Through the mouth of the wicked all the lands are murmuring against the Lord: through the mouth of the good all the lands are making a joyful noise to the Lord.

And what is this joyful noise? Another Psalm exclaims: 'Blessed are the people who know the festal shout!' [Ps. 89:16] It must then be something very important if the experience of it brings happiness. Let us run towards this happiness, let us take careful note how to achieve this joyful noise.

One who is making a joyful noise does not utter words. No words are needed to make his joy heard. It is the song of a soul overflowing with joy, expressing its feelings as it may, above the level of discourse.

We find ourselves in this state of jubilation when we are glorifying God and we feel incapable of speaking of him – when for example we are considering the whole creation which makes itself available for us to know and to act in. The soul then asks: 'Who has made all this? And who has put me here? What are these truths that I am understanding? And who am I that understands? Who is it who has made it all? Who is he?'

If you want some idea of who he is, you must draw nearer to him. To look from a distance is to risk being deceived. It is the spirit that perceives him and the heart that sees him. What sort of heart? 'Blessed are the pure in heart: they shall see God.' [Matt. 5:8]

You must draw nearer to him by becoming like him. You will feel his presence to the extent that love grows in you, because God is Love.

Then you will not be able to do anything but praise him. And if you make a joyful noise to the Lord, you will understand the joyful noise that all the lands make to him.

Augustine
On Psalm 99, 3ff. (PL37, 1271ff.)

25th August

The Creatures Speak through our Voice

Heaven and earth glorify God. All the creatures proclaim his existence. The heaven cries to God: 'You it was who made me: I did not make myself.' And the earth cries: 'You are my creator: you it was who made me.'

But when and how do they proclaim this truth? When humankind reflects on them and on this truth, therein

269

precisely is the answer. It is thanks to your careful examination of them, it is thanks to your voice that they have a voice.

Look at the heavens: how beautiful they are! And look at the earth: how beautiful it is! Both heaven and earth radiate beauty.

God has made them, he directs them, he orders their course, is always present in their history, he determines their importance and arranges them in relation to his nature. That is why all creatures glorify him, those that move and those that are static, the heavens above and the earth below, perennial youth and august old age.

This spectacle which has been given you to admire, the joy with which it inspires you, the impetus with which it raises you up towards the Maker of it all, the revelation of the ineffable Being through whom he created it – all this is the testimony of heaven and earth to which you bear witness when you look at them.

Because he has made every object, because no object is greater than he, all his works are as it were within him, as though contained in him. If you love what he has made, love still more him who has made it all. If the creation is beautiful, God who is reflected in it is infinitely more beautiful.

Augustine
On Psalm 148, 15 (PL37, 1946)

26th August

Wait Till the End and You will Understand

Wait till the end and you will see the outcome of events. Don't fuss, don't worry yet awhile.

Imagine someone who is not of the trade watching a blacksmith start melting down gold and mixing in ashes and straw. If he does not wait till the end, he will think that that poor piece of gold is going to be destroyed.

Imagine someone else, born and bred on the sea, being suddenly landed on terra firma and not having the least notion about agriculture. He sees a farmer collecting grain and shutting it in a barn to protect it from damp. Then he sees this same farmer take the same grain and cast it to the winds, spreading it on the ground, maybe in the mud, without worrying any more about the dampness. Surely he will think that the farmer has ruined the grain, and he will reprove him.

Is such reproof justified? Yes it is, not on grounds of fact, but because of the ignorance, the pride and rashness of the judgment made. Because if this individual, before committing himself, had waited for the summer, he would change his ideas. He would see the corn waving in the fields, he would see the farmer sharpening his scythe to reap the very grain that he had scattered and left to rot, he would see how greatly that grain had multiplied.

Now, if the farmer waits all the winter, so much the more ought you to await the final outcome of events, remembering who it is that ploughs the soil of our souls.

And when I speak of the final outcome, I am not referring to the end of this present life, but to the future life – God's plan for us aims at our salvation and glory.

John Chrysostom
On Providence, 9, 1 (SC79, pp.145ff.)

27th August

The Destiny of the World Depends on the Dignity of Human Beings

Houses, it is said, will no longer have any inhabitants, and the earth will no longer display fertility. Right from the beginning, in fact, in consequence of the sin of Adam, thorns and thistles are destined to cover it.

Why should you be surprised that the human race's wickedness can hinder the fertility of the earth? For our sake the earth was subjected to corruption and for our sake it will be free of it. It exists solely for us, to serve us. Its being like this or like that has its roots in this destiny.

We see proof of this in the story of Noah.

Human nature had fallen into the extreme of wickedness. Everything therefore was destroyed: seeds, plants, animals, earth, sea, air, mountains, valleys, hills, cities, walls, houses, towers. A terrible flood engulfed every object. But because the human race needed to regain its proper course, the earth returned to its accustomed order and clothed itself again in the beauty that it had formerly.

It is easy to understand the meaning of this. What happens to the world, happens to it for the sake of the dignity of the human race. Humankind was raised to a dignity above that of all the other visible creatures, and the earth was created specifically for humanity.

John Chrysostom
On Isaiah, 5, 4 (PG56, 61)

272

28th August

A Different Life will Need a Different World

Some individuals are sharp enough at examining physical facts, but are culpably blind in regard to the knowledge of the truth.

They know how to measure the distance of the stars, to list those that shine in the region of the North Pole and those that are visible only to the inhabitants of the areas round the South Pole, and they know how to track the course of each one with great care.

Of all their abilities only one is missing – that which would enable them to discover God as creator of the universe and as a just judge who will reward each of the actions of our existence as it deserves, an ability that would permit them at the end of the world to have an adequate idea of universal judgment.

It is in fact absolutely necessary that the world should be transformed if our souls are due to be transformed in a different kind of life.

As the present life has affinities with the nature of this world, so the kind of existence which will apply to our souls tomorrow will have to have an environment appropriate to their new condition.

Basil the Great
Hexaemeron, 1, 4 (SC26, p.103)

29th August

New Heavens and a New Earth

The Lord Jesus will return from heaven. He will return in glory, on the last day, at the end of this age. Then will come the consummation of this present age and there will be a new age for us.

The reason is this: corruption, thieving, adultery and sins of every kind have been sown on earth. In the world pure breeding has been corrupted by impure stock. Because this marvellous abode of humankind has not been protected from the slime of iniquity, the world of today will pass away and there will arise an even better one.

If you want this proved to you from Scripture, listen to this: 'The skies shall roll up like a scroll. All their host shall fall as leaves fall from the vine, like leaves falling from the fig tree.' [Isa. 34:4] 'The sun will be darkened and the moon will not give its light, and the stars will fall from heaven.' [Matt. 24:29]

Why are we sorry for ourselves as though we alone will have to die? The stars will be put out too, but perhaps they too will rise again. The Lord will not roll up the heavens to destroy them but to renew them in beauty.

The prophet David says: 'In the beginning, O Lord, you laid the foundation of the earth, and the heavens are the work of your hands. They will perish, but you endure.' [Ps. 102:25-26] Someone may object: then it is clear that they will perish!

Yes, but hear in what sense they will perish. The following words explain: 'They will all wear out like a garment. You change them like a raiment, and they shall be new.'

Human beings are doomed to die: nevertheless, they

await the resurrection. And we are in this way awaiting an undoubted resurrection of the heavens.

Cyril of Jerusalem
Catecheses, 15, 3 (PG33, 872)

30th August

Conclusive Harmony

We think that the harmonious development of the world through the centuries is the work of the divine Word, believing that what is seen is derived from the Invisible.

In the same faith we accept also the Word of God according to which inevitably all things will have an end.

On the question of 'how' we ought not to yield to curiosity. We believe rather that the visible world will find its conclusive harmony in the world that has not yet been revealed, and we refuse to investigate what transcends our understanding.

Because the divine power is sufficient to bring creatures out of nothing into existence, we are convinced that that same power will complete the restoration of all things.

Gregory of Nyssa
The Creation of Man, 23 (PG44, 209)

31st August

God will Make a New Creation for You Too

In every corner of the earth there are trees growing. It is impossible to study them all in all their details: their fruit, their usefulness, their scent, their appearance, their structure, their leaves, their colour, their shape, their height or their smallness, the way to find them, preserve them, cultivate them, the differences in their bark, their trunk and their branches, the healing properties that many of them possess.

But all this exists for you, who are human.

So are the arts for you, cities and countryside are for you, sleep is for you, death is for you and so is life.

This magnificent world exists for you. And it will also exist for you tomorrow when it becomes better. For without doubt it will become better, and it will become so specially for you. Listen in fact to what Paul says: 'The creation itself will be set free from its bondage to decay' [Rom. 8:21] that is, from its own corruptibility. And it will obtain this privilege, this honour because of you. That is really what Paul goes on to say: 'the glorious liberty of the children of God.'

God's providence shines with greater strength than the light of this world. So do not examine events that are above you, do not scrutinize his motives which you cannot understand. For your very existence has been given you out of pure generosity. God had no need of help from us.

Let us rather marvel and give him glory.

John Chrysostom
On Providence, 7, 31 (SC79, pp.127)

September

Wealth belongs to us
that we may belong to God

1st September

'Anyone who will not Work shall not Eat'

Paul writes: 'Anyone who will not work shall not eat.'
[2 Thess. 3:10]

The Apostle himself would have been able not to
work, since he had been entrusted with a great mission.
Notwithstanding that, he worked day and night. All the
more reason for others to do the same.

'We hear that some of you,' St Paul goes on, 'are
living in idleness, not doing any work.' Even if they
were passing the time in prayer and fasting, they would
not be doing the manual work of which the Apostle is
speaking.

He concludes: 'Such persons we command and exhort
in the name of the Lord Jesus to do their work in
quietness and to earn their own living.'

Paul does not say: 'If they are idlers, let the community
keep them.' On the contrary, he demands two things:
that they keep quiet, and that they work!

John Chrysostom
On the Second Letter to the Thessalonians, 5, 2
(PG62, 494)

2nd September

'In the Sweat of Your Brow You shall Eat Bread'

In the beginning God had given us a life free of anxiety
and fatigue. But we misused his gifts, we lost them
through our laziness and have been driven out of paradise. From that moment life has become painful for us.

279

God has explained why, more or less in these words:

'I had granted you a pleasurable life, but in your prosperity you turned to evil. For this reason I am imposing on you pain and sweat. The earth will produce thorns and thistles. You will have to toil with much weariness and pain. I will make you live with suffering all the time, so that it may be a curb to keep you from entertaining an idea of yourself that is above what is right. In this way you will always have with you a realization of your nature that will not let you be deceived a second time.

'When I introduced you into the world, I, God, wanted you to live without suffering, without pain, without weariness, without sweat. I wanted you to live in joy, without the restraint of the body's needs, and therefore in freedom. But since this security does not suit you, I am cursing the ground on your account. It will not yield you its fruits as it did, unless you plough it and work it and suffer. As for food, "In the sweat of your brow you shall eat bread." ' [Gen. 3:19]

John Chrysostom
On John, 36, 2 (PG59, 205); *On Genesis*, 17, 9
(PG53, 146)

3rd September

Work is not Only a Question of Muscle

Of all the trades the one that Adam first practised was the trade of the tailor. Yes, before taking up any other trade he collected some fig-leaves and sewed them together.

Who taught him this skill? How did he learn it? The fact is that he had received from God the gift of intelligence; the fact is that he was the image of God.

You may ask yourselves in what way man arrived at the construction of the first plough, at woodwork, at forging iron, at putting oxen under the yoke, and in what way woman invented the art of spinning.

Where did all this come from?

When a trade comes into being, it is plied with a tool. The hands are not involved in the work as much as the reason, intelligence which arranges different objects in different shapes. It is the intelligence, for example, that manufactures clothes. The shape of the clothes reveals the intelligence of the tailor. When you read in the Bible that God worked in creating the world, do you really think he needed hands for his work?

If you are looking for the origin of a trade, if you are asking how a discovery or an invention could have come about, remember the word that God spoke: 'Let us make humanity in our image.' [Gen. 1:26]

Then you will have the solution at once. Humanity in the image of God. How could humanity possibly fail to use intelligence? Humanity in the image of the Creator. How could humanity possibly fail to imitate him?

Severianus of Gabala
The Creation of the World, 6, 6 (PG56, 492)

4th September

Is Work Humiliating?

Work is not shameful; idleness is. If work were shameful, Paul would not have worked and he would not have boasted of it.

He was the teacher of the Gentiles, to him were entrusted all the inhabitants of the earth, his care embraced all the Churches under the sun, yet he worked day and night without a moment's rest.

We on the other hand on whom not as much as a thousandth part of his responsibilities weigh, we who can scarcely imagine what his concerns were, spend all our life in idleness. I ask you, how can we justify ourselves, what hope have we of forgiveness?

The origin of all the miseries which have fallen on humanity lies in the fact that many people have reckoned it an honour not to have any occupation and have thought work degrading.

Paul was not ashamed to hold a needle in his hand and to sew skins together to make tents, even if he was talking to important people.

On the contrary, he boasted of it. In his letters he has left us a memorial of his trade like a bronze monument.

He had learned that trade when he was a boy, and he did not cease to practise it when he grew up, despite the fact that God had initiated him into his unfathomable mysteries.

John Chrysostom
Priscilla and Aquila, 1, 5 (PG51, 193ff.)

5th September

If We did not Work for One Another Humanity would Disappear

God wanted to unite people among themselves. So he made things in such a way that the good of one is inseparably bound to being useful to others. It is in this way that the world is united.

Think of the trades. If one of them were directed solely to the benefit of the one who was plying it, life could not continue and that trade would disappear. If for example a farmer were to sow only just enough grain for his own use, it would be the death of the others and therefore of him too. If a smith were not prepared to put his skill at the service of his neighbour, he would ruin all the other trades and therefore his own as well. If a baker or a leather-worker were to refuse to let the fruits of his labour circulate, he would damage not only the others, but in damaging the others he would hurt himself.

In short, if all these humble people were to imitate the idle rich who deny their possessions to those who have need of them, there would be very serious consequences.

Giving and receiving – this is the principle of the multiplication of goods. It holds good in agriculture, in teaching, in any sort of trade.

If anyone wished to be the only person to enjoy the benefits of his own work, he would destroy the life of everyone.

John Chrysostom
On the First Letter to the Corinthians, 4 and 25, 4
(PG61, 86ff. and 210ff.)

6th September

If a Human Being Could Outstrip a Horse

Why does the human body not have in itself the means to cope with its own needs?

Human beings come into the world defenceless, in poverty, lacking everything, incapable of satisfying the elementary demands of life. You could say they deserve pity more than envy.

On the other hand, logically speaking, since we are dealing with beings destined to dominate all other living creatures, nature ought to supply them with appropriate means to be independent of outside help.

In my opinion, precisely that which seems to be a deficiency in our nature is a spur to us to dominate the lower creatures. Let us imagine human beings who could outstrip a horse, whose feet hardly touch the ground and so on. They would not try completely to dominate the other creatures, because they would have no need of any help. On the contrary, for the reason I have indicated, the animals have received some good properties which are essential to us. That is why as a result it appears imperative for us to dominate them.

Because their bodies are slow, human beings have tamed the horse.

Because their bodies are bare, they keep sheep whose wool they take every year.

Because they have to obtain the means for their own survival from a long distance away, they have compelled beasts of burden to serve their needs.

Because they cannot, like the animals, feed on grass, they have domesticated the ox to make their life easier.

Gregory of Nyssa
The Creation of Man, 7 (PG44, 140ff.)

7th September

The Rousing of the Sluggard

When the sun rises it spreads its bright rays everywhere and encourages everyone to work. The farmer then grasps his mattock and goes out, the smith takes up his hammer, every worker picks up his own tools.

And the sluggard, what does the sluggard do? He is no sooner up than he rushes to fill his belly, like a pig. Only animals for the slaughter house, those that are only useful as food, behave like him.

Other animals carry weights and give people their help. No sooner is the night over than they too go to work. The sluggard, by contrast, rises when the sun is already at full strength and we are by now worn out with fatigue. He gets up like a fattened pig.

I speak like this to teach you to shun a lazy and useless life. What is sadder than someone who does nothing? What is more depressing and more contemptible?

The soul is active by nature and does not take kindly to inactivity.

John Chrysostom
On the Acts of the Apostles, 35, 3 (PG60, 256ff.)

8th September

Trials of Saint Anthony

When the saintly abbot Anthony was living in the desert, he fell into a state of listlessness and was attacked by a throng of dark thoughts. So he said to God: 'Lord, I want to be saved, but these thoughts will

not allow me to be. What should I do in my misery?
How can I possibly be saved?'

A little later Anthony went out and met a man who
resembled him. The man was sitting down to work.
Suddenly he got up and prayed. Then he sat down
again to twist a rope. Then he stood up again to
pray.

It was an angel sent by God to put Anthony right
and to reassure him. In fact Anthony heard him say:
'Do this and you will be saved.'

At these words the saintly abbot experienced great
joy and much encouragement. He behaved in this way
and was saved.

Sayings of the Desert Fathers (PG65, 76)

9th September

Work or Prayer?

Certain monks, called 'the Prayer People' because they
wanted to dedicate themselves entirely to prayer, went
to pay a visit to Abbot Lucius.

The aged monk asked them: 'What work do you
do?'

They said: 'We don't do work, but we obey Paul's
teaching to pray without ceasing.'

The old man asked them: 'Do you eat?' and they
replied, 'Yes.' The Abbot then demanded to know who
prayed instead of them while they were eating. Then
he asked them: 'Do you sleep?' and they replied, 'Yes.'
The Abbot then demanded a second time to know who
prayed instead of them while they were sleeping. The

monks were at a loss to answer either of the two questions.

Then the old man continued: 'Forgive me, but you are not doing what you say you are. I, on the other hand, succeed in working with my hands and at the same time in praying without ceasing. I start by sitting down in the presence of God. Then I begin my task of making ropes and I say: "Have mercy on me, O God, according to your steadfast love; according to your abundant mercy blot out my transgressions." ' [Ps. 51:1]

Then he asked them if that was prayer and they replied 'Yes.' The old man went on: 'At the end of a day passed in work and prayer, I have earned roughly sixteen shillings. Two shillings I deposit on the ground outside the door and the rest I spend on food. The person who picks up the two shillings prays in my place when I am eating or sleeping. In this way, by the grace of God, I am obedient to the teaching to pray without ceasing.'

Sayings of the Desert Fathers (PG65, 253)

10th September

The Excuse, the Opportunity and the Need

You should not say: 'I am praying' to justify your own laziness, your own fear of weariness. You should rather profit from your work as being an opportunity to struggle, to face painful effort, to practise patience under difficulties.

Not only so. Besides being a necessary discipline for the body, work is a requirement of the love of our neighbour. By means of our service, God grants to our needy brethren the wherewithal for their survival.

The Apostle gives us an example of this love in the Book of Acts: 'I have shown you that one must help the weak.' [Acts 20:35] and elsewhere he says: 'Work honestly with your hands so that you may be able to give to those in need.' If we act like this, we shall be worthy to hear the invitation: 'Come, O blessed of my Father, inherit the kingdom prepared for you from the foundation of the world; for I was hungry and you gave me food; I was thirsty and you gave me drink.' [Matt. 25:34]

It is superfluous to say that idleness is always a fault since the moment that Paul clearly warned us that anyone who does not work has no right to eat. Because daily bread is indispensable for everyone, everyone ought to work as much as possible. It is not for nothing that we read this in praise of the 'strong woman': 'She looks well to the ways of her household and does not eat the bread of idleness.' [Prov. 31:27]

Some people avoid work by putting forward the excuse that they have to pray. Let them remember well, those people, what the preacher says: 'For everything there is a season, and a time for every matter under the sun.' [Eccles. 3:1]

Basil the Great
The Greater Rules, 37 (PG31, 1009)

11th September

'I was Hungry and You Gave me Food'

Anyone working, you should know, ought to work not so much for the satisfaction of his own needs by his efforts, as to fulfil the commandment of the Lord who said: 'I was hungry and you gave me food.' [Matt. 25:35]

Thinking of oneself only is absolutely forbidden in these words: 'Do not be anxious, saying "What shall we eat?" or "What shall we drink?" or "What shall we wear?" The Gentiles seek all these things.' [Matt. 6:31] The aim which everyone ought to have in working is to help the needy, more than to provide for oneself.

In this way we shall avoid the accusation that we are attached to our own personal advantage and we shall receive the blessing that the Lord gives to those who love their brothers and sisters. The Lord said: 'As you did it to one of the least of these my brethren, you did it to me.' [Matt. 25:40]

So anyone who works day and night to succour the destitute is nearing perfection.

Basil the Great
The Greater Rules, 42 (PG31, 1025)

12th September

Four Ways of Loving Money

People seek money, not for its practical usefulness, but because with it they can become slaves to pleasure.

Three reasons for the love of money are pleasure, conceit, and lack of faith. Hedonists love money to spend it on their pleasures, the conceited want it to procure fame, those who are lacking in faith seek money to keep it hidden away out of fear of starvation, old age, or illness. The latter put their trust in their money rather than in God the creator of the universe, whose providence knows no bounds and reaches even the lowest of his creatures.

But there are four kinds of people who put money aside. I have just mentioned three. There are, however, also those who restrict themselves to the administration of goods. Only these last are justified in accumulating money, on the assumption that their aim is to be always in the business of helping the needy.

Maximus the Confessor
Centuries on Charity, 3, 16ff. (SC9, pp.128ff.)

13th September

Don't Say of the Rich: Lucky Things!

You are guilty of over-simplification if you define as fortunate the rich and the powerful. They are on the contrary most unfortunate and miserable because they possess the good things of this world and use them in pursuit of vice and wickedness.

Therefore if you see depraved people wallowing in wealth, don't say, 'What happiness.' They are unfortunate precisely because they have too many opportunities of living in iniquity.

If you see other people who seem upright, imprisoned by adversity and poverty, don't at once think they are unfortunate and don't accuse God of injustice. They will suffer no harm through their misfortune, because they have been educated by it to bear discomfort like the champions of virtue that they are.

For just as dwellers in iniquity pervert even good things to use as weapons of wickedness, so lovers of virtue can adapt even bad things to act as material for true wisdom.

Theodoret
The Cure of Pagan Diseases, 6, 3ff. (SC57, pp.269ff.)

14th September

The Great Eye on your Breast

To admire black or green stones which are the rubbish of the pilgrim sea or waste products of the earth is childish. Children, of course, when they see a fire are attracted by its brightness and go near to it without realizing, from lack of experience, the risk of their being burnt. No better than children are those foolish women who let themselves be seduced by the stones or other jewels of which their necklaces are composed: for instance the amethyst, the jasper, or 'that queen of precious stones, the emerald.'

More prized even than the stones is the pearl. It forms inside the oyster-shell and looks like a great fish's eye. And some women are not ashamed of attaching such importance to the product of a sea shell.

A holy stone would be a far better ornament for them, the Word of God which Scripture has described as a pearl. In it is Jesus in his brightness and his purity, the all-seeing eye, the invisible Logos which

291

took human flesh, whose precious flesh was made regenerate in the water of baptism.

But I ought to reply an objection: if everyone prefers the simple things, who will have the precious ones? My answer is: those who know how to handle them with detachment.

But it is not easy for everyone to be so wise!

Clement of Alexandria
The Teacher 2, 12 (PG8, 540)

15th September

Full Coffers and Empty Conscience

Do you have wealth? It is a good thing. But only if your use of it is good. You will not be able make good use of it if you are evil: wealth is an evil for the evil, a good for the good. Not that it is a good in the sense that it makes you good, but it is converted into good when it is in the hands of the good.

Do you want to have honour? It too is a good. But only if used well. How many are those whom honour has led to a bad end! Yet how many others have been helped by honour to behave well!

Be a good tree. Do not fool yourself that you can produce good fruits if you are a bad tree; good fruit comes only from a good tree. So, change your heart and your actions will change too. Weed out greed and plant love. As 'the root of all evil is greed', [cf. 1 Tim. 6:10] so the root of all good is love.

If only you knew what goodness is! What you want is not good, the good is what you do not want. Look within yourself, seek within. What is not pleasing to your renewed heart, kill off; what is pleasing to it, nourish.

If you find yourself void of good works, why are you so keen to have external goods? What use is a coffer brimming over with money, if your conscience is empty? What use are the things you have, if you do not have the One who gave all?

Do not put your trust in untrustworthy riches. Hope in God, in God alone. He gives you all in abundance: the goods of the earth for your use, the goods of eternity for your pleasure.

Augustine
Sermons, 36, 5ff. (PL38, 217)

16th September

Money itself is not Evil

Isidore said:

'In this fleeting life the rich do not have the satisfaction of permanently enjoying their power, their fame, or their money. Suddenly death carries them off, the abyss swallows them up and they disappear, condemned to eternal torments.

'Greed makes the rich haughty. It does not happen because of their riches, but because of their free choice. Evil does not consist in things, but in the use we make of them.

'Those who spend their riches on beneficial objects are making good use of good things. The same good things are being badly used by those who plan to multiply their wealth or who only do good to their neighbours for reputation's sake.'

Defensor Grammaticus
Book of Sparkling Sayings, 58 (SC86, p.160)

17th September

Owning a Slave is no Measure of Worth

Riches ought to be used in a reasonable way, and it is necessary to overcome avarice and share them generously with others.

The love of beautiful objects must not become purely selfish. If it does, we shall end up not knowing what the true beauty is like. It would be sad indeed if people were to say of us: 'Their land, their slaves and their capital assets are worth fifteen million, but they themselves are only worth three pennies.'

If you separate owners and slaves, you will see that the owners are not different from slaves, in fact they are very like them. If there is any difference, it is that the owners are weaker and more prone to illness than their slaves.

We must continually repeat those amazing words of the Lord: 'Sell what you possess and give to the poor, and you will have treasure in heaven, where there are neither robbers nor rust.' [cf. Matt. 19:21; 6:20]

The truly rich are not those who keep their riches to themselves but those who give to others. Happiness comes not from possessing wealth but from giving it away. Whatever is generously given away becomes a fruit of the soul. It therefore becomes the soul's wealth.

Clement of Alexandria
The Teacher, 3, 6 (PG8, 604)

18th September

When Wealth can Liberate

'No one can serve two masters.' What sort of masters? Christ explains it to you when he continues: 'You cannot serve God and Mammon.' [Matt. 6:24]

It is clear then. Those who make Mammon their master cannot serve God, but they serve the master they have freely chosen. They love to be at Mammon's disposal, they are happy to serve him because they have chosen Mammon, because they have voluntarily subjected themselves to him. Generally people love the masters they have chosen of their own free will more than those to whom they have become subject by compulsion.

A different pattern of behaviour is exhibited by a small number of people who are pleasing to God. They have become the masters of their own wealth. And they have used it, as if it were their faithful slave, to feed the hungry, to clothe the naked, to free the debtors who are insolvent and in prison. Abraham, Isaac, Jacob, Job, Joseph, David acted like this. Money was not the master of these people; they were the masters of their money.

'You cannot serve God and Mammon.' Here then is the commandment to be observed by those who possess riches. Christ, seeing that they were not raising themselves to the height of perfection, came down to their level with his word and established a law which they can keep in the situation in which they are.

In other words, it is as if he had said: 'Seeing that you are not willing to renounce wealth, at least don't become its slave. Become in actual fact its master and use it for all the very best of actions.'

Philoxenus of Mabbug
Homily 8, 226ff. (SC44 pp.225ff.)

19th September

The Beggar's Made-Up Tale Is Evidence of our Inhumanity

It is folly, it is madness, to fill our wardrobes full of clothes and to regard with indifference a human being, a being made in the image and likeness of God, who is naked, trembling with cold and almost unable to stand.

You say: 'But that fellow there is pretending to tremble and not to have any strength.' So what? If that poor fellow is putting it on, he is doing it because he is trapped between his own wretchedness and your cruelty. Yes, you are cruel and guilty of inhumanity. You would not have opened your heart to his destitution without his play-acting.

If it were not necessity compelling him, why should he behave in such a humiliating way just to get a bit of bread?

The made-up tale of a beggar is evidence of your inhumanity. His prayers, his begging, his complaints, his tears, his wandering all day long round the city did not secure for him the smallest amount to live on.

That perhaps is the reason why he thought of acting a part. But the shame and the blame for his made-up tale falls less on him than on you.

He has in fact a right to be pitied, finding himself in such an abyss of destitution. You, on the other hand, deserve a thousand punishments for having brought him to such humiliation.

John Chrysostom
On the First Letter to the Corinthians 21,5
(PG61, 177)

20th September

'Woe to Those who put Bitter for Sweet and Sweet for Bitter'

If you help a poor person in the name of the Lord, you are making a gift and at the same time granting a loan.

You are making a gift because you have no expectation of being reimbursed by that poor person. You are granting a loan because the Lord will settle the account. It is not much that the Lord receives by means of the poor, but he will pay a great deal on their behalf.

'They who are kind to the poor lend to the Lord.' [Prov. 19:17] Do you not want the master of all to be on your side, especially as he is prepared to settle your debt? If a rich person were to promise to pay on behalf of others, would you not be happy to accept the pledge? Why then do you not accept the Lord as surety for the poor?

Make a present of the money you have to spare without asking for interest: it will benefit you and others.

It will benefit you insofar as you have made your money safe. It will benefit the others insofar as they are able to use it.

If all the same you are looking for some profit, be content with what the Lord will give you. He will also give the interest on your gift to the poor. So wait for the benevolence of the one who is truly benevolent.

The profit that you gain from the poor surpasses all bounds of cruelty. You are profiting from misfortune, you are squeezing money out of tears, you are persecuting a defenceless being, you are belabouring someone who is starving.

You think the profit you make out of the poor is just. But 'Woe to those who put bitter for sweet and sweet for bitter!' [Isa. 5:20] 'Are grapes gathered from thorns, or figs from thistles?' [Matt. 7:16] or kindly relationships from usury?

Basil the Great
On Psalm 14 (PG31, 277)

21st September

Portrait of a Money-Lender

The miser sees someone in need kneeling in front of him and entreating him for money, resigned to any act of humiliation, prepared to say anything at all. The miser has no pity on the wretched beggar but remains unbending in his refusal to help. He does not give way to any entreaties, he does not take heed of any prayers, he is not moved by the other's tears. He continues to maintain that he does not have any money, that he also has to look for someone to make him a loan, and he confirms this lie with an oath.

By contrast, when the beggar talks to him about interest and pledges, at once his eyebrows go up and he smiles, he recalls the friendship that linked their parents, he regards the other almost as one of the family, to be treated as a friend.

He says: 'Let's see if by any chance I have a little money. Yes, I have some money belonging to another friend. He lent it to me for a bit of business. Unfortunately, he is asking for a very high rate of interest on it. For you I will make a discount. I will make you the loan at a lesser rate.'

With these lies he traps the unlucky beggar who is promptly shackled with a contract and ceaselessly pestered. In this way, the beggar is freed from distress only to be deprived of liberty. Anyone who submits to paying interest becomes a slave for the rest of his life.

Basil the Great
On Psalm 14, (PG31, 265)

22nd September

Don't Become a Slave of the Money-Lenders

Dogs are pacified if you give them a bone. The money-lender becomes fiercer than ever when you pay him back his money. He keeps on barking, demanding ever higher interest rates. He won't believe your sworn statement. He tracks down what you have at home, he investigates all your business affairs. If you go out of your house he drags you by force to his office. If you stay in hiding at home, he stands in front of the door and knocks and knocks.

In the presence of your wife he makes you blush, he molests you in the presence of your friends, he attacks you in public. He makes your life intolerable by repeating to you: 'I need money urgently and the only possibility of my obtaining it is to secure from you the interest on my loan.'

If he then allows you a deferment, do you hope to derive any advantage from it? Poverty is like a galloping horse. It catches up with you quickly, it begins to chase you again and you find yourself in trouble as before, only further in debt than at first. A loan in fact does not do away with poverty: it only postpones it. Because that is so, put up with the hardships of poverty today and don't put them off till tomorrow.

If you don't ask the money-lender for help, while you are poor today, tomorrow you will be equally poor, but certainly no poorer. If you ask the money-lender, tomorrow you will be worse off than today, because the interest payments will increase your poverty.

Today, no one will blame you for being poor. It is a misfortune, not your fault. But tomorrow, if you become a slave of the money-lender because of the interest payments, everyone will accuse you of folly.

Basil the Great
On Psalm 14 (PG31, 269)

23rd September

The Monster gives Birth to Children without Stopping

It is said that hares when their leverets have been born, at once, while they are beginning to rear them, conceive another brood. The same thing happens with money lent by usurers. At once it conceives more money and has a reproductive capacity that is ever more intense.

You hardly have it in your hands before the current month's interest payments are already due. So that it breeds misery for you continuously as long as you live.

Interest payments are the product of an activity, usury, which is more fruitful than anything. They are also prolific in the sufferings they cause to the person who has incurred the debt. Just as labour pains strike a woman when she is about to give birth, so the interest payment date makes the debtor writhe in anguish.

Piled up interest payments: these fruits of usury ought to be called the offspring of the viper. They say that vipers just before they are born devour their own mother's womb. Interest payments similarly devour the home of the debtor.

Seeds grow slowly with time. Animals have a fairly long gestation period. Interest payments, on the other hand, are produced today and begin at once to produce more.

If animals begin to breed again too soon, they become infertile no less soon. Money committed to the usury, by contrast, besides beginning to breed at once, has a fertility that grows continually greater *ad infinitum.*

Never get entangled with this monstrous animal.

Basil the Great
On Psalm 14 (PG31, 273)

24th September

Only a Gladly Given Gift does not Hurt the Pride of the Poor

It is not enough to help the poor. We must help them with generosity and without grumbling.

And it is not enough to help them without grumbling. We must help them gladly and happily.

When the poor are helped there ought to be these two conditions: generosity and joy.

Why do you complain of giving something to the poor? Why do you display bad temper in the practice of almsgiving? If they see you in that frame of mind, the poor would prefer to refuse your gift. If you give with a brusque demeanour, you are not being generous but lacking gentleness and courtesy. If your face reveals a feeling of hostility, you cannot bring comfort to your brother or sister who is living in the midst of hostility.

Afterwards, you will be happy to see that they do not feel ashamed or humiliated just because you have helped them joyfully. Nothing actually causes shame so much as having to receive something from someone else.

By showing great joyfulness you will succeed in enabling your brother or sister to overcome their sensitivity. They will understand that in your opinion receiving is just as beautiful as giving.

By showing bad temper, on the other hand, far from cheering them up you will be depressing them even further.

If you give gladly, even if you give only a little, it is a big gift. If you give unwillingly, even if you give a big gift, you turn it into a small one.

John Chrysostom
On the Letter to the Romans, 21, 1ff. (PG60, 603)

25th September

Charity with Other People's Money

Augustine said:

'The poor ought to be helped, not with money we have stolen but with money we have earned. What kind of a gift is money which one person receives with joy while the other weeps to lose it, for which one laughs while the other cries?

'You want to make a present from your possessions? The best way is to give back to your neighbour what you owe him. Some people prefer to lose their own belongings by donating them, rather than to present to others what actually belongs to them anyway.'

Jerome said:

'It is a splendid thing for bishops to help the poor. It is shameful for any priest to seek to enrich himself.'

Basil said:

'Don't become pleased with yourself when you help the poor, and don't consider yourself better than those you help.'

Gregory said:

'When we are presenting something to the poor that they need, we are not giving them what would be ours but that to which they have a right.'

Defensor Grammaticus
Book of Sparkling Sayings, 49 (SC86, pp.102ff.)

26th September

Decide the Use of Your Money Together

Consult one another and manage your possessions together, whether it be the treasure you are laying up for yourselves in heaven by helping the poor or the money you have left for your needs and those of your children.

You who are a wife, when it is a matter of disposing of these possessions, or of using them in the way that seems best, ought to discuss it with your husband.

As things are, however, you have behaved in a way I find saddening.

Your marriage had been heading towards great holiness, because you had made the most perfect plans together in common counsel. So much the less, therefore, had you any right to make decisions about your clothes, about gold or silver, about money or any other matter, without consulting your husband.

Your behaviour towards him is a scandal.

Augustine
Letter 262, 4ff. (PL33, 1079ff.)

27th September

A Staff and a Companion for Your Journey

We should possess only what we can carry with us on our journey: a light burden, therefore. Wife and husband should have the same attitude to this. Thrift is a good companion for those who are on the road to heaven.

The limit for our possessions is the body, just as the limit for a shoe is the foot. What is left over – that is to say necklaces and all the gewgaws that the rich collect – is only a nuisance, not a proper adornment for the body.

Any who want to climb the hard path ought to have a good staff, namely the practical helping of the poor. Any who want to share the true rest should show themselves generous to the afflicted.

Scripture in fact says: 'One who is rich has to pay a ransom.' [Prov. 13:8] This means that the rich can be saved by giving away their money to anyone in need whom they may meet.

Look at a well of spring water. We draw some off and the water returns to its previous level. It is the same with true generosity, where the spring is love for one's neighbour. When generosity gives drink to the thirsty, it wells up and is full again at once, just as a mother's milk flows into her breasts the moment the babe has sucked.

Clement of Alexandria
The Teacher, 3, 7 (PG8, 609)

28th September

More Than One Kind of Poverty

Poverty is not always praiseworthy, but only when it represents a free choice according to the Gospel commandment.

Many are poor in terms of possessions and very miserly in spirit, and those people will not be saved through their poverty but damned by their attitude of mind.

Not every poor person therefore is worthy of praise, but only those who of their own choice put the commandment of the Lord before all the treasures of the world.

Those people the Lord says are blessed when he proclaims: 'Blessed are the poor in spirit.' [Matt. 5:3] He does not say the poor in possessions but those who have freely chosen poverty in spirit.

What is involuntary cannot merit blessedness. Every virtue, and poverty in spirit more than any other, must be a free choice.

The same argument applies to Christ. In his own nature he is rich. Everything that the Father has is his. But 'For your sake he became poor, so that by his poverty you might become rich.' [2 Cor. 8:9]

Moreover, everything that can lead us to blessedness has been experienced by the Lord first. He offers himself as an example to his disciples. Reflect on the beatitudes, analyse them one by one, and you will realize that the theoretical teaching in them is drawn from practical experience.

Basil the Great
On Psalm 33 (PG31, 561)

29th September

Naked We Came into the World and Naked We Shall Leave It

It may seem an extraordinary thing to do, to sell all you have and give the proceeds to the poor. Actually, however, it is a natural action. It is like going back to creation, to our own birth itself.

When Job had lost all his possessions he did not think what had happened to him was anything abnormal. He soothed the pain by saying: 'Naked I came from my mother's womb, and naked shall I return.' [Job 1:21] As if to say: 'All that has happened is that I find myself as I was when I was born.'

It is natural for human beings to be deprived of everything, to end up with nothing but their own bodies.

But it becomes much greater than something simply natural if someone does it voluntarily, for the love of God. It is like death. To die for the love of God is martyrdom.

When Adam and Eve were created they did not possess anything. Not only had they no wealth: they did not even have any clothes. They were like a child which comes naked from its mother's womb. They were in the position Job describes. They were as Paul has said: 'We brought nothing into the world, and we cannot take anything out of the world.' [1 Tim. 6:7]

Let people look at their beginning and their end, and try to be like that also during the time between.

Philoxenus of Mabbug
Homily 9, 338ff. (SC44, pp.301ff.)

30th September

Lord, Grant me a Foretaste of Eternity

Lord, when I came into this world, I did not bring anything with me, and when I leave it, I shall not take anything out. So long as I have something to eat and clothes to wear, I am happy.

Because if you want to become rich you fall into temptation, into foolish desires which carry one away and lead towards death. The root of all evil is covetousness. Many who have coveted riches have turned aside from the faith and encountered affliction.

But I will encounter you, you who are truly poor, because although you were rich, for my sake you became poor. Who could possibly have an accurate idea of your riches? And who could have an accurate idea of your poverty?

What poverty, the poverty of my Lord!

You were conceived in a virgin's womb, you were enclosed in the body of your mother.

What poverty!

You were born in a narrow room, they wrapped you in swaddling clothes and laid you in a manger. And then the king of heaven and earth, creator and maker of all things visible and invisible, drinks, eats, cries, grows up, reveals his age and hides his majesty. In the end he is arrested, flogged, mocked, spat on, slapped in the face, crowned with thorns, fastened to the cross, transfixed by a lance.

What poverty!

Lord, when I meditate on your poverty, whatever I may look at loses any attraction for me.

So give me something eternal, grant me a foretaste of eternity.

Augustine
Sermons 14, 7ff. (PL38, 115)

October

*The Church is our light
and leaven for the world*

1st October

Every Page of the Bible is a Hymn to Christ

You have heard the account of the two disciples who met the Lord on the road to Emmaus and yet did not recognize him. When he met them, they had lost all hope of the redemption that is in Christ, they were convinced that the Master was dead like any other man, they did not realize that Jesus inasmuch as he is Son of God was still alive. According to them he had left this life without being able to return, like one of the many prophets.

Then the Lord revealed to them the meaning of the Scriptures. Beginning with Moses and quoting one prophet after another he showed that everything that he had suffered had been foretold.

After that, he appeared to the eleven disciples and they thought they were seeing a ghost. So Jesus let them touch him, the one who had let himself be crucified. He was crucified by his enemies and touched by his friends. He healed them all, the former of their wickedness, the latter of their unbelief.

Yet the Lord did not consider it was sufficient to allow them to touch him. He wanted to appeal to the Scriptures to confirm their hearts in the faith. He saw us in anticipation, who had not yet been born, who do not have a chance to touch Christ but do have the opportunity to read about him.

The Apostles believed because they had touched him. But what can folk like us do? By now Christ is ascended into heaven and will only return at the end to judge the living and the dead. On what base shall we build our faith, unless it be those Scriptures with which the Lord wanted to confirm the faith of those who touched him?

He revealed to them the meaning of the Scriptures and showed how it was necessary that the Christ should suffer and should fulfil all that had been written about him in the books of the Law of Moses, in the Prophets, and in the Psalms. The Lord went through the whole Old Testament. He seemed to span it all in his embrace.

The Scriptures are in fact, in any passage you care to choose, singing of Christ, provided we have ears that are capable of picking out the tune. The Lord opened the minds of the Apostles so that they understood the Scriptures. That he will open our minds too is our prayer.

Augustine
On the First Letter of John, 2, 1 (SC75, 151ff.)

2nd October

Guide to the Discovery of Scripture

By what principle ought one to read and interpret the Scriptures? It is a fact that a number of errors have had their origin in an inability to understand a sacred text in the right way.

For example, many Jews have not believed in our Saviour, because they have been attached to the literal meaning of the prophecies made about him and have not seen them physically fulfilled. They have not seen the prisoners set free, [Isa. 61:1] nor the city of God built in the way they imagined it, [Ezek. 48] nor the chariot cut off from Ephraim, nor the warhorse from Jerusalem, [Zech. 9:10] nor butter and honey being eaten and the good chosen without prior knowledge of evil or preference for it. [Isa. 7:15]

So then the reason for so many mistaken ideas about

312

God consists solely in the inability to interpret Scripture in a spiritual sense. It has been taken in its literal sense only.

Those who receive the Word, even the most literal-minded, know that some truths revealed in the sacred Books are full of mysteries. Wise and humble people recognize that they cannot explain them. What do we say, for instance, about the prophecies? They are packed full of obscure words. And who has not been struck by the unspeakable mysteries contained in the revelation made to John?

The literal-minded person finds edification in the sacred Books. He finds the bare bones, so to say, of the Scriptures. But the person who has made some progress attains to the soul of the Scriptures. The one who is perfect, then, discovers the spiritual law.

Origen
Principles, 4, 2, 4 (PGII, 345)

3rd October

The Two Meanings of the Bible

The reason why the divine power has given us the Scriptures is not solely to present facts according to the literal interpretation of the narrative. If one looks to the letter of the text, some of the facts have not actually happened and would be irrational and illogical.

Granted, the facts that have happened in the literal sense are much more numerous than the facts that have been added and have only a spiritual meaning.

All the same, in the face of certain pages the reader feels embarrassed. Without accurate research it is not possible to discover if a fact that seems historical actually happened according to the literal sense of the words or if it did not happen at all.

By keeping the commandment of the Lord to 'search the Scriptures' [John 5:39], one ought to examine with care and attention where the literal meaning is historical and where it is not.

In Scripture not everything is objectively historical in the literal sense. Sometimes it is obvious that the result of taking it literally is impossible. But the divine Scripture, taken as a whole, has a spiritual meaning.

Origen
Principles, 4, 3, 4 (PG11, 347)

4th October

These Words Are the Word of God

The Scriptures that prophesy about Christ, the words that announce his coming and his teaching are inspired by God. They were proclaimed with power and authority and it is for this reason they have conquered so many people's hearts.

However, only with the coming of Christ have the divine character of the prophetic writings and the spiritual meaning of the books of the Mosaic Law become apparent. Before Christ it was not possible to produce decisive arguments for the inspiration of the Old Testament. The coming of Jesus persuaded even the doubtful that those pages were written under the influence of grace.

Whoever reads the Prophets carefully will be convinced that they are no human achievement. The reader will understand the meaning of divine inspiration.

As far as the books of the Mosaic Law are concerned, a veil has been drawn between their brightness and people's understanding. The coming of Jesus has made that light shine in such a way that it has become possible to recognize clearly those future benefits at which the literal meaning of those books only hinted. [cf. 2 Cor. 3:12-18; Heb. 10:1]

It would take a long time to review the ancient prophecies of events that would be realized in the future. But someone in doubt who did this would be struck by their divine character. He would give up all his uncertainty and dedicate himself to the Word of God with all his soul.

Origen
Principles, 4, 1, 6, (PGII, 342)

5th October

The Fighter's Handbook for the Conquest of the Kingdom

The divine reading of the sacred Books reveals the counsels of the most holy God.

Thanks to reading them each of us knows what he ought to do, and learns the laws of the struggle which he has taken on in order to deserve the kingdom of Christ.

The divine reading of the holy Gospel explains to those who love it zealously what sufferings they must undergo on account of it. The Word comes down from heaven and teaches them ineffable things.

After they have heard it, they gather together among

315

themselves in accordance with it, and in gratitude for their own salvation they offer their testimony; that is, they recite the divine Symbol of faith.

Maximus the Confessor
Mystagogia, 10ff. (PG91, 689)

6th October

God Found a Harlot and Made Her a Virgin

I believe in the holy Church, that holy Church which we are ourselves.

In saying 'we' I do not mean we who are united here, all you who are listening to me now. I mean all the Christians of this local church, those, that is, who live in this city, all the Christians of this region, all the Christians of this province, all the Christians there are beyond the seas, in the whole world, because 'from the rising of the sun to its setting the name of the Lord is to be praised!' [Ps. 113:3] All these are the Church, our true mother, the true bride of the Bridegroom.

We esteem her highly. She is a worthy spouse of so great a Lord. The goodness of the Bridegroom in fact has been exceptional. He found a harlot and made her a virgin.

That she was a harlot she cannot deny: she would be forgetting the forgiveness of the One who set her free. Was she not a harlot? She certainly committed fornication with idols and devils! All were guilty of spiritual fornication. Only a few were guilty of fornication in the flesh, but all of them committed fornication of the heart.

The Lord has come and made the Church a virgin.

The Church is therefore pure. May she remain pure, may she fear the seducer, may she be far from any who could defile her!

Augustine
Serm. Morin I, I (Miscellanea Agostiniana 447ff.)

7th October

There is Life in the Church because in the Church is the Spirit

My brothers and sisters, if you want the Holy Spirit to dwell in you, listen carefully.

Our spirit, by means of which each individual lives, is called the soul. And look what the soul does in the body. It gives life to all the limbs. It sees with the eyes, hears with the ears, smells with the nose, speaks with the tongue, works with the hands, walks with the feet. It is present at one and the same time in all the limbs to make them live. It gives life to all the limbs and to each limb its function. It is not the eye that hears, not the ear that sees, not the eye or the ear that speaks. Yet they are nonetheless alive. The ear is alive, the tongue is alive. Their functions are different, the life is the same.

The Church of God is like that.

By means of some believers she performs miracles, by means of others she teaches the truth; by means of some she keeps virginity, by means of others she respects marital fidelity. The tasks are different, the life is the same.

What the soul is to the body of a human being, the Holy Spirit is to the Body of Christ, the Church. The Holy Spirit does for the whole Church what the soul does for the body of the individual.

Look then and see what you ought to fear and what you ought to avoid. If the body suffers an amputation (for example of a finger or a hand or a foot) does the soul go with the limb that has been cut off? While it was in the body, that limb was alive; when it is cut off it loses its life.

It is like that with Christians. They are alive only while they are in the Body. If they are cut off from the Body, the Holy Spirit is no longer with them.

Augustine
Sermon 267, (PL38, 1231)

8th October

Christ is the Gate that is Humble and Low

Jesus said: 'He who does not enter the sheepfold by the door but climbs in by another way, that man is a thief and a robber.' [John 10:1] He is not, that is to say, the shepherd who enters the sheepfold to guard the flock and keep it safe.

There have been some people of that sort. They gave very subtle lectures on the virtues and the vices, they marked out distinctions and definitions, they drew conclusions from penetrating arguments, they wrote book after book, they puffed out their cheeks to proclaim their wisdom at the top of their voice, and they dared to say: 'Follow me, join my sect.'

Those people, because they did not enter by the gate, were butchers and murderers.

Christ's sheepfold is the Church. Anyone who wants

to enter the fold must enter by using the gate: he must preach the true Christ.

And not only preach Christ. He must also seek Christ's glory, rather than his own. Many, in seeking their own glory, have scattered the flock of Christ, when they ought to have been uniting it.

Christ is the gate that is humble and low. All who want to enter by this gate must humble themselves and stoop low. Any who do not humble themselves, but make themselves important, are clearly proposing to enter by scaling the wall. But climbing the wall means heading for a fall.

Augustine
On the Gospel of John 45, 2 (PL35, 1720ff.)

9th October

The Church, Reconciler of Differences

The holy Church includes many people, men, women and children without number. They are all quite different from one another in birth, in size, in nationality and language, in style of living and age, in trades and opinions, in clothes and customs, in knowledge and rank, in welfare and in appearance. They are nonetheless all of them in the selfsame Church. Thanks to her, they are all reborn, newly created in the Spirit. The Church grants to all of them without distinction the grace of belonging to Christ and of taking his name by calling themselves Christians.

Faith, moreover, puts us in a position which is extremely simple, and incapable of separation, in such a way that the differences between us seem not to exist, because

319

everything is gathered together into the Church and reconciled in her.

No one lives alone any more, no one is separated from the others, but all are mutually joined together as brothers and sisters in the simple and indivisible power of faith.

Of the first Church, Scripture says: 'The company of those who believed were of one heart and soul', [Acts 4:32] in such a way that all the many members looked like a single body, truly worthy of Christ himself, our true Head. And speaking of the action of Christ in the Church, the Apostle asserts: 'There is neither male nor female, neither Jew nor Greek, neither circumcised nor uncircumcised, neither barbarian nor Scythian, neither slave nor freeman, but Christ is all and in all.' [cf. Gal. 3:28; Col. 3:11] Christ with the unique power of goodness and with infinite wisdom reunites everything in himself, as the centre from which the rays go out.

Maximus the Confessor
Mystagogia, 1 (PG91, 664)

10th October

Who Has Peter's Keys?

When you hear the words: 'Peter, do you love me?' [John 21:15] imagine you are in front of a mirror and looking at yourself.

Peter, surely, was a symbol of the Church. Therefore the Lord in asking Peter is asking us too.

To show that Peter was a symbol of the Church remember the passage in the Gospel: 'You are Peter, and on this rock I will build my Church and the gates of hell will not prevail against it. I will give you the keys of the kingdom of heaven. [Matt. 16:18]

Has only one man received those keys? Christ himself explains what they are for: 'Whatever you loose on earth will be loosed in heaven.' [Matt. 18:18] If these words had been said only to Peter, now that he is dead who would ever be able to bind or loose?

I make bold to say that all of us have received the keys. We bind and loose. And you also bind and loose.

Whoever is bound is separated from your community: he is bound by you. When he is reconciled, however, he is loosed, thanks to you because you are praying for him. We all in fact love our Lord, we are all his members.

And when the Lord entrusts his flock to shepherds, the whole number of shepherds is reduced to one individual body, that of the one Shepherd. [cf. John 10:16]

Peter is undeniably a shepherd, but without doubt Paul also is a shepherd. John is a shepherd, Andrew is a shepherd, each Apostle is a shepherd. All the holy bishops are shepherds, without a shadow of doubt.

> **Augustine**
> *Serm. Morin*, 16 (Miscellanea Agostiniana, 493ff.)

11th October

I am Someone Destined to the Service of Unity

All of you must become a unity. Let there be no divisions in your hearts. When I was among you I cried at the top of my voice, with the very voice of God: 'Be united with the bishop, the priests and the deacons.'

Some people thought I cried like this because I foresaw

a schism. He for whose sake I am in chains is my witness that I did not speak in that way because anyone had given me any such warning. I had simply been listening to the Spirit proclaiming:

'Do nothing without the bishop! Keep your body as a temple of God! Love unity, avoid factions! Be imitators of Jesus Christ, as Jesus Christ is of the Father!' [cf. 1 Cor. 3:16; 6:19; 11:1]

With such an aim I have done all I could, as one destined to the service of unity. God does not dwell where there are divisions and bad feeling. I exhort you: never give way to a quarrelsome spirit, but always carry out the teaching of Christ!

Jesus Christ is my criterion. Unassailable grounds of judgment for me are his cross, his death, his resurrection and the faith that comes from him. And it is thanks to them that, with the help of your prayers, I hope to be justified.

Ignatius of Antioch
To the Philadelphians, 6, 2 (SC10, pp.146ff.)

12th October

The Symphony of Your Love

It is right that you should live, as in fact you do live, in unison with the mind of your bishop. Your priests are united in harmony with the bishop like the strings of the lyre. In a similar way your unity of feeling and the symphony of your love raise a song of praise to Jesus Christ.

Every one of you ought to share in this chorus. In the harmony of your mutual agreement, taking the tune from God himself in unity, with the help of Jesus Christ, all of you should sing with one voice to the Father. He will hear you, and will recognize that underlying all your works you are members of his Son.

If your unity is unbreakable, you are always in communion with God.

In a very short time I have struck up a friendship with your bishop which is not just on a human level but is a spiritual relationship. Still more blessed are you who are deeply united with him as the Church is united with Jesus Christ and as Jesus Christ is united with the Father, in the harmony of complete unity.

If the prayer of two people has great power, how much stronger is that of the bishop together with all his Church! [cf. Matt. 18:20]

> **Ignatius of Antioch**
> *To the Ephesians*, 4, 1 (SC10, p.73)

13th October

The Church in the Night of Persecution

If you see the Church scattered and smitten with the severest of trials, if its members are beaten with rods, if he who was entrusted with its government is exiled to far distant lands, do not look only at these tribulations themselves.

Think of their outcome too: the wages, the reward, the prize for the struggle. 'Whoever endures to the end will be saved,' is the teaching of Scripture. [Matt. 10:22]

Our fathers in Old Testament times saw events contradicting the promises of God, yet they were not shocked or worried. They trusted in a Providence beyond their understanding. Knowing the richness and skill of the divine wisdom they awaited the outcome and in the meantime they endured all the adversities, giving thanks to God and singing his praises despite his allowing these trials.

Compare those events of long ago with what is happening now. You will discover your own weakness. You will see how lacking in strength are the people who are shocked. You will understand how their being shocked stems entirely from the fact that they do not trust in a Providence beyond their understanding.

John Chrysostom
On Providence, 9, 6 (SC79, p.149)

14th October

What are Bishops For?

Today we have here a gift of the divine mercy: a bishop is being consecrated, on your behalf. So we ought to speak, to exhort you and also to instruct the man who thereafter will have to teach you.

Whoever is head of the Church ought first of all to understand that he is the servant of all. Do not despise this service, either! Do not be ashamed to be the servant of all, seeing that the Lord of lords was not ashamed to put himself at our service.

Writing to a bishop, the Apostle says to him: 'If anyone aspires to the office of bishop, he desires a noble task.' [1 Tim. 3:1] He does not simply assert that the office of a bishop is a noble task. He teaches that besides the desire for the office of a bishop we should have the desire to perform a noble task.

Therefore, if anyone desires to become a bishop but does not desire to perform a noble task, but rather to call attention to himself, he is seeking the title but not the real thing. 'I want to be a bishop. O, if only I were a bishop!' And if you were? Are you seeking the title or the real thing? You are seeking the real thing only if you are proposing to undertake a noble task.

We have said what we bishops ought to be and what we ought to shun. But does this concern you as well, people of God? Yes, it does concern you as well. Pray for the bishops. The higher the office we hold, the greater is the danger to which we are exposed. We receive honours, but also slander. Many people flatter us, but many others speak evil of us.

And what do we do if the community of the faithful to which we belong happens to have a bad bishop? Our Lord, bishop of bishops, has given you the assurance that your hope is not based on a human being!

Augustine
Serm. Morin, 32 (Miscellanea Agostiniana, 563ff.)

15th October

A Power not Even the Angels Have

If we realize how great a privilege it is to approach the perfect holiness of God while still being only human creatures, mixtures of flesh and blood, then we can understand the grace of the Holy Spirit with which priests are honoured.

They dwell on the earth, they live an earthly existence, and yet have received a power that God has not given even to the angels. 'Whatever you bind on earth will be bound in heaven, and whatever you loose on earth will be loosed in heaven.' [Matt. 18:18]

Earthly rulers also have the power to bind, but they only bind the body. This 'binding', on the other hand, directly concerns the soul and is also valid in heaven. What priests accomplish down here, God confirms on high: what the servants decide, the Master ratifies. 'If you forgive the sins of any, they are forgiven; if you retain the sins of any, they are retained.' [John 20:23]

Is there any power greater? 'The Father has given all judgment to the Son,' and the Son has appointed priests to be full trustees of this judgment. He has raised them to such a high rank as if they had already been taken up to heaven, as if they had already overcome human nature by setting us free from our miseries.

John Chrysostom
On Priesthood, 3, 5 (PG48, 643)

16th October

Pathfinders for Salvation

Priests have been given by God a greater power than a father or a mother has.

The difference between parents and priests is as great as the difference between the present life and the future life.

The former produce children for this life, the latter for the other life.

The former are not capable of saving their children from the death of the body nor of warding off illness.

The latter, by contrast, save the soul that is sick, near to perdition, and they forestall the ruin of souls. They do it by their teaching, their warnings, their prayers.

Parents cannot help their children if they have offended someone important. Priests, by contrast, reconcile a person not with earthly rulers but with God himself.

> **John Chrysostom**
> *On Priesthood* 3, 6 (PG48, 644)

17th October

Words Alone Are not Enough to Teach the Truth

Any in the Church who assume the office of a teacher commit themselves to distributing to others, by means of their words and their works, the greatest benefits that there are. They become mediators of people's intimate and eternal relations with God.

The faithful teacher reflects the true magnificence of the Word, in such a way that others understand the benefits they receive from it derive from the Lord himself. By means of the teaching, the catechumen created in the image of God is transformed into a true human being, a new person who has attained to the possibility of salvation.

True teachers know that they serve their neighbour by the likeness of their own life to their own message. They think the truth and speak it to the advantage of those who hear them and give them their assent. They speak as they think, and they live as they think. They offer themselves as an example to the Church, to the disciples whom they have brought to the faith. Being a friend of God and of people, they bear witness by their life to the truth of their words.

Clement of Alexandria
Miscellaneous Studies 7, 9, 52 (PG48, 644)

18th October

No Luck for the Hunter of Applause

Any who tackle the office of teacher should not be concerned about commendation nor be discouraged if it is refused them. Rather let them prepare their sermons in a way that may please God. This will be their final criterion for judging if they are preaching well.

When they are not commended they must not go looking for praise nor be sorry about it. The consciousness of having done everything possible to communicate a piece of teaching that would receive divine approval will console them for their efforts more than anything else.

On the other hand, if the desire for useless praise is tormenting them, they will not gain any reward for their difficult preparation and the skill of their speech, and after the sermon they will not be in a position to bear with the otherwise fatuous criticisms of the crowd. In consequence, their ardour will cool and they will take less care to devote themselves to the service of the Word.

John Chrysostom
On Priesthood, 5, 7ff. (PG48, 676)

19th October

The Rock where Wild Beasts are Lurking

Pride is a terrible rock where wild beasts lurk that would tear you to pieces every day.

What are these wild beasts?

They are violence, negligence, envy, quarrelsomeness, calumny, lies, hypocrisy, actions to the detriment of the innocent, satisfaction at the misfortunes of colleagues, regret at their success, desire for praise, conceit over honours received (which is the wild beast most fatal to the soul), ostentatious conversation, unworthy flattery, contempt of the poor and obsequiousness towards the rich, coveting favours not altogether commendable which endanger those who grant them and those who receive them, slavish timidity, outbursts of arrogance, unlimited humility in appearance and no humility at all in fact, accusations against those not present and extreme severity towards the weak while not daring to utter a word against the powerful.

All these wild beasts, and others still more numerous, that keep company with one another on the rock of pride are a menace to the soul of the priest.

John Chrysostom
On Priesthood, 3, 9 (PG48, 646)

20th October

For You Too Everything Begins with this Water

Water makes the body clean, the Spirit makes the soul holy. It is in this way that we are able to draw near to God, since, while our body is being washed in the clean water, our heart is being purified by means of the Spirit.

You who are about to go down into the baptismal water must not stop to consider the weakness of this visible element, since you will receive the strength of the Holy Spirit to enter into a new life. Without the two, the water and the Spirit, you would not be able to reach perfection.

It is not I who am telling you this, but the Lord Jesus Christ who has power over these things. He says, in fact: 'No one can enter the kingdom of God without being born of water and the Spirit.' [John 3:5] Look closely: 'Of water and the Spirit.'

Those who wash in the water but do not receive the Spirit do not have the grace that can make them holy. On the other hand they cannot enter the kingdom unless they receive the water, the visible sign, made rich also in good works. This assurance will appear daring, however it is not mine: it was Jesus who spoke in that way.

Let me give you an illustration from Holy Scripture. Cornelius was a just man, proved so by his vision of angels, and he had won favour with God through his prayers and his alms. Peter came to him, and the Holy Spirit was poured out on the believers and they spoke in tongues and prophesied. After the gift of the Holy Spirit, according to the Scripture, Peter commanded them to be baptized in the name of Jesus Christ so that while the soul was being born again through faith, the body might have its share of the gift through water. [cf. Acts 10]

If you want to know why it is by water and not by any other element that grace is given, consult the Scripture. Before the creation of the world 'the Spirit of God moved upon the water'. [Gen. 1:2] Thus at the beginning of the world we have water: at the beginning of the gospels, the river Jordan.

Cyril of Jerusalem
Catecheses, 3, 4 (PG33, 429)

21st October

'O Death, Where Is Your Sting?'

Jesus sanctified baptism when he himself was baptized. Who then is in a position to belittle baptism and still retain the faith after the moment in which the Son of God was baptized?

He was immune from sin. So he did not submit to baptism to obtain the forgiveness of sins. Despite being free from sin, he submitted to baptism in order to bestow grace and dignity on those who would be baptized after him.

He shared our flesh and blood in order that we might be partakers not only of his bodily existence but also of his divine grace. And in the end he conquered death so that all of us might win salvation and be enabled to say: 'O death, where is your victory? O death, where is your sting?' [1 Cor. 15:55]

In fact, the sting of death has been destroyed by means of baptism.

When you go down into the water to be baptized, you take with you your sins. But the grace which is called down upon you marks your soul in a new way.

You go down dead because of your sins: you come up given new life by grace. For if you were planted in the likeness of the Saviour's death, you were also thought worthy of resurrection.

Cyril of Jerusalem
Catecheses, 3, 11 (PG33, 441)

22nd October

The Consecration of Jesus and the Confirmation of Your Faith

Christ was not anointed with ordinary natural oil. The Father anointed him by making him the Saviour of the whole world, and he anointed him with the Holy Spirit, as Peter said: 'God anointed Jesus of Nazareth with the Holy Spirit.' [Acts 10:38]

The prophet David had already sung: 'Your divine throne endures for ever and ever. Your royal sceptre is a sceptre of equity; you love righteousness and hate iniquity. Therefore God, your God, has anointed you with the oil of gladness.' [Ps. 45:6-7]

Christ was crucified, he was buried and he rose again. God's love has granted to you a somewhat similar experience: in baptism, you also are crucified, you also are buried and rise again.

The same thing happens in Confirmation.

Christ was anointed with spiritual oil, that is, with the Holy Spirit, called 'oil of gladness' precisely because he gives spiritual joy. And you also have been anointed with ointment, chrism, so that you may be partakers with Christ, sharing his lot.

And it is no ordinary ointment, either.

The bread of the Eucharist, after the invocation of the Holy Spirit, is no longer ordinary bread: it is the Body of Christ. So this ointment, after the invocation, is no longer ordinary ointment: it is a gift from Christ which is able to confer on you the Holy Spirit.

While the body is being anointed with the visible oil, the soul is being consecrated with the Holy and Life-giving Spirit.

Cyril of Jerusalem
Catecheses, 21 (PG33, 1088)

23rd October

The Daily Miracle of Lazarus

'Jesus came to the tomb of Lazarus; it was a cave and a stone lay upon it.' [John 11:38]

What is the meaning of the Lord's words after that: 'Take away the stone'? That we should preach grace.

The Apostle Paul asserts that 'The New Covenant is not of the letter but of the spirit: the letter kills, but the spirit gives life.' [2 Cor. 3:6]

The letter that kills is like a stone that crushes. 'Take away the stone,' Jesus ordered. Take away the weight of the law, preach grace.

'From heaven the Lord looked at the earth,' sings the Psalmist, 'to hear the groans of the prisoners, to set free those who were doomed to die.' [Ps. 102:19-20] Those doomed to die – it is the forgiveness of their sins that sets them free from the snares of death. What use would it have been to Lazarus to come out of the tomb if Jesus had not added: 'Unbind him and let him go.'

It was the Lord who overcame the weight of the stone and Lazarus came out. He came out thanks to the strength, not of his own feet but of him who had cried out to him: 'Come out!'

The same thing happens in the heart of a penitent. If a person repents of his sins, he is risen from death.

He has hardly laid bare his conscience by confessing his faults before he comes out of the tomb. However, he is not yet free. When and by whom will he be set free?

'Whatever you loose on earth shall be loosed in heaven.' [Matt. 18:18] It is on good authority that the Church sets free the sinner.

Augustine
On the Gospel of John, 49, 22 (PL35, 1756); *On Psalm 101*, 11, 3 (PL37, 1306)

24th October

The Mountain of Your Sins will Never be Too High

Anyone who is a slave to sin should prepare himself for true regeneration by means of faith. He must shake the yoke of sin off his back and enter the joyful service of the Lord. He will be thought worthy to inherit the kingdom.

Don't hesitate to declare yourselves sinners. Thereby you will put off your old humanity that was corrupt because it followed the bait of error. And you will put on the new humanity, the humanity newly clad in intimacy with its Creator.

The regeneration of which I am speaking is not the rebirth of the body, but the second birth of the soul. Bodies are procreated by the father and mother, but souls are recreated by means of faith, since the Spirit blows where it will. [John 3:8]

God is kind and he is kind to an immeasurable extent.

Don't say: 'I have been dishonest, an adulterer, I have committed grave offences innumerable times. Will he forgive them? Will he deign to forget them?' Listen rather to the Psalmist: 'How great is your love, O Lord.' [cf. Ps. 31:19]

Your sins piled one above the other do not overtop the greatness of God's love. Your wounds are not too great for the skill of the Doctor.

There is only one course of treatment for you to follow: rely on him in faith. Explain frankly what is wrong to the Doctor and say with the Psalmist: 'I acknowledged my sin to you, and I did not hide my iniquity.' [Ps. 32:5] Then you will be able to go on with the Psalmist to say: 'Then did you forgive the guilt of my sin.'

Cyril of Jerusalem
Catecheses, 1, 2ff. (PG33, 372)

25th October

His Body and His Blood

Because we are composed of a dual nature, soul and body, we need a dual birth and dual nourishment.

We receive our birth by means of water and Spirit, that is, by Holy Baptism. We find our nourishment in the bread of life, that is, in Jesus Christ himself.

When the moment arrived for him to undergo death for us of his own free will, in the night in which he was to be handed over to his enemies, he established a new covenant with his disciples, and through them with all those who believe in him.

He washed his disciples' feet, offering in this a symbol of Holy Baptism. Then, breaking the bread, he gave it to them saying: 'Take and eat; this is my body which will be broken for you for the forgiveness of sins.' In the same way he gave them the cup with the wine and the water saying: 'Drink, this is my blood.'

If sky, earth, water, iron and air have been created by the Word of God, so much more certainly this noble being called humanity has been formed by him. And if the Word himself became flesh by the pure blood of the Virgin, will he not be able to make the bread his body and the wine and water his blood?

In the beginning God said: 'Let the earth bring forth green grass.' And so after that the earth, watered by the rain, in obedience to God's command, brings forth its fruits.

Then God said: 'This is my body, this is my blood,' adding: 'Do this in memory of me.' After that, all the mystery takes place, thanks to his all-powerful Word, and proclaims its faith in the Lord.

It is a new kind of planting. The rain comes down on it, that is to say, the power of the Spirit comes down, and overshadows it.

John Damascene
On the Orthodox Faith, 4, 13 (PG94, 1137ff.)

26th October

The Eucharist Reveals our Greatness

The sacrifice you are looking at was instituted by Christ our Lord as the sacrifice of his own body and blood. His body was pierced by the spear and there flowed out water and blood, through the medium of which we have obtained the forgiveness of our sins.

Mindful of this gracious gift, approach with fear and trembling to take part in this feast, knowing that God himself is at work in you. Recognize in this bread the body that was hanged on the cross. Recognize in this cup of wine the blood that gushed out from his pierced side. Take and eat the body of Christ, since in the body of Christ you have become Christ's members. Take and drink the blood of Christ.

To counter your tendency to disunity, eat that body which is the bond of your unity. So as not to appear to be without value in your own eyes, drink that blood which is the price that was paid for you.

When you eat this food and drink this wine, they will be transformed into your substance. Equally you will be transformed into the body of Christ, if you live in obedience and faithfulness.

The Apostle reminds us of the prediction in Scripture: 'Two will become one flesh.' [Eph. 5:31] And elsewhere, in reference to the Eucharist itself, he asserts: 'Because there is one bread, we who are many are one body.' [1 Cor. 10:17]

You, therefore, begin to receive what you already begin to be.

Augustine
Serm. Denis (Miscellanea Agostiniana, 18ff.)

27th October

In the Liturgy Christ Gives Himself to Us

The liturgical service takes place on earth, but it belongs to the realm of heavenly realities. In fact it was not instituted by a human being or an angel, but by the Spirit himself, so that those who are still living in the flesh should think of performing the service of angels.

O what mercy, O what love of God for human beings! Christ who is seated with the Father in highest heaven is at that moment grasped by the hands of all and does not hesitate to give himself to anyone who wants to embrace him and be bound to him.

He whom the eyes of faith perceive is possessed by everyone.

You remember how Elijah was surrounded by a great crowd and had in front of him the victim for sacrifice placed on the stone. [cf. 1 Kgs. 18] Everyone stood stock still. The silence was complete. Only the prophet raised a prayer. Suddenly from heaven came down fire on the victim. It was a marvellous spectacle that filled everyone with amazement.

Here, however, something much more than a marvellous spectacle is unfolded. Something is happening that is greater than any marvel. Here the priest draws down not fire but the Holy Spirit himself.

John Chrysostom
On Priesthood, 3, 4 (PG48, 642)

28th October

The Liturgy Makes Present Now the Events of Salvation

We firmly believe, brethren, that the Lord has died for our sins, the just for the unjust, the master for the slaves, the shepherd for the sheep and, still more astonishingly, the Creator for the creatures.

He has preserved what he was from eternity; what he was in time he has sacrificed.

God hidden in the guise of a visible man, giving life with his strength and dying in his weakness 'was put to death for our sins and raised for our justification.' [Rom. 4:25]

All of that happened once and for all, as you know well enough. And yet we have the liturgical solemnities which we celebrate as, during the course of the year, we come to the date of particular events.

Between the truth of the events and the solemnities of the liturgy there is no contradiction, as if the latter were a lie.

The historical truth is what happened once and for all, but the liturgy makes those events always new for the hearts that celebrate them with faith.

The historical truth shows us the events just as they happened, but the liturgy, while not repeating them, celebrates them and prevents them being forgotten.

Thus, on the basis of historical truth, we say that Easter happened once only and will not happen again, but, on the basis of the liturgy, we can say that Easter happens every year.

Thanks to the liturgy, the human mind reaches the truth and proclaims its faith in the Lord.

Augustine
Sermons, 220 (PL38, 1089)

29th October

The Kiss of Peace

The spiritual embrace that all the worshippers give one another during the liturgy symbolizes in anticipation agreement, concord, unanimity in faith and love. It prefigures ineffable future blessings.

By virtue of that embrace, that kiss, those who are worthy receive the gift of union with God and with the incarnate Word.

The mouth in fact symbolizes the word. By means of the mouth all those who enjoy the gift of reason are united with the first and only Word which is the origin of the reason.

Maximus the Confessor
Mystagogia 12, 17 (PG91, 689)

30th October

Is the Veneration of Images Justified?

Some people reprove us for honouring images of the Saviour, of the Mother of God and other holy servants of Christ. But let them think for a moment.

In the beginning God created humanity in his own image. Why ever should we have such respect for one another, if not because we are made in the image of God?

In Basil's words, 'the honour paid to the image is in reality paid to its prototype,' that is to say, to what the image represents. Thus the Jewish people revered the Tabernacle because that, much more than the rest of creation, was an image of God.

The making and the veneration of images are not a novelty. They are based on a very ancient tradition.

God made the first human being as an image of himself.

Abraham, Moses, Isaiah and all the prophets saw God, not in his true being, but in his image.

The burning bush was an image of the Mother of God. When Moses wanted to approach, God said to him: 'Put off your shoes from your feet, for the place on which you are standing is holy ground.' [Exod. 3:5]

If the ground on which Moses saw the image of the Mother of God was holy, how much more holy will the image itself be!

John Damascene
On the Orthodox Faith, 4, 16 (PG94, 1168ff.);
Discourses on Images, 2, 16ff. (PG94, 1301ff.)

31st October

Christians in the World Are What the Soul Is in the Body

Christians are not distinguishable from other people either by nationality or by language or by the clothes they wear.

Their way of life has nothing peculiar about it. They conform to local customs, but they show how extraordinary and paradoxical the laws of their spiritual state are.

They live each in his own country, but as a foreigner.

They fulfil all their civic duties, but as foreigners.

Every foreign country is to them the home country and every home country is to them a foreign country. They live in the flesh but not according to the flesh. They spend their lives on earth but they are citizens of heaven.

They love everyone and everyone persecutes them. Misunderstood, they are condemned and put to death, but in such a way that they attain life.

They are poor and make many others rich. They are deprived of everything and have a superabundance of everything.

Despised, they find in this contempt their glory. While they do nothing but good, they are punished as offenders. When they are punished, they taste the joy of those who are born to life.

To sum up, what the soul is in the body, Christians are in the world.

Letter to Diognetus 5, 1ff. (SC33, 63ff.)

November

Speak to me, O Lord,
then I shall know how to answer you

1st November

Our Father

Anyone with a bit of good sense would not make so bold as to call God by the name of Father until he had come to be like him.

It is impossible for God who is goodness in his very being to be father to someone of evil will. It is impossible for the Holy One to be father of a depraved person. It is impossible for the Giver of life to have as a child one whose sin has subjected him to death.

So if one of us, in examining himself, discovers that his conscience is covered in mud and needs to be cleansed, he cannot allow himself such familiarity with God. First he must be purified.

Then why, in this prayer of his, does the Lord Jesus teach us to call God by the name of Father? I suppose that, in suggesting this word, he is only putting before our eyes the holiest life as the criterion of our behaviour.

Gregory of Nyssa
On the Lord's Prayer, 2 (PG44, 1141)

2nd November

Who Art in Heaven

These words I think have a very deep meaning. They remind us of the homeland we have abandoned, of the citizenship we have lost.

In the parable of the young man who left his father's house, went off the rails and was reduced to living with pigs, the Word of God shows us human wretchedness.

That young man did not find his one-time happiness again until he had realized his moral degradation, had looked into his own heart and had pronounced the words of confession.

These words almost agree with the Lord's Prayer, because the prodigal son says: 'Father, I have sinned against heaven and against you.' [Luke 15:21]

He would not confess himself to be a sinner against heaven if he were not convinced that the homeland he had left at the time of his going astray were not in actual fact heaven.

By this confession of his he makes himself worthy once again to stand in the presence of his father who runs towards him, embraces him, and kisses him.

The conclusion is this. To return to heaven there is only one route and that is to admit one's sinfulness and seek to avoid it. To make the decision to avoid it is already to be perfecting one's likeness to God.

> **Gregory of Nyssa**
> *On the Lord's Prayer*, 2 (PG44, 1144)

3rd November

Hallowed be Thy Name

What is the meaning of the words 'name' and 'hallow'?

'Name' denotes the proper and exclusive nature of the being that carries it and indicates the general effect of its qualities. In human beings these qualities can change, and with them their names too. Abram came to be called Abraham, Simon became Peter, and Saul's name was changed to Paul. By contrast in the case of

God who is immutable, who never changes, there is but one name, the 'I am' that was given him in Exodus. [Exod. 3:14] We all endeavour to reflect on God to understand his nature, but they are few indeed that succeed in sensing his holiness.

Jesus' prayer teaches us that God is holy. It helps us to discover the holiness of the Being that creates, provides, judges, chooses and abounds in generosity, welcomes and rejects, rewards and punishes equally. This is what characterizes the quality that belongs to God, the quality that the Scriptures call by the name of God.

Therefore in the Scriptures we read: 'You shall not take the name of the Lord your God in vain,' [Exod. 20:7] and again: 'May my teaching drop as the rain, my speech distil as the dew, as the gentle rain upon the tender grass, and as the showers upon the herb, for I will proclaim the name of the Lord.' [Deut. 32:2]

Anyone who prays ought therefore to ask that the name of God may be hallowed, as is said also in the Psalms: 'Let us exalt his name together.' [Ps. 34:3] The Psalmist hopes that we may arrive, in harmony of spirit, at a true understanding of the nature of God.

Origen
On Prayer 24, 1 (PG11, 492)

4th November

Thy Kingdom Come

'The kingdom of God is within us,' that is, on our lips and in our hearts. [Luke 17:21] Therefore anyone who prays that the kingdom of God may not delay its coming is praying that it may be consolidated, extended, and reach its fullness within him. Our Lord in fact dwells in all holy people who recognize God as their king and obey his spiritual laws. The Father is present in the perfect soul and Christ reigns together with the Father, according to his own actual word 'If someone loves me ... we will come to him and make our home with him.' [John 14:23]

The kingdom will not reach its fullness in each of us until wisdom and the other virtues are perfected in us. Perfection is reached at the end of a journey, so we ought to be 'forgetting what lies behind and straining forward to what lies ahead.' [Phil. 3:13]

In other words, on the one hand the believer is a tireless traveller and on the other hand the kingdom of God will reach its completion in us only when the words of the Apostle are fulfilled: 'When he has subjected all things, Christ will deliver up the kingdom to the Father, that God may be all in all.' [cf. 1 Cor. 15:24-28]

Let us subdue our members to produce the fruits of the Spirit. Then the Lord will walk with us as in a spiritual paradise. He alone will reign in us, together with Christ. And we shall already possess the benefits of the new birth and of the resurrection.

Origen
On Prayer, 25 (PG11, 498ff.)

5th November

Thy Will be Done on Earth as It is in Heaven

We who are praying are still on earth ourselves. And since we reckon that all the inhabitants of heaven fulfil the will of God in heaven, it comes naturally to us to ask that we too on earth should succeed in fulfilling the divine will. That will come about, logically, if we do nothing outside that will.

When we have perfectly accomplished it, although we are still remaining on earth we shall be like the heavenly beings and will bear equally with them the image of the heavenly Being. [cf. 1 Cor. 15:49]

In the end we shall inherit the kingdom of heaven. Those who come to take our place on earth will ask that they too may become like us who are then in heaven.

In addition it is recorded that our Lord after his resurrection said to the eleven Apostles: 'All authority in heaven and on earth has been given to me.' [Matt. 28:18]

Jesus claimed in short to have received authority on earth equal to that which he has in heaven. The things of heaven, at the beginning, have been illuminated by the Word. And at the end of time, thanks to the authority granted to the Son of God, the things of earth will be like those of heaven which is already perfect.

So then it is clear that Christ is calling his disciples to work faithfully with him by means of their prayers. That all earthly events may come to be transformed by the authority that Christ has received both in heaven and on earth, this ought to be our prayer.

Origen
On Prayer, 26, 1 (PG11, 500)

349

6th November

Give us this Day our Daily Bread

Bread represents life, and bread is easy to get. Moreover, nature herself gives us something to put on it to make it more tasty. The best thing to eat with bread is the peace of a good conscience. Then the bread is eaten with gusto, because it is being eaten in holiness of life.

But if you want to experience the taste of bread otherwise than in symbolic description, in the physical sense in fact, you have hunger to eat it with. Therefore, first of all, don't eat too much: you would lose your appetite for a long time. And then, let your dinner be preceded by sweat. 'In the sweat of your brow you shall eat bread,' is the first commandment mentioned in the Scriptures. [Gen. 3:19]

The Lord's Prayer speaks of 'daily' bread. In saying that, let us remember that the life in which we ought to be interested is 'daily' life. We can, each of us, only call the present time our own. Why should we worry ourselves by thinking about the future?

Our Lord tells us to pray for today, and so he prevents us from tormenting ourselves about tomorrow. It is as if he were to say to us: 'He who gives you this day will also give you what you need for this day. He it is who makes the sun to rise. He it is who scatters the darkness of night and reveals to you the rays of the sun.'

Gregory of Nyssa
On the Lord's Prayer, 4 (PG44, 1173)

7th November

Forgive us our Trespasses as we Forgive those who Trespass against us

The mercy of God is beyond description. While he is offering us a model prayer he is teaching us a way of life whereby we can be pleasing in his sight.

But that is not all. In this same prayer he gives us an easy method for attracting an indulgent and merciful judgment on our lives. He gives us the possibility of ourselves mitigating the sentence hanging over us and of compelling him to pardon us. What else could he do in the face of our generosity when we ask him to forgive us as we have forgiven our neighbour?

If we are faithful in this prayer, each of us will ask forgiveness for our own failings after we have forgiven the sins of those who have sinned against us. I mean those who have sinned against us, not only those who have sinned against our Master.

There is, in fact, in some of us a very bad habit. We treat our sins against God, however appalling, with gentle indulgence: but when by contrast it is a matter of sins against us ourselves, albeit very tiny ones, we exact reparation with ruthless severity.

Anyone who has not forgiven from the bottom of the heart the brother or sister who has done him wrong will only obtain from this prayer his own condemnation, rather than any mercy. It will be his own action that draws a much more severe judgment on himself, seeing that in effect by these words we are asking God to behave as we have behaved ourselves.

Cassian
Conferences, 9, 22 (SC54, 59f.)

351

8th November

And Lead us not into Temptation

The request 'Lead us not into temptation' raises a difficult problem. If we pray God not to allow us to be tempted, what opportunity shall we have to give him proof of our steadfastness and fidelity? For it is written: 'Blessed is the one who endures temptation and overcomes it.' [cf. Jas. 1:12]

Then what is the meaning of this phrase? It does not mean: do not allow us to come into temptation. It means: when we come into temptation, let us not be defeated by it.

Job was tempted but he did not give way to the temptation. In fact, he did not accuse the divine Wisdom, he did not go down the road of blasphemy to which the Tempter wanted to attract him.

Abraham was tempted, and Joseph was tempted. But neither one nor the other yielded to the temptation, because neither of them said 'yes' to the Tempter.

So praying the Lord's Prayer is like saying: 'Together with the temptation, give us also the strength to overcome it.' [1 Cor. 10:13]

Cassian
Conferences, 9, 23 (SC54, 59ff.)

9th November

But Deliver Us from Evil

The Lord's Prayer has an ending which neatly summarizes the different requests. We say actually at the end: 'But deliver us from evil,' understanding by such an expression everything that the Enemy can devise against us in this world.

One certain conviction we have: that God is a powerful support since he grants his help to anyone who asks for it.

Consequently, when we say: 'Deliver us from evil,' there is nothing else left for us to ask. Invoking the protection of God against evil means asking for everything we need.

This prayer secures us against any kind of machination of the devil and of the world. Who could be afraid of the world if he has God as his protector?

You see, brothers and sisters, how amazing the Lord's Prayer is. It is truly a compendium of all the requests we could possibly make.

Our Lord Jesus Christ who came for all people, for the wise as for the ignorant, without distinction of sex or age, reduces the precepts of salvation to the essential minimum. He wants even the simplest to be able to understand and remember them.

Cyprian of Carthage
On the Lord's Prayer (PL4, 538)

10th November

A Prayer that Contains the Fullness of Perfection

The 'Our Father' is a short formula, a model prayer. It does not contain requests for riches, or any suggestion of honours sought. There are no demands for authority or power. There is no mention of the health of the body nor of temporal life. The Architect of eternity does not want us to ask for anything fleeting, and it would be an insult to his generosity to neglect the riches of eternal life and ask for something transitory instead. Such baseness of mind would earn the wrath rather than the favour of the Judge.

The 'Our Father' prayer contains all the fullness of perfection, inasmuch as the Lord himself has given it to us, both as a model and also as a precept. Those who are familiar with this prayer are raised by it to a very lofty condition, namely that 'prayer of fire' which very few know by direct experience and which it is impossible to describe.

The 'prayer of fire' transcends all human feeling. There are no longer sounds of the voice nor movements of the tongue nor articulated words. The soul is completely imbued with divine light. Human language, always inadequate, is no use any more. But in the soul is a spring bubbling over, and prayer gushing out from it leaps up to God. The soul expresses in a single instant many things which could only be described or remembered with difficulty when it has returned to its normal condition.

Our Lord has traced an outline of this mystical state in this formula, the 'Our Father' that contains various supplications, and also in the hours he spent alone on the mountain side, and in the silent prayer of his agony in the moment when he even sweated blood through the unique intensity of his unity with the Father.

Cassian
Conferences, 9, 24ff. (SC54, 61ff.)

11th November

Hymn in Praise of Prayer

Prayer is union with God and colloquy with him.

Prayer maintains the equilibrium of the world, reconciles people to God, produces holy tears, forms a bridge over temptations, and acts as a buttress between us and affliction.

Prayer drives away the struggles of the spirit. It is the blessedness to come. It is an action that will never come to an end.

Prayer is a spring of the virtues, it is an illumination of the mind, it is a curtain to shut out despair, it is a sign of hope, it is victory over depression.

Prayer is a mirror in which we see our steps forward, it is a signpost of the route to follow, it is an unveiling of good things to come, it is a pledge of glory.

Prayer, for one who prays truly, is the soul's tribunal, it is the Lord's judgment on that person now, in advance of the final judgment.

Prayer is the queen of the virtues which summons us with a loud voice and says to us again: 'Come to me all who labour and are heavy laden and I will give you perfect rest! Take my yoke upon you! You will find peace for your souls and healing for your wounds! For my yoke is easy and can restore the greatest fall.' [cf. Matt. 11:28-30]

355

Let your prayer be very simple. For the tax-collector and the prodigal son just one word was enough to reconcile them with God.

John Climacus
Stairway to Paradise, 28 (PG88, 1129)

12th November

Prayer is Answering the Word of God

Isidore said:

'Anyone who wants to be always united to God must pray often and read the Bible often. For in prayer it is we who are speaking to God, but in the readings it is God speaking to us.

'All spiritual progress is based on reading and meditation. What we do not know, we learn in the reading; what we have learned, we preserve by meditation.

'Reading the Bible provides us with a two-fold advantage. It instructs our minds, and introduces us to the love of God by taking our attention off vanities.

'None can understand the meaning of the Bible if they do not acquire familiarity with it through the habit of Bible reading.'

Augustine said:

'Nourish your soul with Bible reading. It will prepare a spiritual feast for you.'

Jerome said:

'Anyone who is assiduous in reading the Word of God becomes weary while reading, but afterwards is happy because the bitter seeds of the reading produce sweet fruits in the soul.

'Let us study while we are on earth that Reality which will stay in our minds also when we are in heaven.'

Defensor Grammaticus
The Book of Sparkling Sayings, 81 (SC86, 308ff.)

13th November

Even if a Thousand Trumpets Were to Sound in the Ears of the Dead

Anyone who is assiduous in reading the Word of God but does not put it into practice would be bound to hear himself accused by the reading itself. So he would necessarily deserve an even more serious condemnation for despising and dishonouring what he was reading every day.

Sadly he is like a dead person, like a soulless corpse.

Even if a thousand trumpets were to sound in the ears of the dead, they would never hear them. That is how it is with a soul that is dead in sin, a soul that has lost all memory of God, a soul that never thinks of God all day: it does not hear the sound of the Word that is calling it. The trump of the Word does not wake it. It is sunk in the sleep of death and this sleep is pleasant to it.

Being a dead soul, it is not conscious of its state and is not moved to ask for life. It is like one who has died of natural causes, or who on the level of practical obedience to the Word of God has committed suicide. It does not suffer as a result of its death and the idea of asking for a return to life does not enter its head.

The soul is dead when it never thinks of God, when it has lost all memory of God. Its powers of discernment are dead. Its desires for the things of heaven

357

are dead. Its nature is alive, but its will is dead and its freedom has disappeared.

> **Philoxenus of Mabbug**
> *Homily 1*, 5ff. (SC44, 28ff.)

14th November

The Psalms: Voice of the Church and Medicine for Hearts

Any part of the Scriptures you like to choose is inspired by God. The Holy Spirit composed the Scriptures so that in them, as in a pharmacy open to all souls, we might each of us be able to find the medicine suited to our own particular illness.

Thus, the teaching of the Prophets is one thing, and that of the historical books is another. And, again, the Law has one meaning, and the advice we read in the Book of Proverbs has a different one.

But the Book of Psalms contains everything useful that the others have. It predicts the future, it recalls the past, it gives directions for living, it suggests the right behaviour to adopt. It is, in short, a jewel case in which have been collected all the valid teachings in such a way that individuals find remedies just right for their cases.

It heals the old wounds of the soul and gives relief to recent ones. It cures the illnesses and preserves the health of the soul.

Every Psalm brings peace, soothes the internal conflicts, calms the rough waves of evil thoughts, dissolves anger, corrects and moderates profligacy.

Every Psalm preserves friendship and reconciles those who are separated. Who could actually regard as an enemy the person beside whom they have raised a song to the one God?

Every Psalm anticipates the anguish of the night and gives rest after the efforts of the day. It is safety for babes, beauty for the young, comfort for the aged, adornment for women.

Every Psalm is the voice of the Church.

Basil the Great
Commentary on Psalm 1, 1 (PG29, 209)

15th November

Continually Before the Face of God

Be mindful of God, so that in every moment he may be mindful of you. If he is mindful of you, he will give you salvation.

Do not forget him, letting yourselves be seduced by vain distractions. Do you want him to forget you in your times of temptation?

Stay near him and obey him in the days of your prosperity. You will be able to rely on his word in difficult days, because prayer will keep you safe in his continual presence.

Remain constantly before his face, think of him, remember him in your heart. Otherwise, if you only meet him from time to time, you risk losing your close friendship with him.

Familiarity between people comes about through physical presence. Familiarity with God, by contrast, is built on meditation and self-abandonment to him during prayer.

Those who would see the Lord should purify their

hearts with the continual remembrance of God. They will reach the contemplation of God in every moment, and within him all will be light.

Isaac of Nineveh
Philocalia

16th November

We Pray as We Live

For prayer to have the fervour and the purity it ought, certain conditions are necessary.

First of all, suppress any kind of desire for the things of the flesh. Then, shut the doors of the spirit not only to anxiety, but even to the recalling of any kind of business matters or affairs. Next, renounce evil speaking, vain words, long high-sounding discourses, scurrilous witticisms. Conquer the agitation that comes from anger or melancholy. Cut off greed and attachment to money at the roots.

After we have destroyed these vices, not to mention other defects equally serious and evident, after we have made this purification which results in simplicity and innocence, we ought to lay solid foundations for a deep humility capable of supporting a tower that reaches to heaven.

After that, there is the building of the spiritual edifice of the virtues.

Finally, it is necessary to prevent the soul being allowed to wander off into distractions and anything that would divert it from its aim. Only then will it begin to be exalted to the contemplation of God and to the intuition of spiritual realities.

In fact, everything that we have in our minds before the time of prayer is inevitably brought back by memory when we are praying. So whatever kind of people we want to be in our prayer time, we need to be before we begin to pray.

Cassian
Conferences, 9, 3 (SC54, 41ff.)

17th November

If Moses did not Take off his Shoes

Moses was prevented from approaching the burning bush until he had taken off his shoes. You are aspiring to stand in the presence of the One who is greater than every thought and every passion. How then can you refuse to strip yourself of every passionate thought?

Praying means rejecting pleasures and banishing anger.

Do not open your heart to fleshly longings. They stir up emotions that trouble the eye of the mind and therefore destroy prayer.

Your prayer ought to be steadfast and fervent. So dispel all distractions and wandering thoughts the moment they present themselves. They disturb you and worry you so that your fervour is weakened.

During your prayer, try to keep your mind deaf and dumb. Only so will you be able to pray.

Do not be content with external attitudes of prayer. Turn your mind to the prayer of the spirit, with awe and fearfulness.

Evagrius of Pontus
Sentences on Prayer 479ff. (PG79, 1167ff.)

18th November

Strange Yoke Fellows

What is prayer? It is the mind detached from earthly things and the whole heart pointed to that in which it hopes.

We need to have both these qualities evenly matched. Otherwise, we are imitating a farmer who yokes together to pull the plough not two oxen or two asses, but an ox and an ass.

In order that prayer should not be disturbed by distractions it is essential for the mind to be constantly directed towards God. Through this continual recollection God dwells in us, provided that there is in us a loving search for his will.

Then our soul under the action of the Holy Spirit is truly purified. Through this, prayer becomes the symbol of our future state. Prayer raises human nature above all the excitements that are stirred up in the heart by the thought of earthly things.

The gift of the Holy Spirit makes us capable of practising prayer continually. When the Holy Spirit has established his temple in a person, that person cannot but pray without ceasing. Whether waking or sleeping, prayer does not fade from his soul.

Isaac of Nineveh
Philocalia

19th November

Freedom and Joy, Signs of True Prayer

Perfect prayer consists in speaking to God without distraction, holding all the thoughts and all the senses quietly concentrated. We come to the point of being dead to humanity, to the world and to all the objects in the world.

When you pray, you only have to say this: 'Lord save me from evil! Your will be done in me!'

Concentrate your spirit on the presence of God and speak to him. True prayer is recognized by the fact that an individual is free from all kinds of distraction and is full of joy under the influence of the illumination of the Lord.

And you can tell that someone has reached this freedom and this joy from the fact that he is not worried even if the whole world assails him.

Anyone who is dead to the world and to its pleasures can pray without distraction. On the other hand, there is no other way of mastering all the passions than to call on the name of God.

Barsanuphius
Philocalia

20th November

The One who Prays is Safe from Despondency and Discouragement

Prayer is an ascent of the mind to God.

If you love God, you converse with him continually as you would with your father, banishing every passion from your mind.

If you want to pray in the right way, try not to make anyone unhappy: otherwise your prayer is vain.

'Go, sell all you possess and give the proceeds to the poor; then take up your cross, renounce yourself.' [cf. Matt. 16:24; 19:21] Act in this way so as to be able to pray without anything to distract you. Renounce yourself continually and endure all your trials wisely, through love of prayer.

In the time of prayer, you will receive the fruit of every suffering that you have endured wisely.

Prayer is born of joy and gratitude.

Prayer makes gentleness blossom in the heart.

Prayer saves us from despondency and discouragement.

Evagrius of Pontus
Sentences on Prayer 14ff. (PG79, 1169)

21st November

On the Threshold

Grace acts on people in different ways.

Some, spurred on by great enthusiasm, redouble the number of their prayers. Others, on the contrary, are led by inner peace to reduce the number of their prayers until they are only saying one.

In some cases, the words of prayer become extraordinarily sweet. Then it comes naturally to repeat the same word continually, without any feeling of satiety making us pass on to the next word.

In other cases, vocal prayer acts as a stimulus to contemplation, in such a way that the words disappear little by little from the lips and the soul enters into ecstasy, becoming unconscious of the world.

In this development of prayer, the movements of the tongue and of the heart are like household servants. On the threshold of the house the tongue falls silent, the lips become mute. However, the heart and the reason must be silent too and also the senses and the mind. They have to be, because the Master of the house, that is the soul, is about to enter.

Once there in the house, the object of the prayer is forgotten. The activity of the spirit is immersed in a sea of elation. The soul no longer knows the outside world. Holy, happy ignorance!

Isaac of Nineveh
Philocalia

22nd November

Spreading Arms to Heaven

To describe it with the boldest expression, prayer is a conversation with God.

Even if we speak with a low voice, even if we whisper without opening the lips, even if we call to him only from the depths of the heart, our unspoken word always reaches God and God always hears.

Sometimes, however, besides speaking, we lift our head and raise our arms to heaven.

In this way we are underlining the desire that the spirit has for the spiritual world. We are striving with the word to raise the body above the earth. We are giving wings to the soul for it to reach the good things on high.

Clement of Alexandria
Miscellaneous Studies, 7, 7, 39ff. (Stählin III, 30ff.)

23rd November

Don't Rack your Brains

When you are praying, don't rack your brains to find words. On many occasions the simple, monotonous stammering of children has satisfied their Father who is in heaven.

Don't bother to be loquacious lest the mind is bewildered in the search for words. The tax-collector gained the Lord's forgiveness with a single sentence, and a single word charged with faith was the salvation of the robber.

Loquacity in prayer often fills the head with foolish fancies and provokes distractions. Brevity on the other hand – sometimes only one word is enough – in general favours recollection.

John Climacus
Stairway to Paradise, 28 (PG88, 1132)

24th November

Better the Silence of the Heart than Distracted Words

Isidore said:
'Prayer is a work of the heart, not of the lips. For God does not pay attention to the words of the one who is praying to him, but rather to his or her heart. It is better to pray in the silence of the heart than to pray only with words, without the mind paying attention.

'It is useless to pray when trust and hope are missing.

'Our spirit contemplates God perfectly only if it is not obstructed by earthly anxieties.'

Defensor Grammaticus
The Book of Sparkling Sayings, 7 (SC77, 132ff.)

25th November

'Your Will be Done in Me'

Pray to obtain the gift of tears.

Pray that the Lord may soften the hardness of your soul.

Pray that the Lord may forgive the sins you confess to him.

Don't pray that what you want may come to pass. It does not necessarily coincide with the will of God.

Pray rather as you have been taught, saying: 'Your will be done in me!'

Pray that the will of God may be done in everything. He, in fact, wants what is good and useful for your soul, while you are not always seeking that and only that.

Evagrius of Pontus
Sentences on Prayer 479ff. (PG79, 1167ff.)

26th November

Do not Seek Special Favours from the Lord

'I sought the Lord and he heard me.' [Ps. 34:4] If someone has not been heard it means he has not sought the Lord.

Pay particular attention to this point. The Psalm does not say: 'I asked the Lord for riches and he heard me. I asked for a long life and he heard me. I begged for this or that and he heard me.' Seeking to obtain something from the Lord does not mean seeking the Lord himself. 'I sought the Lord and he heard me.'

You yourself, when you pray, what do you say to him?

Maybe you request him to remove so-and-so whom you detest from the world! If so, you are not seeking the Lord but setting yourself up as judge of your enemy and demanding that God should execute your sentence. Are you sure the person whose death you are requesting is not better than you? In this, at least, he is probably better than you: he can plead that he is not praying for your death.

When you turn to God, do not seek some favour from him. Seek the Lord himself and he will hear you.

He will interrupt your prayer saying:

'Here I am. Yes, surely, here I am, here. What do you want? What is your request? Everything I can give you is nothing in comparison to the gift of myself. Accept me, find your joy in me, talk with me. Touch me with the hands of your faith and you will be united to me.

'I will make all your burdens light. So, when your mortal body is clothed in immortality, you will be able to be united with me also in your body. Then you will continually see my face. You will be full of joy, and no one will take that joy away from you.'

Augustine
On Psalm 33, 9 (PL36, 313)

27th November

Glorify God who Needs no Glory

'In his temple all cry: Glory!' Let all those who like long speeches heed these words of the Psalmist.

God knows the prayer of each person. So he knows very well who is seeking heavenly things only in appearance and who is seeking them from the depths of his being. He sees quite clearly who says the words of his prayer merely with his lips while his heart is elsewhere. He sees who asks for physical health, earthly riches, or the praise of others.

There is no need, as Scripture teaches, to ask for these things. Rather: 'In his temple all cry: Glory!'

All creation, in heaven and on earth, singing or silent, continuously praises the Creator.

On the other hand, human beings, wretched creatures, leave their homes and go to church almost as if they were merchants going to swing a good deal. They pay no attention to the word of God: 'In his temple all cry: Glory.'

You have a tongue: praise the Lord with it! You have intelligence: meditate on the words you use! Give praise with your voice but also with your mind.

God in himself has no need to receive glory from you. But he wants you to become worthy to receive glory from him.

Basil the Great
Commentary on Psalm 28, 7 (PG29, 301).

28th November

Alleluia, Praise the Lord!

Here on earth our task is the praise of the Lord, because in eternity our blessedness will consist there also in the praise of the Lord. No one, in fact, can be fit for such a future without some practice in it beforehand.

So today, at once, let us praise the Lord.

Let us praise him and implore him. Our praise will be a hymn of joy, our invocation will be lamentation.

Promises have been made which have not yet been fulfilled, and he who made them is true. So we are hoping and we are happy. But because these promises have not yet been fulfilled, besides hoping, we weep. We have to wait for our promises to be fulfilled and our weeping to cease. Then only our praise will resound. I exhort you, brethren, to praise God.

This is the meaning of the salutation which we exchange these days: 'Alleluia, praise the Lord!' You say this to your neighbours and they say this in reply. All of us have these words on our lips, all of us are praising God.

But we need to praise him with all our being: not only with our lips, not only with our voice, but with our thoughts, with our whole life, with all our works.

Doubtless when we meet one another in church we praise him. But then, when we return to our occupations, we seem to forget the praises of God.

Live a holy life and you will be praising God with your whole life. But you are ceasing to praise God when you depart from righteousness and from the works that are pleasing to God.

Augustine
On Psalm 148, 1 (PL37, 1937)

29th November

Is Unceasing Prayer Possible?

How is unceasing prayer possible? When we are singing the Psalms, when we are reading the Scriptures, when we are serving our neighbour, even then it is easy enough for the mind to wander off after irrelevant thoughts and images.

Yet the Scriptures do not require impossibilities. St Paul himself sang the Psalms, read the Scriptures, offered his own apostolic service, and nonetheless prayed uninterruptedly.

Unceasing prayer means to have the mind always turned to God with great love, holding alive our hope in him, having confidence in him whatever we are doing and whatever happens to us.

That is the attitude that the Apostle had when he wrote: 'Who shall separate us from the love of Christ? Shall tribulation, or distress, or persecution, or famine, or nakedness, or peril? Neither death nor life nor any other creature shall be able to separate us from the love of God in Christ Jesus.' [cf. Rom. 8:35-38]

Thanks to this attitude of mind, Paul prayed without ceasing. In all that he did and in all that happened to him, he kept alive his hope in God.

And like him all the saints, so as to be able to attain to the love of God, are cheerful in their trials.

It is for this reason that the Apostle himself wrote: 'I will all the more gladly boast of my weaknesses, that the power of Christ may rest upon me. For when I am weak, then I am strong.' [cf. 2 Cor. 12:9-10]

Maximus the Confessor
Ascetics, 25 (PG90, 929)

30th November

Christ who Offers and Is Offered

O great and glorious King, whoever is a slave to desires and passions is unworthy to present himself before you, to approach you or to serve you, for your service is a great and awesome work.

But you, of your immeasurable and unspeakable mercy, when you made man, became our High Priest, and you have entrusted to us, O Lord of the Universe, the task of offering to you this bloodless sacrifice.

You only, O Lord, reign over things in heaven and on earth. You alone are the Holy One and make your dwelling among them that are holy.

To you alone therefore do I pray, who are gracious and quick to hear me. Behold me a sinner and an unworthy servant. Purify my mind and my body from evil desires. By the power of the Holy Spirit, grant that I may be clothed in the grace of the priesthood and enabled to present myself at this your table to consecrate your spotless Body and your precious Blood.

Turn not your face far from me; reject me not in your service. Grant me, albeit an unworthy sinner, to offer these gifts to you.

You, O Christ our God, indeed are he who makes the offering and is offered; you are he who receives and is received. To you do we give glory, you who are one in unity with the eternal Father and with the all-holy, good and life-giving Spirit, now and for ever.

Byzantine Liturgy of John Chrysostom

December

Amen! I believe, I hope, I love,
O lord!

1st December

As the Eye Needs Light

To see visible objects we need the eyes of the body.

To understand intelligible truths we need the eyes of the mind.

To have the vision of divine things we cannot do without faith.

What the eye is for the body, faith is for reason.

To be more precise; the eye needs the light which puts it in contact with visible things; reason needs faith to show it divine things.

Theodoret
The Cure of Pagan Diseases, 1, 78 (SC57, 124)

2nd December

Even Learning the Alphabet Needs Faith

Let no one speak against faith. For Aristotle faith is the principle of science. Epicurus considers faith to be the first movement of the reasoning faculty. This movement is followed by the activity of cognition and the result is the understanding of truth. Faith requires knowledge, but in its turn knowledge has need of faith. As there cannot be faith without knowledge, so there cannot be knowledge without faith.

Faith comes before knowledge: knowledge is subsequent to faith. Thereafter purpose is allied with knowledge and purpose determines action.

Therefore: first of all, one must believe, then learn.

Once the truth is known, a decision has to be made and action taken in conformity with it.

Not even the letters of the alphabet can be known without faith, without trust in the teacher. If someone suddenly began to contradict his teacher by refusing to believe that 'A' is the first letter of the alphabet, he would never learn to read or write. On the other hand, if anyone shows faith in his teacher and follows his teaching, he will very quickly acquire knowledge in addition to faith.

Theodoret
The Cure of Pagan Diseases, 1, 90ff. (SC57, 128)

3rd December

At the Garden Gate

'All Scripture is inspired by God and is profitable for training in righteousness.' [2 Tim. 3:16] The soul therefore gains great advantage from the reading of the Bible.

'Like a tree planted by streams of water,' [Ps. 1:3] the soul is irrigated by the Bible and acquires vigour, produces tasty fruit, namely, true faith, and is beautified with a thousand green leaves, namely, actions that please God.

The Bible, in fact, leads us towards pure holiness and holy actions. In it we find encouragement to all the virtues and the warning to flee from evil.

The Bible is a scented garden, delightful, beautiful. It enchants our ears with birdsong in a sweet, divine and spiritual harmony, it touches our heart, comforts us in sorrow, soothes us in a moment of anger, and fills us with eternal joy.

Let us knock at its gate with diligence and with perseverance. Let us not be discouraged from knocking. The latch will be opened.

If we have read a page of the Bible two or three times and have not understood it, let us not be tired of re-reading it and meditating on it. Let us seek in the fountain of this garden 'a spring of water welling up to eternal life.' [John 4:14] We shall taste a joy that will never dry up, because the grace of the Bible garden is inexhaustible.

John Damascene
On the Orthodox Faith, 4, 7 (PG94, 1176ff.)

4th December

Four Winds Blowing on the World

There are four gospels and only four, neither more nor less: four like the points of the compass, four like the chief directions of the wind. The Church, spread all over the world, has in the gospels four pillars and four winds blowing wherever people live.

These four gospels are in actual fact one single Gospel, a fourfold Gospel inspired by the one Spirit, a Gospel which has four aspects representing the work of the Son of God.

These aspects are like the four cherubs described by Ezekiel. In the prophet's words: 'The first had the likeness of a lion,' symbolizing the masterly and kingly role of Christ in priesthood; 'the second had the appearance of an ox,' the beast of sacrifice, recalling the perfect sacrifice of Christ; 'the third had the face of a man,' undoubtedly referring to the coming of the Lord in human nature; 'and the fourth had the aspect of a flying eagle,' with a clear allusion to the grace of the Spirit hovering over the Church. [cf. Ezek. 1:10; Rev. 4:7]

The four Gospels correspond to these symbols. Christ is at the centre of them.

John actually speaks of his kingly and glorious Sonship to the Father in his opening words: 'In the beginning was the Word.' [John 1:1] Luke begins with Zaccharias offering sacrifice. Matthew chooses first of all the Lord's human genealogy. And Mark leads off by calling on the prophetic Spirit which invests humanity from on high.

Irenaeus
Against Heresies, 3, 11, 11 (Harvey II, 46)

5th December

Beyond the Husk of the Literal Sense

The sacred Scripture, taken as a whole, is like a human being. The Old Testament is the body and the New is the soul, the meaning it contains, the spirit.

From another viewpoint we can say that the entire sacred Scripture, Old and New Testament, has two aspects: the historical content which corresponds to the body, and the deep meaning, the goal at which the mind should aim, which corresponds to the soul.

If we think of human beings, we see they are mortal in their visible properties but immortal in their invisible qualities.

So with Scripture. It contains the letter, the visible text, which is transitory. But it also contains the spirit hidden beneath the letter, and this is never extinguished and this ought to be the object of our contemplation.

Think of human beings again. If they want to be perfect, they master their passions and mortify the flesh.

So with Scripture. If it is heard in a spiritual way, it trims the text, like circumcision.

Paul says: 'Though our outer nature is wasting away, our inner nature is being renewed every day.' [2 Cor. 4:16] We can say that also of Scripture.

The further the letter is divorced from it, the more relevance the spirit acquires. The more the shadows of the literal sense retreat, the more the shining truth of the faith advances.

And this is exactly why Scripture was composed.

Maximus the Confessor
Mystagogia, 6 (PG91, 684)

6th December

A Magnet that Only Attracts Those who Want to be Attracted

A magnet has the property of attracting iron. Sometimes we see a piece of iron suspended. It is not resting on any support underneath it, and it is not tied to any object above it. It is only attached, with invisible bonds, to the strength of the magnet acting on it from above.

Something similar happens with the Holy Scriptures.

Many people, if not all, have heard them. Only those who have faith, however, are attracted by them. Those people do not rest on material prosperity nor are they bound to heaven by any visible tie, but they nourish their spirit solely on invisible hope.

A magnet, while it compels iron to fly towards it,

leaves every other kind of material stationary.

The grace of the Scriptures is slightly different. While it attracts some people, it does not reject others. It pours out water on all who want to drink.

The difference between the reactions depends rather on free will. Some feel thirsty and approach the spring. Others, on the other hand, freely decide to suppress their desire for water.

The Doctor of souls does not compel anyone who does not wish to use this medicine. He has created human nature free, its own master. He dissuades it from evil and angles it towards good, but he never forces it.

It is up to each one of us to decide whether or not to share in a better destiny. God does not do violence to our nature. He confines himself to launching a proposal: 'If you want, if you obey me, you shall have many blessings.' [cf. Isa. 1:19]

Theodoret
The Cure of Pagan Diseases, 5, 1ff. (SC57, 226)

7th December

The Word which is Brief and Effectual

Plato made lengthy discources to demonstrate the immortality of the soul, yet he did not succeed in persuading even his own disciple Aristotle. Here, on the other hand, are fishermen like John and a tax collector like Matthew and a tentmaker like Paul, and they have persuaded Greeks, Romans, Egyptians, the whole world. Thanks to them very many people are now convinced that the soul is immortal, that it is gifted with reason, that it has the power to control the passions, that if it breaks the commandments it does so through negligence and not through absence of freedom, that after having sinned it is able to turn back to righteousness, to free itself from vice and to recover the mark of God on itself.

These principles are known, not only to the doctors of the Church, but also to shoemakers, smiths, weavers, and every kind of workman. And it is the same among women. These principles are known not only to those who have studied but also to spinners, dressmakers and household servants. They are known to city people and also to country folk. We find miners and drovers and farmers talking of the threefold nature of God.

All of these, moreover, practise virtue, cleanse themselves from vice, are afraid of future punishment, await the final judgment, reflect continually on eternal life, and gladly accept weariness and trials of every sort for the sake of the kingdom of heaven.

So compare the vain chatter of the philosophers with the simple teaching of the fishermen and reflect on the difference. The fables of the poets and the maxims of the philosophers are not followed by anyone. The Word of God on the other hand commands admiration for its brevity and praise for its effectiveness.

Theodoret
The Cure of Pagan Diseases, 5, 67 (SC57, 248)

8th December

First: Do not Imitate Worms!

Some people have tireless tongues and are very skilful at digging up amusing and recondite expressions. But they would do better to busy themselves with the right way to act. We should have fewer sophists then!

There is not the slightest spirit of faith in their behaviour. They are interested only in difficulties to raise or resolve. They are anxious only to make a good impression on the ignorant and to provoke applause.

Look out for them! They are not all concerned with arguing about God. To reach him it is necessary to pay a very high price, and first of all to stop crawling like worms.

Not everyone is capable of discussing God, but only those who have purified their souls and their bodies, or at least are striving to purify them.

Gregory Nazianzen
Oration 27. 1ff. (PG36, 12ff.)

9th December

Scholarship is a Help to Faith

It is possible to be a faithful Christian without knowing how to read. But it is impossible to understand the doctrine of the faith without having studied it.

Accepting the right ideas, rejecting erroneous theses: this cannot be done by simple faith, but only by faith that has been ripened by scholarship.

Virtue, too, is more easily and more speedily attained with the help of knowledge.

It is true that knowledge is not indispensable. Just as one can live an honest life amid riches or in penury, so one can make progress along the road of virtue either with scholarship or without it.

All the same, it is an advantage to have completed

some study and 'to have one's faculties trained by practice to distinguish good from evil.' [Heb. 5:14]

Clement of Alexandria
Miscellaneous Studies, 6, 2 (SC30, 71)

10th December

Only a Faint Ray for Now

What God is like in his own nature and in his own being no one on earth has ever discovered nor will ever be able to discover. We shall only discover this when what is similar to God, namely, our soul, is united to the Supreme Being – only when the image attains to the prototype to which it is now straining. Yes, one day 'we shall know as we are known.' [1 Cor. 13:12]

For the time being, all we can possibly grasp is a mere feeble reflection, a faint ray of the great Light.

One can come to a certain knowledge of God, a knowledge superior to that of others. If we call that perfect knowledge, however, it is not perfect in an absolute sense, but only when compared with the knowledge of other people.

On this subject, in short, it is hard to face a discussion or to attempt an explanation. We are tackling an enormous task with a tiny tool. We want to attain to the spiritual realities, but we have to make use of our senses from which we cannot be parted and which carry us in another direction. They lead us into error.

Gregory Nazianzen
Oration 28, 17ff. (PG36)

11th December

The Foundation Stone of the Soul

Let the truth of God sink into your soul to be its foundation stone.

God is One, without beginning and without change. There was no one before him who caused him to be, and he will not have anyone after him. He has not had a beginning and he will not ever have an end. He is good and just.

God is One and he has created souls and bodies, heaven and earth.

He is the maker of everything, yet the Father of an only Son before time began: our Lord Jesus Christ through whom he has made all things visible and invisible.

God the Father of our Lord Jesus Christ is not restricted to any one place: not even the heavens can contain him. On the contrary, the heavens are the work of his fingers and it is he who holds the universe in his hands.

He is in everything and yet also beyond everything.

Do not imagine that the sun can shine more brightly than he or be as great as he. It was God who created the sun and therefore he is proportionately more magnificent and more brilliant.

He knows what will happen in the future.

He is more powerful than anyone.

He knows everything and does everything in accordance with his own will.

He is not subject to the vicissitudes of time; he does not depend on others; he is not the victim of destiny.

He is perfect in everything and possesses all the virtues in their fullness.

He it is who has prepared a crown for the righteous.

Cyril of Jerusalem
Catecheses, 4, 4ff. (PG33, 47)

12th December

The Nameless One who Has All Names

The theologians extol God as the Nameless One, because he himself reproved Jacob for having asked him: 'Tell me, I pray, your name.' [Gen. 32:29] The very same God who replied to Jacob: 'Why do you want to know my name?' said to Manoah: 'Why do you ask my name, seeing it is wonderful?' [Judg. 13:18]

It is truly wonderful, this name that transcends every name, this nameless name 'above every name that is named, not only in this age, but also in that which is to come.' [Eph. 1:21]

On the other hand, theologians attribute many names to him, appealing again to God himself who said: 'My name is "I-am-who-I-am." ' [Exod. 3:14] He is also given the names 'God', 'Life', 'Light', 'Truth.' [cf. John 8:12; 14:6]

They praise the Universal Cause, examining his effects, giving him the names Goodness, Beauty, Wisdom, Loveliness, Lord of Lords, Holiest of Holies, Eternal, Being, Origin of Time, Giver of Life, Word, Holder of all the treasures of all knowledge, Mighty, King of Kings, Ancient of Days, Everlasting Youth, Immutable, Salvation, Righteousness, Sanctification, Redemption.

They assert, moreover, that God is present in minds, souls and bodies, in heaven and on earth, and that he is in the universe, around the universe, beyond the universe. They call him Superessential, Sun, Star, Fire, Water, Spirit, Dew, Cloud, Rock.

To sum up, they say that he is all that exists and also not one of the things that exist.

Pseudo-Dionysius the Areopagite
On the Divine Names, I, 6 (PG3, 629)

13th December

God is Life

We ought to celebrate Life eternal, from which comes all other kinds of life. Every being that participates in life in some way, receives life from it, each according to its capacity.

This divine Life, which is higher than any other kind of life, provides and preserves life. Any kind of life and any kind of vital movement proceed from this Life which transcends every life and every beginning of every life.

To that Life souls owe their incorruptibility, just as it is thanks to that Life that there is life in all the animals and in all the plants, which have life's weaker echo.

To human beings, creatures made of spirit and matter, that Life gives life. If then we chance to forsake our lives, then that Life, from the overflowing of his love towards humanity, converts us and recalls us to himself.

More than that: he promises us he will bring our souls and bodies to the perfect life, to immortality.

It is not enough to say that this Life is alive; it is the Beginning of life, the only Cause and Fountain of life. Every living thing ought to contemplate him and praise him. He is Life that overflows with life.

Pseudo-Dionysius the Areopagite
On the Divine Names, 6, 1ff. (PG3, 856)

14th December

God is Wisdom

God, besides being eternal Life, is Wisdom: Wisdom which substantiates all wisdom, transcends all wisdom, exceeds any possibility of comprehension.

Indeed, not only does God overflow with wisdom and 'there is no limit to his wisdom.' [Ps. 147:5] He transcends all mind, all intelligence, all wisdom as well. This is what Paul amazingly understood when he wrote: 'The folly of God is wiser than human wisdom.' [1 Cor. 1:25]

On the other hand, the divine Wisdom is the cause of all intelligence, of all wisdom, of every possibility of comprehension. From it souls receive the power to reflect, that is, the power to approach in thought and, as it were, sail close to the very truth of things, and the power to reduce multiplicity to unity.

Pseudo-Dionysius the Areopagite
On the Divine Names, 7, 1 (PG3, 865)

15th December

God is Peace

God is Peace, the principle of all kinds of communion. Let us extol peace with songs of peaceful praise.

It is God-who-is-Peace who brings all things into unity, who is the cause of every agreement, who is the author of all harmony. All people strive for this Peace, so as to transform their multiplicity and their divisions into perfect unity and so as to be able to live in peaceful co-existence.

Peace, in fact, sheds its fullness on all beings. It unifies every situation by binding one extreme with the other and submitting the whole to the unity of a friendship which makes the extremes homogeneous.

This Peace makes even the farthest confines of the earth share in its own blessedness. It unites everything together by means of a thousand unities, a thousand identities, a thousand conjunctions, a thousand communions.

This Peace allows the superabundance of its peace-making fruitfulness to overflow its source all the time.

Pseudo-Dionysius the Areopagite
On the Divine Names, 11, 1ff. (PG3, 96off.)

16th December

God is Light

John writes: 'God is light and in him is no darkness at all.' [1 John 1:5]

Although he is speaking of light, the words are obscure. The sun is also light, the moon is also light, a lamp is also light. There must be in God something very greatly superior to these lights in grandeur, in brightness, in quality.

Just as God is superior to his creation, as an author is superior to his work, as Wisdom is superior to any object made with wisdom, so this Light ought to surpass all the other lights.

Perhaps we shall approach it if we do all we can to be illuminated by it. The Light does not humble us if we humble ourselves.

Who are they who humble themselves? Those who know they are sinners.

Who are they who are not humbled by the Light? Those who are illuminated by it.

Who are they who are illuminated by it? Those who, seeing how sin darkens them, long for it to enlighten them and who come close to it.

It is as the Psalmist says: 'Look to the Lord, and be radiant so your faces shall never be ashamed.' [Ps. 34:5]

No indeed! The Light will not make you blush with shame when it shows you your filthiness, but this filthiness will make you sad and the Light will enable you to perceive its beauty.

Augustine
On the First Letter of John, 1, 4 (SC75, 121)

17th December

God is Father

If you want to know why we call our God Father, listen to Moses: 'Is he not your Father who created you, who made you and established you?' [Deut. 32:6]

Listen too to Isaiah: 'O Lord, you are our Father; we are the clay, and you are the potter; we are all the work of your hand.' [Isa. 64:8] Under prophetic inspiration, Isaiah speaks plainly. God is our Father, not by nature, but by grace and by adoption.

Paul too was a father: father of the Christians in Corinth. Not because he had begotten them according to the flesh, but because he had regenerated them according to the Spirit.

Christ when his body was fastened to the cross saw Mary, his mother according to the flesh, and John, the disciple most dear to him, and said to John: 'Behold your mother.' and to Mary: 'Behold your son.' Christ called Mary John's mother, not because she had begotten him, but because she loved him. [John 19:26-27]

Joseph too was called father of Christ, not as pro-creator in a physical sense, but as his guardian: he was to nourish and protect him.

With greater reason God calls himself Father of human beings and wants to be called Father by us.

What unspeakable generosity! He dwells in the heavens; we live on the earth. He has created the ages; we live in time. He holds the world in his hand; we are but grasshoppers on the face of the earth.

Cyril of Jerusalem
Catecheses, 7, 8ff. (PG33, 613)

18th December

The Door that Opens the Way to the Father

Those who believe in one God the Father Almighty ought to believe in his only-begotten Son. Jesus says: 'I am the door. No one can come to the Father but by me.' [John 10:9; 14:6]

Anyone who does not accept the door cannot possibly reach the Father. Anyone who wishes to pray to the Father should adore the Son, or his prayer is not accepted.

The Son is called Christ, which means anointed, that is consecrated. He was not anointed by human hands but consecrated by the Father to become a priest for ever. He died, but he did not remain, as all human beings do, in the underworld. He is the only one free among the dead.

The Saviour becomes all things to all, according to the need of each: to those who ask for joy, he becomes the vine; to those who wish to enter, he becomes the door; to those who are under the weight of sin, he becomes a lamb, a lamb slain for them. He becomes all things to all, but he remains nonetheless what he is.

He is called by a twofold name: Jesus because he gives us salvation, and Christ because he is priest.

He is the healer of bodies and the doctor of souls.

As he made whole those who were physically blind, so he gave light to their minds. As he gave the lame the chance to walk, so he urges the steps of sinners in the direction of the way of penitence.

Cyril of Jerusalem
Catecheses, 10, 1ff. (PG53, 660)

19th December

Gabriel's Song

Gabriel was invited to Nazareth to bring to the Virgin the glad annunciation from the Father. The angel found Mary at home and greeted her with these words:

'Rejoice, you that are full of grace; the Lord is with you.

Rejoice, you that are the first and only one to conceive a babe free from sin.

Rejoice, you that bring into the world the beginning of life.

Rejoice, O Virgin Mother.

393

Rejoice, O Mother unmarried yet not without child.

Rejoice, O Mother unwed but not unfruitful.

Rejoice, you that await the birth yet shall not travail.

Rejoice, you that bear the deliverer from your father Adam.

Rejoice, you that without wearying sustain the sustainer of creation.

Rejoice, you that without pain are intermediary between God and humanity.

Rejoice, you that give birth to a God who is not only God, to a man who is not just a man.

Rejoice, you that are full of grace: the Lord is with you.'

The Virgin did not give importance to the exhortation to rejoice but reflected on this greeting and said: 'What can this salutation be? And who is this who entered our home without an invitation?'

The angel explained: 'Fear not, Mary. You have acquired the grace that the first woman lost. She, alone, yielded to the tempter's guile. Now you, alone, are bearing the conqueror of temptation. You will bring forth a son and shall call his name Jesus.'

Antipater of Bostra
Homily on the Forerunner, 9 (PG85, 1763ff.)

20th December

She Bore in her Womb the Bread of Heaven

A great mystery has been performed through Mary, a mystery that exceeds all understanding and knowledge.

The Mother of God has received tremendous powers,

in virtue of which she is greater than all the saints we honour.

Christ conferred on some of his servants grace to heal the sick not only by touching them but even by just letting their shadow fall on them: in Jerusalem people laid their sick friends in the street so that the shadow of Peter might heal them. [Acts 5:15] That being so, what powers should he have conferred on his Mother?

And if Christ declared the Apostle Peter blessed by entrusting the keys of the kingdom to him, is it conceivable that he should not have proclaimed Mary most blessed of all, since she was considered worthy to give birth to him whom Peter recognized as the Son of the living God? [cf. Matt. 16:17]

And if Paul was marked out as 'a chosen instrument', [Acts 9:15] because by his preaching he had carried to every part of the world the name of Christ, what sort of instrument will the Mother of God be, she who carried in her womb the Bread of Heaven that would be distributed to the faithful to be their food and their strength?

> **Basil of Seleucia**
> *Homily on the Mother of God*, 6 (PG85, 425ff.)

21st December

We Think of Him as Human, We Adore Him as God

The care of the Creator for his creatures is well known to us, and it explains why the Redeemer became incarnate.

It was consistent with his love not to leave the human race to go to perdition, from the moment he had constructed the universe and given existence to non-existent beings.

The Lord of the world did not consider it right to allow human beings, for love of whom everything had been made, to be besieged by sin and to be sold like slaves to death.

For this reason he assumed human form, hid his invisible nature under visible guise, and kept the visible nature free from the stain of sin.

Undoubtedly, it would have been easy for him to save the human race without assuming the garment of the flesh. He could have overthrown the power of death by a simple act of will. He could have made the father of that power, sin, disappear by exiling it from earth in such a way that no trace of it would remain on the earth.

Instead of that, he chose to demonstrate the holiness of his providential care.

To restore salvation to human beings he did not employ as his servants the angels and archangels, nor cause a piercing voice to resound from heaven. He preferred to build for himself a chamber in the womb of the Virgin and from there to come among us.

For this reason we think of him as man and adore him as God. Begotten of the Father before the beginning of time, he took of the Virgin a visible body. He is the Being who is both new and pre-existent.

Theodoret
The Cure of Pagan Diseases, 6, 74ff. (SC57, 281)

22nd December

If Christ had not been Born of Woman

A God who was not only God, and a man who was not simply man, was born of woman.

By being born he formed the gate of salvation from what had at one time been the way in for sin. Where in fact the serpent by exploiting human disobedience had infused his poison, there the Word entered through obedience and built a living temple. From the womb of a woman had come forth the original son of sin, Cain; and from the womb of a woman, without seed, there came into the light the Christ, the redeemer of the human race.

Let us not be ashamed that he was born of a woman. That birth was for us the beginning of salvation.

If Christ had not been born of woman, he would not have died either, and would not 'by death have destroyed him who had the power of death, that is, the devil.' [Heb. 2:14]

Proclus of Constantinople
Homily on the Mother of God (PG65, 679ff.)

23rd December

The Foolish Cross is the Power of God

Every action of Christ glorifies the Church, but the cross is the glory above all glory. Paul understood that well when he said: 'I will glory in nothing else but the cross of Christ.' [cf. Gal. 6:14]

That a blind man should have been able to regain

his sight by the pool of Siloam is certainly a marvellous fact. But what does this single episode add up to, when you think of the blind all over the world?

The resurrection of Lazarus who had already been dead four days was a miraculous event, overcoming all the forces of nature. But this favour granted to him alone could not be any comfort to all those who had died through their own sin.

It was a miracle to feed the five thousand with five loaves. But what use could that be for all the ignorant people starved of truth?

The glory of the cross, by contrast, has enlightened all those who were blinded by ignorance. It has set free all those who were slaves of sin. It has redeemed the whole human race.

Let us glory in the cross of the Saviour. 'The word of the cross is folly to those who are perishing, but to us who are being saved it is the power of God.' [1 Cor. 1:18]

Cyril of Jerusalem
Catecheses, 13, 1ff. (PG33, 772)

24th December

One Day from the Womb Today from the Tomb

Death was swallowed by the fight
as from the dead you woke, O Christ our God.
And we, now glorying in your Passion,
rejoice and thrill with gladness,
celebrate and cry with delight:
the Lord is risen!

The Lord is risen indeed.
And though the tomb guards were paid
to keep their mouths tight shut,
the very stones cry out
that with no touch of mortal hand
the mountain-hewn rock was lifted up:
as one day from the Virgin's womb,
so today from the tomb,
the Lord is risen!

Yes, O Saviour, from the Virgin's womb you came
  indeed,
born without seed, in birth keeping her virgin;
so too this day in death you slaughter death;
the shroud and Joseph you left by the grave,
by the same grave giving life to the progenitor of
  Joseph;
behind you came Adam and Eve followed after,
Eve now servant of Mary.
All the earth falls down before you
and to you proclaims a hymn of victory:
the Lord is risen!

Romanus Melodus
Resurrection Hymn 2

25th December

Let Every Day be Love's Christmas

In the Song of Songs the Bride, that is the Church,
cries to her maidens, that is to humanity: 'I adjure
you, daughters!' [cf. S. of S. 2:7] Why ever does she

adjure the maidens? 'I adjure you, daughters: waken my love, and make him arise.'

It is as though the Bride were saying: 'How long is love asleep in you? In me love is not asleep, for I am wounded by love. But in you, in you love for your spouse, for Christ, this love is asleep.

'I adjure you: waken the love which is in you, and after you have woken it make it rise up!

'When the Creator of all things created you, he planted in your hearts the seeds of love. But now in you love is asleep.'

The Word of God is asleep in those who do not believe and in all those of doubtful heart, while it is awake in the saints. It sleeps in those who are shaken by storms, but it awakes the moment they cry out – those who want to be saved and who are looking for this to waken their spouse.

When he is asleep there is tempest, death and despair. The moment he is awake, peace returns. The raging of the waters is hushed. He commands the adverse winds and the wrath of the waves falls silent.

Origen
Homily on the Song of Songs, 2, 9 (SC37, 96ff.)

26th December

The Feats of the Spirit

The Holy Spirit was present in the act of creation. For this reason the creaturely perfection of the beings made is not the fruit of any action of theirs. The Spirit was present and gave them perfection.

Exactly the same thing can be said of the design

of salvation which was carried out by our God and Saviour Jesus Christ in complete agreement with the love of the Father for the human race. Who could be in any doubt that the perfect accomplishment of this design depends on the Spirit?

But let us look back to the time before Christ.

The blessings granted to the patriarchs, the help secured by the gift of the Law, those things that prefigure New Testament truths, the prophecies, the wonderful events of Israel, the miracles achieved by the righteous, the preparation for the coming of the Lord in the flesh: all this was accomplished by the Spirit.

The Spirit was present in the body of the Lord. He was his anointing and his inseparable companion.

The Church itself is the work of the Spirit.

Basil the Great
Treatise on the Holy Spirit (PG29, 140)

27th December

The Thousand Languages of the One Church

When the Holy Spirit came down from heaven and filled with his presence those who had believed in Christ, they began to speak in all the languages. At that time, if one spoke in all the languages it was a sign that he had received the Spirit.

What did the Holy Spirit want to show by this miraculous feat? And why does he not do it now as well? Obviously, he wanted to teach us something.

He wanted to teach us that the Gospel should be spread in all languages. Well then, I dare to assert:

today also the Church speaks in all languages and in all languages is proclaiming the Gospel.

The Church is like a body. In a body the eye can say: 'The foot walks for me,' and the foot can say, 'The eye sees for me.'

So I would say: Greek is my language, Hebrew is my language, Syriac is my language. There are all these different languages and one single faith which gathers them all together, a bond of love that unifies them all.

Augustine
Serm. Denis, 19 (Miscellanea Agostiniana, 109ff.)

28th December

Their Death is More like Dreaming

We ought to honour the saints. They are Christ's friends, children and heirs of God. This is the teaching of the theologian and evangelist John: 'To all who received him ... the Word gave power to become children of God.' [John 1:12]

The Creator of all things is called in Scripture Lord of lords, King of kings, God of gods. The saints are precisely lords, kings and gods, not in their own nature but because they have become lords over themselves, they have ruled their passions, they have kept intact that image of God in which they were created.

Indeed, the saints of their own choice are united to God, they have welcomed him as a guest in their hearts, and by sharing with him have become what he is by nature. They have become God's servants, friends and children. The honour given to his faithful servants of which they are the witness is a test of our love for our Lord and theirs.

He has found in them a spotless dwelling place and has performed his promise: 'I will make my abode among you . . . and I will walk among you and will be your God . . . ' [Lev. 26:11-12]

It is of the saints that Scripture says: 'The souls of the righteous are in the hand of God and the torment of death shall not touch them.' [Wisd. 3:1] In fact, their death is more like dreaming than dying. God is life and light, and those who are in the hand of God are themselves life and light.

By means of the Spirit, God is dwelling in the bodies of the saints. Why then should we not honour the temple of the living God?

John Damascene
On the Orthodox Faith, 4, 15 (PG94, 1164ff.)

29th December

The Kingdom and The Fire

The God who gives peace is the same God who prepares the everlasting fire. Our one and only Lord has told us that in the judgment he will divide the human race 'as a shepherd separates the sheep from the goats.' To the righteous he will say: 'Come, O blessed of my Father, inherit the kingdom prepared for you.' To the wicked, on the other hand, he will say: 'Depart from me, you cursed, into the eternal fire.' [Matt. 25:31-41]

So it is one and the same God 'who makes weal and creates woe,' [Isa. 45:7] who will give to each of them what they deserve.

403

Our Lord taught the same truth by the parable of the weeds. 'Just as the weeds are gathered and burned with fire, so will it be at the close of the age. The Son of Man will send his angels, and they will gather out of his kingdom all causes of sin and all evildoers and throw them into the furnace of fire, where there will be wailing and grinding of teeth. Then the righteous will shine like the sun in the kingdom of their Father.' [Matt. 13:40-43]

It is therefore the Father who has prepared either the kingdom for the righteous, into which Christ will admit those who are worthy of it, or the fire, into which the angels sent by the Son of Man will cast the wicked at God's command.

Irenaeus
Against Heresies, 4, 66 (Harvey II, 302)

30th December

And your Clothing will be Pure Wool

Jesus said: 'When the Son of man comes in his glory, and all the angels with him, then he will sit on his glorious throne. Before him will be gathered all the nations . . . ' [Matt. 25:31-32]

The entire human race will be there. Think only of those who have lived down the centuries from Adam till today: an immense crowd. Besides them, the angels will be there too. It is impossible not to feel awestruck. And aside from the punishment to which we may be condemned, the idea that God will judge us in front of so many witnesses is frightening.

Jesus goes on to say: 'The Son of man will separate

them one from another as a shepherd separates the sheep from the goats.' [Matt. 25:32]

How will he set about separating them? Will he leaf through some sort of register?

No. He will judge on the basis of what he sees. Wool characterizes sheep: a shaggy wrinkled skin marks goats by contrast.

You, if you have been cleansed from your sins, will put on clothing woven from your holy deeds, and that clothing will be pure wool.

Cyril of Jerusalem
Catecheses, 15, 24ff. (PG33, 904)

31st December

You are Above All that Is

You, O God, are above all that is.
These words cannot contain all that could be sung of
        you.
What hymn can ever celebrate your praise?
And on what shall the mind rest
since you are above the reach of all comprehension?

You only are unknowable
yet all that we can think comes forth from you.
All beings give you praise, those that think and those
        that have no thought.
All that is makes prayer to you.
To you every thinking creature sends up a song of silent
        praise.
All that moves has its motion from you.
All that stays still has its rest in you.

You are the end of all beings.
You are the all and yet are nothing of what created
    beings are.
You are not one among many and you are not the
    totality of all beings.
You have all names there are.
Yet for me it is not possible to name you for you are
    the only one to whom no name can be given.

Have mercy, O God!
You are above all that is.
These words cannot contain all that could be sung of
    you.

Gregory Nazianzen
Poems, 1, 1, 29 (PG37, 507ff.)

On Authors and Texts

AMBROSE (339-397) Born probably at Treviri. Started on a political career and became a governor. His seat was at Milan. Not yet baptized when he was elected Bishop. Received baptism and consecration in the same week. He gave away his inheritance to the poor and dedicated his energies to listening, counselling, helping everyone. He took a stand against various heresies, e.g., Arianism. Pastor of souls as well as a scholar. Eloquent style, sometimes poetic. Chief works: *Hexaemeron*, *On the Gospel of Luke*, *On the Holy Spirit*, *The Mysteries, Penitence*.

AMPHILOCHIUS (d. after 394) A lawyer in Constantinople; became bishop of Iconium. Fought against Arianism and some heretical sects of Manichaean origin. Only a little of his vast output remains, for example, eight of his sermons.

ANTIPATER OF BOSTRA (d. before 378) Bishop of the capital of the Roman province of Arabia. Composed four books against the Manichees, showing himself a seasoned polemicist. Fragments of his Homilies on Luke and a sermon on the Epiphany are extant.

ATHANASIUS (295-373) Native of Alexandria. Deacon, and secretary to his bishop at the Council of Nicaea (325) where he disputed effectively with the Arians. In 328 was elevated to the episcopal See of Alexandria. Because he refused to readmit Arius to the Church, he was deposed by the Synod of Tyre and exiled by the emperor. He was able to return to his See when the emperor died, but was exiled again four times until the people rose up to compel the authorities not to interfere with Athanasius' theological and pastoral position. His literary output, which was enormous, was in great part devoted to the defence of the theses for which he was fighting. Their form is somewhat casual, with frequent repetitions, but his thoughts are always clearly expressed. Works include: *Three Discourses against the Arians*, *Defence against the Arians*, a legendary *Life of St Anthony* and exegetical works.

AUGUSTINE (354-430) Born at Thagaste in Tunisia. An undisciplined youth, during which an illegitimate son was born to him. Despising the Christian faith which his mother Monica professed, he joined the Manichees. Became a teacher of the liberal arts. Secured a position in Rhetoric at Milan. There, listening to the sermons of Ambrose the bishop, assimilating the neoplatonic philosophy of Plotinus and reading the letters of St Paul, he came back to Christianity. In the autumn of 386 he gave up teaching, retired into the country and was prepared for baptism which Ambrose bestowed on him during the Easter Vigil of 387. For some years he led a monastic life with some friends. In 391 he was ordained priest, four years later he was consecrated auxiliary to the Bishop of Hippo, Valerius, and on his death inherited his See. Even as a bishop he continued to live in community. Tireless in the care of the poor, a forceful preacher, and as a writer – his style is particularly evocative – very involved in the theological controversies of the age. Besides his *Confessions*, some of his main writings were *The Soliloquies*, *The City of God*, *On the Trinity* and commentaries on Genesis, Psalms, the Gospels.

BARSANUPHIUS (died c.540) Monk near Gaza. 396 of his letters of an ascetic-pastoral nature remain.

BASIL OF SELEUCIA (d. 460) Metropolitan, showed some inclination to monophysitism, but after the Council of Chalcedon took the side of orthodoxy. About fifty homilies are attributed to him, some of them doubtfully.

BASIL THE GREAT (330-379) Teacher of Rhetoric, then a monk, afterwards a priest at Caesarea and bishop of the same city. He too found himself at grips with Arianism and acted patiently as a mediator to restore unity after a schism occurred in 362. His devotion to his pastoral charge and to the cause of the poor – whom he defended from the fiscal claims of the civil authority – won for him the title 'Great' while he was still alive. Together with Gregory Nazianzen he composed two *Monastic Rules*. We also record his *Against Eunomius*, *On the Holy Spirit*, nine homilies *On the Hexaemeron*, *Homilies on the Psalms*.

BERNARD (1091-1153) Cistercian monk, reformer of the Abbey of Clairvaux. Author of sermons, tracts and letters which reflect his mystical bent and his emotional character. He wrote some 86 expository sermons on the first two chapters of the Song of Songs.

BOETHIUS (480-524) Student of philosophy and Greek literature. Entered the service of the Ostrogoth government and became consul. Suspected of treason, he was condemned to death by King Theodoric. By his writings he made a notable contribution to the spread of Aristotelianism in the West and its application to the theological field. *The Consolation of Philosophy* is his most famous work.

CASSIAN, John (360-430) Born somewhere in the East. Received his religious upbringing in a monastery at Bethlehem and then lived for ten years with Egyptian monks. Ordained priest, founded a community for men and women at Marseilles. His writings greatly influenced the development of the monastic life in Europe. His works: *Organization of Communities and Remedies for the Eight Principal Sins*, *Conferences of the Fathers in the Desert*, *The Incarnation of the Lord*.

CLEMENT OF ALEXANDRIA (Titus Flavius Clemens) (died before 215) Born to pagan parents, perhaps at Athens, became a Christian. After many travels, took direction of the Catechetical School at Alexandria. In 202 the persecution under Septimius Severus compelled him to more journeying. He died in Asia Minor. Is reckoned 'the first Christian Scholar'. With an expert knowledge of the Bible, an attentive observer of social life, well-informed on the principal cultural trends of the age, he set himself to confront Revelation with all branches of knowledge to show that the partial truths expressed by Greek thinkers find their unity and their consummation in Christianity. Of his numerous writings only three remain in their totality today: *Warning to Pagans*, *The Teacher*, *Miscellaneous Studies*.

CYRIL OF JERUSALEM (died 386) Consecrated bishop, came into conflict with the Arians. Twice deposed by the Synod and the third time also sent into exile by the emperor. Returned finally in 378. In 381 took part in the Council of Constantinople. Famed for his 24 *Catecheses*, preparations for baptism, the last five of which have particular importance for sacramental theology.

410

DEFENSOR GRAMMATICUS (after 600) From Ligugé in France, influenced by Gregory the Great, composed an anthology of patristic texts, predominantly ascetic, the *Book of Sparkling Sayings* which was to have enormous influence all through the Middle Ages and in every country.

DIADOCHUS OF PHOTICA (5th c.) Bishop, author of *A Hundred Chapters on Spiritual Perfection* an important work for the history of mysticism and asceticism.

DOROTHEUS OF GAZA (6th c.) Disciple of Barsanuphius and abbot of a monastery near Gaza. Left 23 *Spiritual Discourses* much prized in the monastic world and 8 short letters addressed to his fellow monks.

EVAGRIUS OF PONTUS (346-399) Ordained deacon by Gregory Nazianzen, attracted many followers in Constantinople by his eloquence. Realizing how much his inner life was at risk through his popularity, he left the city and went to live with the monks in the mountains of Nitria. There he became a friend and disciple of Macarius the Egyptian. He copied books for a livelihood. His thoughts owed much of their inspiration to Origen, whose works he tried to spread among his fellow monks. He is the first monk to develop a considerable literary activity. Some of his works: *Gnostic Problems*, *On Prayer*, *Mirror for Monks*, *Mirror for Nuns*, commentaries on the Psalms and Proverbs.

GREGORY NAZIANZEN (330-390) Son of a bishop, lived in various places to study until he was thirty. Became a friend of Basil. Returned home, received baptism. Against his will, through pressure from the local church, he was ordained priest by his father. Infuriated at this 'violence' he fled to solitude. Returned not long after to help his father. Basil consecrated him Bishop of Sasima, but he never set foot in that diocese. When his father died, he exercised his episcopate for a little while at Nazianzus. Then he again embraced the contemplative life. In 379, complying with a pressing invitation, he assumed the governorship of the Nicene community of Constantinople. A succession of problems, intrigues, struggles led him to resign. He looked after the diocese of Nazianzus for two years, retiring in the end to the country and devoting himself to the ascetic life and literary output. His was a nervous and sensitive nature, not much suited to practical activity. He excelled in learning and elegance of form and has left a collection of discourses, many letters and poems.

GREGORY OF NYSSA (died 394) Younger brother of Basil. At first studied rhetoric and founded a family but then, chiefly at the instigation of his friend Gregory Nazianzen, retreated to the solitary life. Later again, at the insistence of Basil, he agreed to become Bishop of Nyssa in Cappadocia. He was then visitor of the churches of Pontus, finally patriarch of Sebaste. He had remarkable speculative qualities. Chief works: *Major Catechetical Discourse, Against Eunomius, Dialogue on the Soul and Resurrection, The Creation of Man, The Life of Moses*, homilies on the Song of Songs, Ecclesiastes, the Beatitudes, the Lord's Prayer.

GREGORY THE GREAT (540-604) From a senatorial family, became Prefect of Rome. In around 575 he resigned all his offices, turned his palace into a monastery and founded six other communities in Sicily. His asceticism was so excessive as to affect his health permanently.

After four years of monastic life he became special envoy to Pope Pelagius II as his legate at Constantinople. In 585 he returned to Rome and took up community life again although he remained adviser to Palagius. On Pelagius' death he was elected Pope against his will. During the years of his papacy he gave the See of Rome a pre-eminence hitherto unknown and laid the foundations for the temporal power of the Church as a state. He refused to be called 'universal pope' and gave himself the name 'servant of the servants of God.' Among his works, the *Book of the Pastoral Rule* and an ample commentary on *Job* are best known.

HESYCHIUS OF SINAI (died after 450) Monk and priest at Jerusalem. Outstanding biblical scholar, he interpreted the Bible in an allegorical manner. He seems to have explained the whole of Scripture. His theology is entirely based on the Bible. He distrusted having recourse to philosophical categories or systems. His commentaries on Leviticus, Job, Isaiah and the Psalms survive.

IGNATIUS (died c. 110) Bishop of Antioch. By order of the Emperor Trajan, he was led as a prisoner to Rome and there thrown to the wild beasts in the amphitheatre. During the journey he wrote seven letters to certain local churches and to Polycarp, Bishop of Smyrna. In impassioned tones, he urged kindness among believers and exalted the ministry of bishops.

IRENAEUS (died c. 202) Coming from Asia Minor, disciple of Polycarp, he was a priest at Lyons and then bishop of the same city. He showed himself a skilled polemicist in confrontations with false 'gnosis'. On the other hand, when Pope Victor I excommunicated the churches of his native country, he urged the Pope to re-establish unity. According to a sixth-century historian he died a martyr's death. Irenaeus wrote in Greek. From his many works there survive *Against Heresies* and *Demonstration of Apostolic Preaching*. In them he put the emphasis on tradition: anyone seeking orthodoxy should inquire into the teaching handed down by the apostles and living in the body of the Church. The Churches of apostolic foundation are privileged witnesses to the faith.

ISAAC OF NINEVEH (7th century) Elected bishop, after only five months he resigned the office to become first a solitary and then a member of a community of monks in the mountains. An important ascetical and mystical author. However, his literary position is hard to establish because of the confusion which occurred in the past between many other authors of the same name.

LETTER TO DIOGNETUS Composed probably at the beginning of the 3rd century. Only one manuscript existed and that was destroyed by fire in 1870. Addressed by an unknown writer to an eminent pagan person called Diognetus, after refuting paganism and Judaism, it illustrates and defends Christianity in an attractive style with lively language. The dominant theme of the letter is love for God and for one's neighbour.

JOHN CHRYSOSTOM (354-407) Born at Antioch, baptized when 18 years old. Completed serious studies in philosophy and theology. For some years he led a life of severe asceticism, first in his mother's home, then under the direction of an aged anchorite; finally on his own in a mountainous region not far from the city. Ill health forced him to return to Antioch. Ordained priest in 386, for 12 years he fulfilled the office of preacher in the cathedral, gaining wide notoriety through his ringing eloquence and the close agreement of his subject matter both with the Scriptures and with daily life. In 398 he was consecrated patriarch of Constantinople. He was popular at once through his simplicity and practical interest in the poor. He tried to remove many abuses among the clergy. At the Synod of Ephesus he deposed various simoniacal bishops and drew on himself the hatred of the empress. Implacable opposition sprang up as a result. He was himself deposed and exiled, but at once recalled. The people welcomed him back with victory celebrations. However, the quarrel with the empress and a wearisome struggle with powerful ecclesiastics went on. He survived an attempt on his life and was again sent into exile where death overtook him. He was above all a pastor of souls and a preacher who knew how to combine the biblical message with the stylistic elegance of the great literature of Greece. Appropriately his gifts of oratory secured for him the title of Chrysostom, that is 'golden mouth'. His output was enormous, among which, for example are his homilies on Genesis, the Psalms, Isaiah, the Gospels of Matthew, Luke and John, the Acts, the Pauline Letters and besides them the treatise *On Priesthood* and the work *On Virginity*.

JOHN CLIMACUS (575-649) Monk on Mount Sinai, author of *Stairway to Paradise* in which he analyses in 30 chapters (or steps) the vices that threaten monks and the virtues that distinguish them. The work was very popular.

JOHN DAMASCENE (675-749) Descended from a distinguished family he quickly took on an important post in state administration. He left it to enter the monastery of St Saba near Jerusalem. Ordained priest, he was very active as preacher and writer. He is the last great theologian among the Greek fathers, and is a religious poet of undoubted talent. Chief works: *The Fount of Knowledge*, the third part of which (entitled *The Orthodox Faith*) is the classical manual of dogmatics of the Greek and the Orthodox-Slav churches.

MAXIMUS THE CONFESSOR (580-682) Belonging to a distinguished family in Constantinople, first became secretary of the emperor, then went into a monastery near Scutari. Fleeing from the Persians he moved to Alexandria and possibly to Carthage. Held violent disputes with monophysites and monothelites. He persuaded some Synods and in the end the Lateran Synod at Rome to condemn monothelitism. He was taken as a prisoner to Constantinople where he was condemned to exile in Thrace. A second trial restricted him to Colchis after having cut out his tongue and amputated his right hand, limbs which symbolize commitment as 'Confessor', as a witness to the true faith. He died soon after as a result of the suffering caused by the amputation. He was the most brilliant theologian of his time. He was concerned also with mystical, exegetical and liturgical problems. His works are often hard to understand and written in a bombastic style.

METHODIUS OF OLYMPUS (died c. 311) After living some time in Lycia, which contains the city of Olympus, he became Bishop of Philippi in Macedonia. He died as a martyr. Famous for having combated Origenism. He wrote many works, for the most part in the form of the Platonic dialogue, written in elegant style, for example: *The Feast of the Ten Virgins*, *The Resurrection*, *Free Will*.

NICETA STETHATUS (1005-1090) While very young he went into the monastery of Studios, where he carried on the trade of copyist. During the visit of the Legate of Rome to Constantinople in 1054, he acted as spokesman for the Greeks in the anti-Latin controversy. Although he was comparatively moderate in his arguments and in the tone of them, the Roman legate replied to him with violence. Niceta submitted and actually became his friend. In complete agreement with Simeon the New Theologian he followed the same ideal with him: the monk ought to reach the height of divine knowledge and then teach in the name of the Spirit. On the literary plane there survive his *Life of Simeon*, *The Centuries*, and various small works and letters.

ORIGEN (185-254) Born probably in Alexandria. The death of his father as a martyr deeply affected him. When not even twenty years of age he was nominated Director of the Catechetical School, which under him acquired enormous prestige. He was greatly concerned with philosophical and especially biblical studies. He led a life of rigorous asceticism. Moreover, misinterpreting the Gospel phrase 'Some have chosen to be eunuchs for love of the kingdom of heaven' he castrated himself. He was ordained priest, despite the impediment of mutilation. For this reason and perhaps for some theses not accepted by the Church, two Synods of Alexandria deposed him from office and the local community expelled him. He went to Caesarea, where he founded a school similar to that at Alexandria. He was put in prison and died after appalling torture. His preference for the allegorical interpretation of Scripture led him into some errors or equivocal expressions. Besides his *Hexapla* – an attempt to reconstruct the exact text of the Septuagint – we have his *Principles*, *Against Celsus*, *On Prayer*, *Exhortation to Martyrdom*, not to mention homilies and scriptural commentaries.

PROCLUS OF CONSTANTINOPLE (died 446) Bishop of Cyzicus and then patriarch of Constantinople, successor at one remove from Nestorius whose heresy he was among the first to oppose in his famous Marian Sermon. On various occasions he acted as mediator in conflicts dividing the churches. Under his name 27 sermons and 7 letters have been handed down.

PSEUDO-DIONYSIUS THE AREOPAGITE (5th century) Unknown author taking the name of Dionysius the Areopagite, a convert of St Paul. Profoundly influenced by neoplatonism which he wished to reconcile with Christianity. His style is obscure, including neologisms. Works: *The Divine Names, Mystical Theology, The Heavenly Hierarchy, The Hierarchy of the Church.*

PSEUDO-MACARIUS (4th century) Under this name there have come down to us *The Great Letter* which inspired Simeon the New Theologian, and 50 *Spiritual Homilies.*

ROMANUS MELODUS (490-560) The greatest of the old Byzantine poets. Exercised his priesthood at Constantinople. Composed a thousand hymns, only 65 extant ones are certainly by him. Some have found their way into liturgical use. His hymns on the Nativity and on Easter are particularly impressive.

SAYINGS OF THE DESERT FATHERS (Possibly compiled at the end of the fifth century) A collection of edifying sayings and examples of virtue taken from the lives of famous monks.

SEVERIANUS OF GABALA (died after 408) A Syrian bishop, highly thought of as an orator. His unusual familiarity with the Scriptures is attested by the rhyming

418

fragments of his *Commentary on the Letters of St Paul* and by 23 homilies.

SIMEON THE NEW THEOLOGIAN (949-1022) Born in the country, he repaired at a very early age to Constantinople to study. Under the guidance of a monk, Simeon the Pious, he was prepared to enter a monastery: he was received there in 977 and very soon nominated as abbot. He lived a very intense life: prayer, direction of the religious, re-establishment of conventual discipline, administrative business. In 1005 he resigned his charge. One of his controversies with the ex-metropolitan of Nicomedia ended in his condemnation to exile. He retired near Scutari, where he built an oratory and collected some disciples. He stayed there even after his rehabilitation. Among his works: *Theological and Ethical Questions and Discourses.*

TERTULLIAN (160-220) From Carthage, son of a pagan Roman centurion. He received a thorough scientific education, including particularly law and rhetoric, and practised as a lawyer in Rome. After a period of depravity, he was converted to Christianity and returned to Carthage. There he began an intense literary activity in the service of the Church. However, around 205 he broke with the official Church, joined the sect of the Montanists and gave rise to a theological trend called specifically Tertullianism. His chief works are: *To the Pagans, Apologetic, The Soul, The Testimony of the Soul, Against Marcion, Against Praxeas, The Flesh of Christ, The Resurrection of the Flesh,* and *Chastity.*

THEODORET (393-460) Born at Antioch. Nominated, against his will, to the see of Cyrrhus. Even so he performed his pastoral office with admirable zeal. Took an active part in the Christological controversy instigated by Nestorius. He is one of the most prolific authors of the Greek Church, and he wrote, for example: the *Exposition of the True Faith*, *Discourses on Providence*, *Cure of Pagan Diseases*, commentaries on the Psalms, the Song of Songs, the Prophets, the Pauline Letters, and his *History of the Church*.

General Index

April: *Ah, my heart is a battlefield*

May: *Come to me, O God, that I may come to you*

June: *My house, O God, is your church*

July: *Many, but one heart, one soul*

August: *The world: joy for humanity and glory for God*

September: *Wealth belongs to us that we may belong to God*

October: *The Church is our light and leaven for the world*

November: *Speak to me, O Lord, then I shall know how to answer you*

December: *Amen! I believe, I hope, I love, O Lord!*

Index of Sources

CISTERCIAN PUBLICATIONS, INC.

TITLES LISTINGS

CISTERCIAN TEXTS

THE WORKS OF BERNARD OF CLAIRVAUX

Apologia to Abbot William
Five Books on Consideration: Advice to a Pope
Grace and Free Choice
Homilies in Praise of the Blessed Virgin Mary
The Life and Death of Saint Malachy the Irishman
Love without Measure. Extracts from the Writings
  of St Bernard (Paul Dimier)
The Parables of Saint Bernard (Michael Casey)
Sermons for the Summer Season
Sermons on the Song of Songs I - IV
The Steps of Humility and Pride

THE WORKS OF WILLIAM OF SAINT THIERRY

The Enigma of Faith
Exposition on the Epistle to the Romans
Exposition on the Song of Songs
The Golden Epistle
The Nature of Dignity of Love

THE WORKS OF AELRED OF RIEVAULX

Dialogue on the Soul
The Mirror of Charity
Spiritual Friendship
Treatises I: On Jesus at the Age of Twelve, Rule for
  a Recluse, The Pastoral Prayer

THE WORKS OF JOHN OF FORD

Sermons on the Final Verses of the Songs of Songs I - VII

THE WORKS OF GILBERT OF HOYLAND

Sermons on the Songs of Songs I-III
Treatises, Sermons and Epistles

OTHER EARLY CISTERCIAN WRITERS

The Letters of Adam of Perseigne I
Baldwin of Ford: Spiritual Tractates I - II
Gertrud the Great of Helfta: Spiritual Exercises
Gertrud the Great of Helfta: The Herald of God's
  Loving-Kindness
Guerric of Igny: Liturgical Sermons I - II
Idung of Prüfening: Cistercians and Cluniacs: The
  Case of Citeaux
Isaac of Stella: Sermons on the Christian Year
The Life of Beatrice of Nazareth
Serlo of Wilton & Serlo of Savigny
Stephen of Lexington: Letters from Ireland
Stephen of Sawley: Treatises

MONASTIC TEXTS

EASTERN CHRISTIAN TRADITION

Besa: The Life of Shenoute
Cyril of Scythopolis: Lives of the Monks of Palestine
Dorotheos of Gaza: Discourses
Evagrius Ponticus:Praktikos and Chapters on Prayer

The Harlots of the Desert (Benedicta Ward)
John Moschos: The Spiritual Meadow
Iosif Volotsky: Monastic Rule
The Lives of the Desert Fathers
The Lives of Simeon Stylites (Robert Doran)
The Luminous Eye (Sebastian Brock)
Mena of Nikiou: Isaac of Alexandra & St Macrobius
Pachomian Koinonia I - III
Paphnutius: A Histories of the Monks of Egypt
The Sayings of the Desert Fathers
Spiritual Direction in the Early Christian East (Irénée
  Hausherr)
The Syriac Fathers on Prayer and the Spiritual Life
(Sebastian Brock)

WESTERN CHRISTIAN TRADITION

Anselm of Canterbury: Letters I - III
Bede: Commentary on the Seven Catholic Epistles
Bede: Commentary on the Acts of the Apostles
Bede: Gospel Homilies I - II
Bede: Homilies on the Gospels I - II
Cassian: Conferences I - III
Gregory the Great: Forty Gospel Homilies
Guigo II the Carthusian: Ladder of Monks and
  Twelve Mediations
Handmaids of the Lord: The Lives of Holy Women in
  Late Antiquity and the Early Middle Ages
Peter of Celle: Selected Works
The Letters of Armand-Jean de Rance I - II
The Rule of the Master

CHRISTIAN SPIRITUALITY

Abba: Guides to Wholeness & Holiness East & West
A Cloud of Witnesses: The Development of
  Christian Doctrine (D.N. Bell)
Athirst for God: Spiritual Desire in Bernard of
  Clairvaux's Sermons on the Song of Songs
  (M. Casey)
Cistercian Way (André Louf)
Drinking From the Hidden Fountain (Spidlék)
Fathers Talking (Aelred Squire)
Friendship and Community (B. McGuire)
From Cloister to Classroom
Herald of Unity: The Life of Maria Gabrielle
  Sagheddu (M. Driscoll)
Life of St Mary Magdalene and of Her Sister
  St Martha (D. Mycoff)
The Name of Jesus (Irénée Hausherr)
Penthos: The Doctrine of Compunction in the
  Christian East (Irénée Hausherr)
Rancé and the Trappist Legacy (A.J. Krailsheimer)
The Roots of the Modern Christian Tradition
Russian Mystics (S. Bolshakoff)
The Spirituality of the Christian East (Tomas Spidlék)
Spirituality of the Medieval West (André Vauchez)
Tuning In To Grace (André Louf)

MONASTIC STUDIES

Community & Abbot in the Rule of St Benedict I - II
  (Adalbert De Vogüé)
Beatrice of Nazareth in Her Context (Roger
  De Ganck)
Consider Your Call: A Theology of the Monastic Life
  (Daniel Rees et al.)
The Finances of the Cistercian Order in the Fourteenth
  Century (Peter King)

TITLES LISTINGS

Cistercian Publications is a non-profit corpora-
tion. Its publishing program is restricted to
monastic texts in translation and books on the
monastic tradition.

North American customers may order these books
through booksellers or directly from the warehouse:
Cistercian Publications
St Joseph's Abbey
Spencer, Massachusetts 01562
(508) 885-7011
fax 508-885-4687

Editorial queries and advance book information
should be directed to the Editorial Offices:
Cistercian Publications
Institute of Cistercian Studies
Western Michigan University
Kalamazoo, Michigan 49008
(616) 387-8920
fax 616-387-8921

A complete catalogue of texts in translation and
studies on early, medieval, and modern monasticism
is available at no cost from Cistercian Publications.

.